Outsider
at the
Heart of Things

Outsider at the Heart of Things

Essays by R. P. Blackmur

Edited and with an Introduction by
James T. Jones

University of Illinois Press
Urbana and Chicago

This book is printed on acid-free paper.

Library of Congress Cataloging-in-Publication Data

Blackmur, R. P. (Richard P.), 1904–1965.
    Outsider at the heart of things: essays/by R. P. Blackmur;
edited and with an introduction by James T. Jones.
       p.   cm.
    Bibliography: p.
    Includes index.
    ISBN 0-252-01579-7 (alk. paper)
    I. Jones, James T., 1948–   . II. Title.
PS3503.L266A6   1989
814'.52—dc19   88-17401
                                                                      CIP

The author wishes to thank the Southwest Missouri State University
Foundation for its grant for permissions fees for some of the essays in
this collection.

Grateful acknowledgment is also made to the following publications, in
which the essays previously appeared, for permission to reprint
copyrighted material:

"Chaos Is Come Again," first published in *Southern Review* 6 (1941),
658–74, reprinted with permission; "The Enabling Act of Criticism,"
by R. P. Blackmur from AMERICAN ISSUES, ed. Willard Thorp,
copyright 1941 by Harper & Row, Publishers, Inc.; "The Undergraduate Writer as Writer," first published in *College English* 3
(1941), 251–64, copyright © 1941 by the National Council of Teachers
of English, reprinted by permission of the publisher; "The State of
American Writing," first published in *Partisan Review,* vol. 15, 1948, no.

For Robert H. Henigan
A model teacher, colleague, and man of letters

Contents

Acknowledgments

I would like to thank the Southwest Missouri State University English department for release time to prepare this collection and the University Foundation for a grant to pay for word processing of the manuscript. Dr. Paul Toom, associate vice-president for graduate studies, helped me secure both funding and research assistance. I am especially grateful to Robert H. Henigan and J. Hillis Miller, who read the introduction and the essays and commented on my selection and arrangement. I also appreciate the editorial help of my research assistant, Valerie Turner.

Introduction:
Outsider at the Heart of Things

In his introduction to the *Selected Poems* of John Brooks Wheelwright, published by New Directions in 1941, just a few months after the poet's death, R. P. Blackmur has this to say about the work of his lifelong friend:

> It is when the flux has been arrested that character begins to emerge, unmoving, perhaps, but unimpeded; imperfect, certainly, as art must be, but undiverted. What had seemed fragmentary, adventitious, disorderly, generally out of bounds, becomes within the bounding lines of death, the very chorus or commentary of the only order of which poetry is capable.

Wheelwright's death was far fresher in Blackmur's mind at that moment than Blackmur's death, over twenty years ago, is in ours now. Yet it is only now, after twenty years, that Blackmur's real value begins to show clear. Thanks to the work of scholars such as the eminent Joseph Frank, Denis Donoghue (certainly one of the most important critics writing in America today), Russell Fraser, Veronica Makowsky, Robert Boyers, Gerald Pannick, William Cain, and others, we are now able to find the order, as he himself found it in Wheelwright, of Blackmur's work. Further, we have come to the point at which we can assent to Blackmur's judgment of his friend that whatever a writer takes out of his work by dying was "never an actual part of it." As half a dozen posthumous collections, a biography, and three critical monographs have demonstrated, much more meaning had been actualized in Blackmur's works than anyone suspected at the time of this death in 1965.

Because we crave more of such actual meaning—for whatever reasons: nostalgia, homesickness, or mere change in weather—I have gathered here some twenty-two essays published by Blackmur during the four decades of his career. These essays, presented in chronological order from 1928 to 1964, were never included by Blackmur in his books, which regrouped and reprinted his more popular and more pivotal writing on a regular basis. The pieces gathered here, published either in periodicals or topical collections, or as introductions, represent thoroughly finished writing of Blackmur's unique variety. What they add, as a group, to our appreciation of the body of Blackmur's writing has to do with the order he speaks of in reference to Wheelright. In the past fifteen years the details of that order have been filled in, clarified, and rearranged; we are now approaching a full version. How these pieces contribute to and nearly complete that order will be seen shortly.

First, however, I should point out three major omissions. Two groups of Blackmur's published essays do not find a place among these twenty-two. One group includes five published essays on Henry Adams, three of which were purposefully omitted from Makowsky's redaction of Blackmur's book on the historian because they failed to take more recent scholarship into account. None of these essays would make sense in the present context, except in terms of the author's inimitable style and devotion to their subjects. A second group would be out of place for a very different reason. This includes four "catalogue" essays, in which Blackmur reviews the work of anywhere from nine to twelve poets at once. While the judgments rendered of individual writers in these pieces reflect Blackmur's biases, the catalogue obviates the necessity for an instrinsic form. Consequently, the considerable drama of Blackmur's other essays, where he attempts to create a still point from which to move his discussion, is missing from them. Three essays recently collected in *The Legacy of R.P. Blackmur* are also omitted. Besides these twelve published essays, a hundred-odd book reviews and very short essays remain uncollected. It may be, as Donoghue has noted, that Blackmur worked best in the twenty- to twenty-five-page format, so these very brief works can be omitted on that ground alone. However, the reader of this book will find some relatively short essays in which Blackmur manages amazingly well to use his preferred strategy and make his point without the additional room. Perhaps a collection of reviews is warranted, as it has been for Allen Tate and Yvor Winters. All Blackmur's unpublished work, however, including his fiction and drama, can probably be left in its present state, available to the interested party at the Princeton University Library. The essays collected here represent not a coda to the critic's work, like those gathered in *The Primer of Ignorance* (1967), but an entirely new thread, a new element in the design of Blackmur's order of criticism. Let me say why.

This collection, on analysis, will break itself handily into three groups of essays. First, there are pieces that deal with cultural topics, including writing. Among these are "Politikon" and its postscript, "The Discipline of Humanism," "Psyche in the South," "Chaos Is Come Again," "The Undergraduate Writer as Writer," "The State of American Writing," and "Religious Poetry in the United States." The second group includes those essays that treat the work of a single author. The third group consists of theoretical essays in criticism: "The Enabling Act of Criticism," "The Language of Silence: A Citation," and "The Chain of Our Own Needles." Each of the groups adds to our store of information about Blackmur in a slightly different way, but together they add up to a new perspective. They show us, first, the essentially social bias of Blackmur's criticism. The dogma of tradition Blackmur received from T. S. Eliot and his application of that dogma to language and convention result in a fundamental persuasion and criterion of judgment that always place the individual in a relation to his society, an artist in a relation to this tradition, and the present in a relation to the past. In fact, if any one insight about Blackmur can be singled out from all the insights contained in these essays, it is his insistence on the presence of the past in all rational—that is, imaginative—human behavior. This should encourage those contemporary critics who want to hold on to the methods of the New Criticism that one of its leading proponents is not only not ahistorical, but indeed, profoundly historical. To generalize the message: any thorough investigation of the works of any New Critic will explode any or all of the myths surrounding the New Criticism, an "ism" as various as Romanticism.

The second group of essays teaches us a valuable lesson about the difference between theory and practice. After looking at the first group of essays it will become obvious to the reader that Blackmur is attempting in them to apply his method of literary criticism to an analysis of culture. Whether this has beneficial or useful results will be up to the reader to decide. After reading the pieces in my second group, the reader may be left wondering about my categories, because what Blackmur displays even more clearly there than in his more famous essays is his propensity to use pointed discussion, even explication, as the setting for theoretical pronouncements. The distinction between theoretical and practical criticism is one I address at length in my book on Blackmur, but I can summarize here. Our usual understanding of those terms has to do not so much with theory as with system. A theoretical critic for most of us is somebody like Kenneth Burke or Northrop Frye who articulates a system independent of specific judgments and then applies various elements of the system to given works or authors. In that sense, Blackmur should never be taken for a theoretical critic. His principles of provisionality and rational imagination militate against critical systems, and his methodology—what Donoghue in the foreword to *Henry Adams* calls Blackmur's "supplication of texts"—makes it impossible to sustain the superstructure of a system with rhetoric and dramatic gesture. He keeps outside a system to stay inside the text.

Blackmur is one of the few critics who is able to replicate in the drama of a critical essay the excitement of meaning in literature. So his "practical" essays are found to be encrusted with "theoretical" gems, which, removed from their settings and arranged according to size, shape, and color, might form a crown to dazzle all but the greatest cynic. One doctrine found in "The Enabling Act of Criticism" is essential to an appreciation of Blackmur. That is that criticism, for him, is an imitation, but no less important for that fact, because by submitting to the authority of the texts it limns for us the exact manner in which the artist submits to the authority of the actual. It is not that the text is stable; far from it. For Blackmur, the text is always an abyss within the abyss, and the critical act conducive, at best, to vertigo. But the critic *accepts* the text, as the artist accepts the world, so that selection may function as judgment. If you cannot accept the fundamental analogy between critical and creative acts, then Blackmur's work will seem erratic, arrogant, monstrous. But I am running ahead of myself, as Blackmur often said of himself.

Let us take examples from each group to see if we can clarify what, together, they add to our understanding of Blackmur, the New Criticism, and American literature in general.

Two essays from the first group have overt biographical significance. Veronica Makowsky begins her introduction to *Henry Adams* by quoting a paragraph from "Politikon" to show how closely Blackmur indentified with Adams, so closely that this piece might have been an addendum to *The Education*. By appending to it the "Postscript," we discover an additonal fact: Blackmur's instinctive ability to distance himself from Adams, witnessed by the immediate shift in style after the election of Hoover. A second essay, "The Undergraduate Writer as Writer," is valuable as biography *and* for what it says about its topic. Often, we forget that one of the primary charcteristics of the New Criticism is that its practitioners turned from independent men of letters to university teachers. Blackmur went to Princeton in 1940 as Allen Tate's associate in the new creative arts program; he spent the rest of his career, a quarter-century, teaching there. Among his colleagues and students were many younger poets: Berryman, Kinnell, Merwin. The problems he indentifies in this essay are problems he helped them solve.

The phenomenon of the writer or critic as teacher is one he addresses in his response to a *Partisan Review* questionnaire on "The State of American Writing." His answers, unlike those of John Berryman and some of the others who replied, are woven into a coherent, and hopeful, essay about the alternatives faced by the academic writer: he may fail all around, he may become wholly a teacher, or he may succeed. Blackmur found the conditions not that much different from those confronting authors in any society, certainly no worse. What is more, he found them inevitable. He approaches the religious element in American poetry in much the same way: in terms of writers struggling to accept and use the conventions given them by their society. The difficulty with religion in poetry is a typical difficulty, as Blackmur sees it. "What is actual, when we would be religious," he says, "invades us like a nightmare of our own behavior suddenly seen, and it is our own monsters that keep us from God." More than a simple survey of religious writers or religious topics in American literature, it is this personal human substance that interests him.

Two other essays in this group reveal even more about Blackmur's central concerns. "Psyche in the South," a pamphlet from the Tryon series, which included an essay by John Crowe Ransom and poetry by Yvor Winters, is a remarkable document. It offers a critique of Southern Agrarianism—a political and economic movement led by Ransom and Tate and other Southern men of letters—which flourished in the 1930s. Not only does Blackmur discuss *I'll Take My Stand,* the 1930 Agrarian manifesto, but he entirely dismantles two essays by Donald Davidson, one of Tate's Nashville associates. And he dismantles them for reasons he learned from Eliot: the interaction between past and present, society and the individual. Using Eliotic religious terminology to describe the social issue, Blackmur calls Southern sectionalism a heresy, which, like "Communism and Humanism . . . under the head of their single insights, attempt to hypothecate absolute disciplines which if effective would destroy the very spirit which animated them." Much of the Agrarian program he finds acceptable, especially its emphasis on tradition. However, this emphasis results in an overemphasis that, in the long run, damages the ability of Southern culture, or any culture, to produce objective works of art. "The heresy," Blackmur asserts, "is that poetry gets put in the second place." Really, this essay turns out to be not much more than a plea for the necessity for change in any given tradition, but I like to think of it in terms of the relation between Southern and Northern New Critics, and I also like to think that it may have influenced the change of values apparent in Allen Tate's essays on the Southern literary imagination, where he finally rejects purely sectional literature.

Blackmur's objections to "-isms" in literature become clearer in his critique of *Humanism in America* (essays by students and disciples of Irving Babbitt and Paul Elmer More), which appeared alongside similar attacks by Malcolm Cowley, Edmund Wilson, Kenneth Burke, Tate, and Winters. He assails the "elevated vacuity" of the younger humanists for the "foreign and irrelevant discipline" that amounts to a censorship of literature. The Humanist "higher will," Blackmur contends, "has nothing to do with either the making or meaning of art in general. . . . It is the last weapon we should use in criticism or judgment." The Humanists, like the Communists, the Sectionalists, the psychologists, and sociologists, have committed the greatest transgression in Blackmur's hierarchy: They have subordinated literature to an extrinsic set of values. Like art, criticism must also be kept free of dogma, otherwise it becomes brittle, self-proclaiming, useless. Literature and criticism, in Blackmur's view, must be kept outside systems.

The final essay in this set, "Chaos Is Come Again," carries Blackmur's insistence on the purity of literature to the cultural level. He takes the occasion of an American Philosophical Society conference to set forth the problem as he, and Eliot, see it: "Getting along without conviction and without faith as we are used, as humans, to enjoy these." This is dissociation of sensibility, American style. The result: we are cast back on the human imagination. Here we discover how all-embracing the imagination is for Blackmur. It guides reason, intellect, and intuition. "We have now as the chief critical task of the imagination," he claims, "the labor of making reason flexible by rational means alone. A frankly provisional, avowedly conventional imagination is the only superrational authority we can muster." This is literary theory applied to the criticism of culture.

Next we come to the second set of essays, which are directed toward and by the authors they propose to discuss. By supplicating the texts of Aiken's novels, which profoundly influenced Blackmur's unpublished novels, Blackmur urges himself to make theoretical statements as well as practical judgments. It is the same with his discussion of the short novel, where a serial treatment of James, Melville, Crane, Twain, Stein, Williams, and Wylie leads to a disquisition on allegory, "not taken here as a mode of interpretation, but as one of the great traditional creative modes of the mind, which it sometimes dominates."

So it is with Blackmur on Poe, Hawthorne, Holmes, Hueffer, and Read. Not till we arrive at Dickinson must we consider an explicit comparison with an earlier essay, "Emily Dickinson: Notes on Prejudice and Fact," included in *The Expense of Greatness* (1940). The earlier essay, after referring to Allen

Tate's seminal work "Emily Dickinson" (1928), where Tate first applied his concept of poetic tension, turns a discussion of the "rational imagination," Blackmur's "omnicompetent" creative faculty, into a manipulation of Tate's idea of "the perfect literary situation" to Blackmur's own ends. It is really, he insists, partly to Tate, partly to us, the poet who makes the age, not the other way around. Any given age tends to disappear into the meaning of its great writers; so with Dickinson. He concludes: "So far as poetry goes, then, the influence of intellectual or other abstracted considerations can be measured only as it effects the choice and arrangement of words—as it richens or impoverishes the texture of the imaginative vehicle of poetry." So, like Marx and Hegel, Blackmur turns Tate on his head, with the opposite result that history is seen to result from literature.

In the later (1956) essay included here, Blackmur takes up the question of poetic identity in a demand for the need to reproduce Dickinson's eccentric punctuation accurately in print. Words, he tells us, are like notes in a musical score, only partially adequate to reproduce the music. Intimacy makes up the difference. That is how we account for the mystery, delineated in the earlier essay, of Emily Dickinson's identity. Blackmur compares her with Herrick and Rilke, an unlikely combination. Her main characteristics are multiplicity, freedom, and spontaneity. Johnson's edition allows us to see these for ourselves, but more, it allows us to recognize that "her disorder is her own. Also, which is more significant, her order is almost only her own." Our access to poetic identity, in short, comes through the words of the revised edition of the poems. That which is most objective is most revealing.

"The Substance That Prevails" fits into a similar, though more complex, relationship with previous essays. One of the most noted essays of Blackmur's early career is "Examples of Wallace Stevens" (1931). He followed this with briefer negative pieces in the 1940s, so the essay presented here makes a fitting conclusion, and a postitive one, for the critic's formal relationship with the great poet. Like Aiken, Stevens is seen to be apt at reinvigorating cliches. Beyond that, Blackmur identifies five main qualities in Stevens: (1) "a superior person making a fundamental product: himself"; (2) the idea of a vocabulary of rare words; (3) the protection of attitudes both of disdain and acceptance; (4) the protection afforded by foreign words; and (5) studied carelessness amid elegance. Together these qualities produce "the sketch of Stevens," but Blackmur is not content with a sketch. He moves toward a definition of thought: "the sum of human activities engaged in ordering, demolishing, and reconstructing the sensibility." Again, he searches for the identity of the poet, this time in terms of style. Finally, he produces a dialectic: the community of understanding and the identity of style. He has come full circle in his judgment of Stevens; set this essay beside the other three reproduced in *Form and Value in Modern Poetry* and you can follow him around.

The essay on Eliot combines two essays that appeared in consecutive numbers of the Harvard little magazine *Hound & Horn* in the same way that the essays were combined in a 1928 *Hound & Horn* pamphlet (except that the pages have been numbered serially). "T. S. Eliot" must also be read against other published and collected essays, "T. S. Eliot: From 'Ash Wednesday' to 'Murder in the Cathedral'" (1935) and "Unappeasable and Peregrine: Behavior and the 'Four Quartets'" (1951), also reproduced in *Form and Value.* The present essay complements the others by providing a reading of *The Waste Land,* "Gerontion," "Prufrock," and other poems not treated in them, as well as offering a thorough analysis of Eliot's criticism. The essay runs fifty-four pages in the original, its bulk being an outward sign of its pressing significance for Blackmur. The first half treats the poems, the second half the criticism.

In the first part Blackmur makes what now sounds like a needless assertion: "T. S. Eliot altered the sensibility of his age." In 1928, however, people were still in a position to object to such apparently extravagant statements, and in fact, one *Hound & Horn* reader wrote immediately to complain. Only figures like Rousseau, this reader said, might be thought to change the sensibility of an entire age. Nevertheless, Blackmur forged on, without recanting his opinion. He traverses *The Waste Land* without even stumbling, manages to address himself to four other poems in addition, and concludes that Eliot, far from being obscure, "has perhaps not risked failure enough." If anything, the age is to blame for failing to provide (as Tate claimed the post-Puritan age had provided for Dickinson) adequate conventions.

The second part of the essay is a compendium of Blackmur's critical debt to Eliot: it covers nearly all his important concerns—provisionality, autonomy of literature and criticism, technique, convention, tradition, art and morality, felt thought (an obsession created in Blackmur by a 1926 letter from Eliot), emotions in art, and these more or less in the order of presentation. The conclusion is a *tour de force:* Eliot is a critic in his poetry and in his criticism; his influence on modern poetry comes through his writing about the literature of the past; and his only drawback is that his criticism cannot be applied to the content of a work (which is not as serious a drawback to Blackmur as it might appear to us). Blackmur insists that the critic never knows all the facts, because the facts of literature are not susceptible of complete apprehension, so judgment must always remain, in the end, tentative, provisional. Again, he draws the analogy between the critic and the artist: "Most great criticism occurs in the mind of the artist at the moment of creation." Finally, with a great flourish, he demolishes completely the boundary between criticism and art by saying, "Literature is its own judge."

The most frequently reprinted piece in this collection is "A Poetics for Infatuation" (1961), an essay published in the *Kenyon Review* and reprinted in *Venture* magazine and in the anthology *The Riddle of Shakespeare's Sonnets*. If the Eliot essay provides a good example of a younger, more radical Blackmur, the Shakespeare piece is a showcase for his later, more complex style. And only Shakespeare was capable of eliciting more theory than Eliot in a discussion of his poetry. Blackmur begins by thanking his lucky stars for the arbitrary order in which the sonnets have been received (much as Roland Barthes thanks his for alphabetical order). Then he divides them into groups to show the development of the theme: 1 through 17 are a preparatory exercise; 18 through 126 explore the theme; 127 through 152 reveal a new phase of the theme; and 153 through 154 give a light echo of the theme in fashionable rhetoric. And what is the theme? The creation of another self, another identity, by the poet. "The last illusion," he maintains, "would be to create or find the second self of second sight. For this, a poem is our nearest substitute and furthest reach." At one point in the essay, Blackmur wants to stop his discussion, but he can't; more themes remain to be treated. He has more theories to expound, more beautiful words to say. He goes on to comment on the effect of repetition in poetry. Then, at the last, he takes up the complicated question of intentionality, a New Critical commonplace. "The clearer the intention," Blackmur says of the poet, "the greater the uncertainty of his knowledge must be; and besides, the words may modify and even correct his intention, as well as ruin it." Words make the poet, or at least his mind, as well as the poem. The net effect of this homage to the sonnets is, if not to make Shakespeare into a modern poet, at least to make his poetry into modern poetry (poetry about poetry). This is Blackmur receiving and modifying the dogma of tradition from Eliot; this is Blackmur proclaiming his own heretical version of the dogma; this is the outsider at the heart of things.

So much for the group of essays about individual writers; now on to the third group and then a brief summation. I already quoted from "The Enabling Act of Criticism," which appeared as the last essay in Willard Thorp's *American Issues* of 1941, directly after Tate's "Tension in Poetry." Besides what I previously noted about the imaginative, yet ancillary, nature of criticism, Blackmur argues for a two-stage critical methodology: first, concentration on the text and its technique; second, submission to the authority of the text. As I also pointed out, the text is far from stable. Here is Blackmur: "In the very degree that the work of literature does focus the interests you want it will be difficult—indeed an inexhaustable labor—to grasp the text." Further, he wants to extend the identity of creative and critical imagination to make it the keystone of criticism. As such it would reveal "the primary aspect of literature: that aspect in which it represents the experience of the actual which is beneath and beyond merely moral experience, and which alone grounds or situates moral experience."

If he rearranges the ordinary priorities in "The Enabling Act," then he retrenches in "The Chain of Our Own Needles: Criticism and Our Culture," which follows an excellent essay on the New Criticism by Father Ong in a book called *The Critical Matrix* (1961). After discussing the great risk that criticism, feeling its imaginative oats without recalling its status subsidiary to literature, may become "an independent mode of the mind," he remarks that different relations between literature and its audience demand different types of criticism to bridge the gap (Blackmur's oft-repeated phrase with regard to critical activity). He posits four categories of criticism: the first deals with the relation between the audience and literature, the second deals with literature in relation to itself, the third deals with the relation between literature and society, and the fourth is not really a type, but relates the first three types of criticism to one another. This last kind of criticism Blackmur calls "great criticism."

One more "find" remains; that is "The Language of Silence: A Citation" (1955), as I read it, a companion piece to "Language as Gesture" (1942). In the earlier essay, one of his most thrilling, Blackmur advises that "when the language of words fails we resort to the language of gesture." There he avers that "poetry is the meaning of meaning"; here, in the later piece, he says, "Meaning is what silence does when it gets into words." It is pretty much the same idea come upon from another direction. "The Language of Silence" provides a glossary of touchstones: Augustine's *De Musica* (subject of another Blackmur essay), Lu Chi's *Wen Fu,* Pascal, Heller's *The Hazard of Modern Poetry,* Eliot's "Dry Salvages," George Eliot, Conrad's *Nostromo,* Forster's *A Passage to India,* Smollett's *Humphry Clinker,* Whitehead on style, and so on, all exemplifying the salutary virtues of silence. Translation, for instance, would be impossible without silence, Blackmur claims. Silence illustrates the gap between thoughts and words: "If there were no gaps between our words . . . we should never find our thoughts." And Blackmur says in "A Critic's Job of Work" (1935), discussing the difference between words in poetry and words about poetry, "The gap is absolute."

The last three essays I cited here make a definite extension of Blackmur's well-known theoretical essays, "A Burden for Critics," "A Critic's Job of Work," "A Featherbed for Critics, "Notes on Four Categories of Criticism," and "Language as Gesture." Together, indeed, they total eight, and perhaps may form the foundation of a system, if not the system itself. I am suggesting, simply, that Blackmur's tendency toward theory is made clearer by the collection at hand.

Other matters are also clarified. Blackmur's four main influences, for instance, march like ringmasters through these essays—Eliot, James, Adams, and the philosopher George Santayana. Several myths about Blackmur are also exploded here. First, the notion that Blackmur became ennervated by academic life; sixteen of these pieces were published after he arrived at Princeton. A corollary to that, the notion that Blackmur turned away from poetry, toward fiction, in his later years also falls. It is now clear, as well, despite the absence here of any essay-length comment on the great European novels (Donoghue's *Selected Essays* includes a previously uncollected essay on *The Charterhouse of Parma* published in 1964) that Blackmur's criticism of fiction was diverse, thorough, and lifelong. Among many minor points of interest, this new collection reveals the details of Blackmur's interest in the little magazine. Many of these essays appeared first in the periodicals that have been so influential this century. Besides *Hound & Horn*, there were *Larus* (Sherry Mangan's publication), *Southern Review, Partisan Review, Kenyon Review,* and *Sewanee Review.* The sheer number and variety of the venues of his publications, the number of reprints of some essays, added to what we already know about Blackmur's penchant for republication and reorganization of his essays, enforce the conclusion that one of the primary reasons for his influence was a relentless energy, almost evangelical in spirit. This energy kept his ideas before the eyes of the literary public.

In terms of theory, what takes us by surprise in considering the essays collected here as a group is their insistence on the importance of poetic identity. That is an insistence that one finds in none of the collections Blackmur made for himself. And it strikes me as an odd insistence, coming from one who accepted wholeheartedly Eliot's doctrine of the impersonality of art. Perhaps I have been reading Blackmur too long, supplicating his writing as he supplicated other texts. Perhaps I have been looking too hard to find what Denis Donoghue has called the "sublime Blackmur," teaching myself to read these difficult essays for enjoyment and reward, without ever fully realizing, until this moment, what I hope the reader of *Outsider at the Heart of Things* will also realize, that in reading Blackmur, you find yourself. That is surely the most valuable function of an outsider at the heart of things. By insisting that literature stand outside any discipline that would subordinate it, Blackmur places literature squarely at the heart of culture. By demanding that criticism—his own and that of others—remain aloof from systematization, Blackmur ensured continued intimacy in its judgments. Learning more about both criticism and literature through the elegant medium of Blackmur's mind, we gain new insight into our own hearts' delights. After stepping out of life nearly twenty-five years ago, Blackmur now lives again at the center of American literature.

Notes on the Criticism of Herbert Read

Experience provides few footholds in the upper reaches of the mind, and there the beginning of a new thought is always rash, always a leap in the dark. There is something giddy and supremely difficult in the movement; a sense of existence as vertiginous and as arbitrary as God. But there is also the balance—however momentary it is yet eternal—of achieved rightness: the solidity is recorded and the vapor blown away. Something is certain. Something is true.

Such is the occasional result of the application of reason and insight to experience and the problems the arrangement of its knowledge suggest. It is a metaphysic; it is dogma. It is faithful and courageous: acting as much on instinct and the knowledge of the heart as your ready-made savage—only with more order, more discipline.

This escape from confusion to order, from lively but loose and inconsequent appreciation to disciplined criticism is as important, and as difficult, among the arts as in politics or mathematics; and the main difference in the problems to be attacked is in their application. We deal in any case with creatures of the mind. Politics tends to control our sense of experience so as to shape it towards our chosen ends. The arts transfigure experience while it is yet alive: the arts tend to control our sense of the meaning of experience, to name the risen ghost. Control is law. And if there are laws governing our faculties in these moods they will be as valid and of the same intrinsic force as those governing the moods of science; they will be laws relating to our apprehension of the forms of knowledge. Laws may not ever control substance, but they will always regulate our sense of its order. And the absence or the denial of law, which for many reasons must often happen, only controls us without our consent and beyond our intelligence: as we are strangers in death's house and are moved there willy-nilly.

There are today certain critics of literature whose attitudes and whose aims bring them at least enough together to be classed as philosophical critics. These are men bent on discovering true forms for knowledge in the field of literature: but forms having relation to the whole body of experience. The excitement of discovering such forms is the supreme adventure of the mind, and I may best begin a brief discussion of one of these critics, Mr. Herbert Read, by saying that his work provokes an almost ubiquitous sense of just such an excitement.

II

At the outset of his one volume of collected essays, *Reason and Romanticism,* he shows himself very definitely as a metaphysical critic; and his main interest is in the assertion and criticism of dogma, in the creation and clarification of concepts.

He is a little rigid in his primary assertion. "The fear that dogmas infringe liberty should not deter us for a moment, for the final object of criticism is the criticism of dogma, and only those dogmas which express values above and beyond liberty need or will survive the assaults of the critical spirit."

This sentence is the text of his whole labour. The belief that there are dogmas "which express values above and beyond liberty" is at once a major note of faith and a commonplace of ordinary experience, and there is an imaginative identity between them. The act of faith has to do with the complete acceptance of the authority of reason where reason is relevant— namely, in that class of idea or dogma whose truth is so nearly coincident with the existence of the mind that without it there is no mind at all. For instance, the dogma that the ideas in the mind refer to their objects and may be true of them, and that these ideas are not themselves the objects; or for another example, the dogma that art is a translation of experience and not experience itself: these are acts of faith and commonplaces without which the mind could not exist.

In connection with this I quote another phrase from the same essay: "For an opinion or judgment is never uttered except as the offspring of a total attitude." He adds that this belief involves not merely the science of writing but also the philosophy of being.

Mr. Read is an example of what I should call if he himself had not somewhat spurned the phrase, the classical spirit. He is on the side of experience subjected in all its constituents to reason, to intelligence. He desiderates direct apprehension of the object by and in relation to the whole mind, but without that false vivification of emotionalised thought or conventionalised feeling. Some of the constituents of this direct apprehension are expressed in a sympathy for the new physics, the new mathematics, the new psychology. I do not mean that he thinks in mathematics or in terms of it, but that there is in his mind a feeling for the beauty and daring of this method of thinking. He would perhaps translate something of the miraculous equipoise of the quantum theory into the consideration of the arts and morals. He would at least bear it in mind; for the more things borne in mind at a given moment the better for the unity of thought. The idea of unity is necessary not only for a mental frame of things but also in order that experience itself should have a sense beyond its spectacle. And it may be that the most intelligent form of unity will be precisely of the kind that mathematical physics suggests: a perfect equilibration and interrelation of concepts consistent with a single logic or a total attitude.

The unity desired is that unity to which all experience can adhere. It is a unity which is a myth of time, space, and thought, which will remain essentially the same while its incidents change with the seasons of the imagination. It is the myth of the universal mind.

A universal mind is a mind which is intelligent to any data in which instructed: a mind of which the very structure is foreign to prejudice in the acquisition of experience, but which is full of courageous prejudice in assigning meaning and order to that experience. This may be an "ideal" mind; and perhaps it may not ever be the property of one body; perhaps it is the property of the sum of articulate minds at a given time, and is in the individual no more than a sense, a feeling, a deeply faithful attitude towards experience. It is the bottomless honesty, liable to many failures but yet the chief vehicle of success, of the wakened mind.

A mind of this order, or a mind trying to reach this order at all consciously, will have the remarkable double advantage of an agile versatility upon the basis of a positive attitude. We will find, in such a mind, a definite feeling for values, for facts, for reason, and for the concepts of all these. The errors of such a mind, *within its system, its order,* will lie in mistaken apprehension. The system itself will not be prone to correction but only to disposition among possible systems; and there is no immitigable cause why some one system might not be finally right. It is a question of limits, of skill, of imagination and insight. In a sense the mind is but the cumulation of all the attitudes of the body to the field of its experience; so that within the limits of this attitude, which are the furthest limits we know, the mind may have true knowledge, and may issue true judgment.

III

The essay on the nature of metaphysical poetry begins with a distinction between "the concrete character of the lyric" and the abstract character of metaphysical poetry. The distinction is made in the two words "perception" and "concept." A second distinction is made between emotional thought and the "mental process in which emotion is the product of thought." The two distinctions are related and upon them are based the important parts of the essay.

The content of metaphysical poetry will not necessarily have the emotional unity of the "lyric" but a unity of conception; it is the poetry of universals and is the arrangement of emotions understood and translated to symbols:—or I should say translated to that plane of the mind where the meaning of things is established symbolically. Mr. Read defines poetry on this plane as "the emotional apprehension of thought." The original thinking of the poem, that is, will be metaphysical in the ordinary sense; but that same thinking must be fused in poetry—"there exists at one and the same time abstract thought and feeling for the thought, expressed in poetry." To describe the process the following figure is employed. "We might represent thought and emotion as two separately revolving pulleys: one, emotion, has a revolution a thousand times greater than the other; but by the operation of a lever the two pulleys are connected, and immediately thought is accelerated to the speed or intensity of emotion." Poetry is that lever. With this last it is possible to agree; and in fact one can do little but recommend the reader to so much of essay as is concerned with the relation between thought and emotion. But to the other distinction there are perhaps certain exceptions; and exceptions exactly in the light of his own observations. He says, truly indeed, that Cavalcanti, Dante, and their company, were able by the metaphysic foundations of their poetry to make abstract concepts as near and real and personal to them as their loves for particular women. But when he implies, as I think—perhaps mistakenly—that he does, that the lyric which is based on a simple perception and has to do only with phenomena, will not have the peculiar merits of metaphysical poetry, I think he is wrong in principle. I mean to attack the opposition of perception and concept as Mr. Read appears to make it. I can see no reason why such poetry need be limited to concepts or submitted to the reign of universals—either mediaeval or platonic. Or put in another way, it may be paradoxically, it seems to me that one of the chief aptitudes of metaphysical poetry ought to be the seizure into the mind of simple perceptions *as* concepts. Such concepts could not be named or catalogued;

but I think they might be "universal" even so in a reasonably technical sense. Just as most of the experience we communicate trembles and clings around the words we use to express it and is alive without definition—so it may be in the realm of essence, which includes the realm of concepts. I think Mr. Read does very much of this same thing in his best poetry. There is a double quality in his verse, and in Donne, Chapman, and Dante—and in others more modern: I mean there is by turns, and some times at once, evidence that the mind has felt an abstract idea with all the shock and nervous devastation of a cold shower, and again evidence that the same mind has reversed its position and felt the immediate sensation with all the implacable clarity and logical force of the abstract idea. It will be remembered that Eliot distinguishes in his paper on Dante between feeling and emotion: to the end, as I interpreted it, that a feeling was particular and essential and an emotion general and conventional; so that, to be very valuable in poetry, an emotion had to be "felt" anew if it was old and habitual, by the force of the imagination, or else had to be constructed out of feelings. The process of such construction would depend wholly on the arrangement of feelings; would emerge but at no particular point. (I do not wish to accuse Mr. Eliot of saying all this; only that to my mind it seemed implicit in a certain paragraph.) In other words, although new conventions, or new concepts, would be continually established—at no time would any of them take nameable form; except of course such as were but modified shapes of those already named. The bulk of experience known is only hinted at in our articulate expression; and one frequent cause for failure in articulation is surely the attempt to force foreign material into our trivial collection of misfit frames—concepts and conventions already existing and limited. That this attempt is necessary cannot be denied; but I think it ought to be made more flexibly, from the point of view of a more flexible attitude:—to make the vague particular precise by aligning it with the existing concept rather than by identifying or merging it. Poetry as much as science ought never to obfuscate any chance for experience; ought rather to maintain itself ready for any experience. Limits will refer only to the *mode* of translation applied to that experience, not to the datum itself. The one type of convention which is immitigable is the principle of structure; which once known is final:—as in mathematics the details of structure are irrevocable because always possible. The structure of things and events in the mind is only less so; we have created that much completely: it is an *order*. What I have to quarrel with in Mr. Read's opposition of perception and concept is that he seems so to limit the order (or structure) of metaphysical poetry as to interfere with the substance. What he says might be true of all the metaphysical poetry ever written (which it is not) and yet predicate nothing for the future. I am content to insist that to the mind properly keyed, and with an appropriate intellectual habit, no item of experience *must* fall outside of metaphysical poetry. It is a question of aptitude and attitude. And I think Mr. Read and I have only said the same thing in a different way. He is more rigid and clear; I would also be rigid and I am afraid I have been vague beyond the necessities.

Near the end of his essay Mr. Read proposes an attitude towards and a task for metaphysical poetry. "Science and poetry have but one ideal, which is the satisfaction of the reason. Aesthetic satisfaction is not, as is too often assumed, the satisfaction of the senses (the senses are never satisfied), but *is* the satisfaction of the co-ordinating judgment of the intellect—in symmetry, in rhythm, and in all the properties of universal truth." He concludes the essay with these sentences. "Science has established a large number of 'phenomena'; but these phenomena remain discrete. They lack harmonic unity. Perhaps mathematical philosophy is working in one direction to establish this unity; metaphysical poetry, working in a different direction, can, without presumption, aim to the same end." Before commenting I should like to quote a definition of reason made in another place. "Reason should rather connote the widest evidence of the senses, and of all processes and instincts developed in the long history of man. It is the sum total of awareness ordained and ordered to some specific end or object of attention." This is religious; a dogma of the soul, to which one assents with the soul and by an act of faith. It is one of those dogmas beyond and above liberty of which Mr. Read speaks in his introductory essay; one of those essential dogmas of the mind which assert and define the capacity of the mind for knowledge:—whereby ordered knowledge, judged knowledge, alone is meant.

I think the ideal is plain and a good one; to which an unconditioned assent can be given by individuals. Whether interpretations of such an ideal fail to agree in concrete instances is not nearly so important as the authority of the ideal itself. Authorities, for the mind, are in the end always ideal and subject to choice and assent; the choice once made and the assent finally granted, a whole body of ideas, a whole skeleton of experience, issues complete. The question of the ideal named is provisioned by temperament as well as wisdom, and in defending the choice Mr. Read makes we are forced to summon in all those who agree with us in the character of their minds, in the leanings of their blood: we choose their company, and their collaboration, with the ideal. And perhaps we shall satisfy the reason, if but momentarily and on the run: the reason which none possesses wholly, but in which all assume joint title.

But, coming back to poetry; "the senses are never satisfied," says Mr. Read. Now it seems to me that a correction is in order here. So far as the senses in their connexion with the mind can be separated from the mind, we can say that the experience of the senses does not ever include a capacity for satisfaction. It is in their nature to be always alert, moving, ravenously in flux. Yet from a different but entirely respectable point of view, is not poetry of the kind we here consider, and by our own definition, an activity of the mind working through the senses? And is not just what we are aiming at a satisfaction of this total awareness which is reason in the medium of the senses? Is not the process of intuition (which is a considerable part of the *process* of metaphysical poetry) an act of the reason *in,* so to speak, the senses? The separation of the faculties is a fiction; and a good one only when employed to accent a *kind* of feeling:—so that I think Mr. Read's distinction appropriate only insofar as it distinguishes the senses, the reason, the whole mind in the act of seizing abstract objects from the mind directed on the concrete or perceptual. So we have returned to the distinction with which I presumed to quarrel first—between perception and the concept as they have to do with metaphysical poetry. I have every reason to recommend the discipline he proposes as relevant and salutary, and I have objected to this point so strongly only because my endorsement is otherwise so hearty.

The poetry which harmonises our abstract concepts, and dramatises our ideals, giving them vivid form in the imagination, so that the remotest reality attacks the senses with the insistence of the specious phantom—is metaphysical poetry. And I can think of nothing more interesting today in our own peculiar intellectual predicament; where the parts of the mind at all instructed are imaginatively at the ends of the earth; for nothing can so satisfy this predicament—which is really a hunger of the soul—as metaphysical poetry.

IV

The kinds of reality assault us, or seduce us, differently; though each is true in its own kind and for itself, the significance, the virtue peculiar to the meaning of each, is unique and in its class; and no where is there more confusion than in the classifications we commonly make among them. For instance, in literature, the idea of realism applies, for various critics, to such disparate works as *Main Street* and *King Lear, Bouvard and Pecuchet* and *Faust*—to choose pairs opposing each other for very different reasons. Now it is plain that the reality of art differs from that of science, not in its subject matter, which may be the same, but in the mode of feeling that subject. Ramon Fernandez insists that art qualifies, individualizes, where science schematizes and collects relations. Seizing the individual from the flux, the valid from the specious, is an act of imagination. Any qualification, any evaluation, whether in morals or art, is imaginative.

In the course of his essay on Charlotte and Emily Brontë, Mr. Read finds suddenly that he has referred to the "fundamental experience upon which she (Charlotte Brontë) built her whole conception of imaginative reality." He is worried lest he may have used a word, *imaginative,* to cloak a lack of thought; so he is compelled to define the word for literature specifically. "True imagination is a kind of logic; it is the capacity to deduce from the nature of an experienced reality, the nature of other unexperienced realities. And upon the depth and totality of the original experience will depend the reach and validity of the imaginative process. And if the process is kept to a quasi-logical rigidity, it may be observed that merely one kind of experience, sufficiently realized, will suffice for an almost unlimited progression of imaginative analogies: the one experience will be ballast enough to carry the author through any fictive evocation of feelings and actions."

It is possible to construct an idea of imagination, parallel to the one here expressed, equally logical but after a different fashion; an excellent idea to bear in mind while considering Mr. Read's own idea. On a psychological plane the imagination—that is, the flux of images in the consciousness—may be said to move logically, in that one feeling-state produces another; a process of which the best evidence is in ordinary day-dreaming. The use of the word logical is there possible because the connections between a sequence of images are, so far as we can observe, like those implied in a sequence of numbers; where the sequence 1, 2, 3, . . . implies infinity.

Mr. Read's idea of logic is here of course very far in intention from either mathematical infinity or day-dreaming; but it has an implicit relation with *both.* Not one, or either one, but both.

But the important part of Mr. Read's definition is the sentence: "And upon the depth and totality of the original experience will depend the reach and validity of the imaginative process." A statement insusceptible of proof except by example and common observation. T. S. Eliot says somewhere, speaking on the same matter, that a poet will do as well or better to write on an experience which he has never had than to limit himself to experience with which he is most familiar. It comes back to the notion that art understands its subject matter without losing itself in it, without any loss of its own identity. The difficulty is that the artist must have a disciplined aptitude for imagining the whole of an experience where his actual perception of it has been in the merest suggestion. Such a disciplined aptitude is gained only through a previously complete experience. It is as if we asserted that an hour of a man's life is a microcosm, is all life; which is what the church, in different terms, has always taught. And this suggests the idea that very few have the genius to understand even a moment; it takes a universal mind—spoken of elsewhere in these notes—a mind having been so thoroughly intelligent to one set of data, that it cannot help, logically, being equally intelligent to any other set with which it may become acquainted.

Different orders of mind will express appropriate realities, and if we insist that the artist's reality is imaginative in the way that we have been defining imaginative, it is not to injure the truth of that reality but rather to perfect it.

V

In the essay on Psycho-Analysis and Criticism Mr. Read notes down several instances whereby psychology is useful in the consideration of literature, where psychology helps to construct a basis for reasoning. It is hardly at all a question of applying the tests of psychology to finished works. The significance of a novel as psychological material is only the significance of its origins; its origins are the flux of the artist's mind, conscious and unconscious, the nature of the particular symbolic process he employs, etc. It has very little to do with the significance of the novel as literature, as a translation of reality to a plane more germane to the understanding. Psychology and literature are interested in two different sets of conventions. Literature employs the first to further the second, which is permissible. Psychology has sometimes judged the second in terms of the first, which is unwarrantable and irrelevant *in so far as it is literature* that is being judged.

As critics what we wish to do with psychology is very simple—to relate the body of its relevant doctrines to the appropriate body of critical ideas upon which we construct our concept of the *nature* of literature or art. And this will be, as you choose to look at it, a very large or a very small affair. The physiology of thought must underlie equally the concept of god and the idea of breakfast. But it is also true that the physiology of the two ideas has very little to do with the validity in a moral or intellectual sense of either. Keeping this in mind it will be seen that in most cases the relation between psychology and criticism will not be very precise or very direct; it will be rather by analogue and intuition. Sometimes the *possibility* of a relationship is more fertile than any actual relationship could be in producing thought.

A single exception on which Mr. Read lights is the problem of Classicism and Romanticism. He takes the theory of types as expounded by Jung—namely the classificaton of all minds into degrees of the Extravert and the Introvert—and suggests that if we substitute the terms of Jung a good part of the problem solves itself. "You will find, for example, that the romantic artist always expresses some function of the extraverted attitude, whilst the classic artist always expresses some function of the introverted attitude . . . He (the critic) must see the romantic and classic elements in literature as the natural expression of a biological opposition in human nature. It is not sufficient to treat the matter one way or the other as a question of intellectual fallacy; it is a question, for the individual, of natural necessity; and criticism must finally, for its general basis, resort to some criterion above the individual." Earlier in the essay is a passage from M. Andre Gide, from which I quote a part, as in a measure corrective of Mr. Read's own remarks. "The classic work of art relates the triumph of order and measure over an inner romanticism. And the wilder the riot to be tamed the more beautiful your work will be. If the thing is orderly in its inception, the work will be cold and without interest."

I do not see why, in the light of both quotations taken together, whatever the decision may be upon individuals, the judgment from any possible criterion would not be against the romantic, or extraverted work if we employ the type of perfect art as criterion, and surely there is none other even relevant, then only the "classic" or introverted artist could produce work to satisfy that criterion. A possibility exists that the artist's mind might be so complex, so properly variegated, as to have a talent for arranging the experiences of an extraverted character in the orderly forms of the "classic" mind; which is just what M. Gide says; and perhaps that is just the "type" of the artist's mind. The difficulty is to establish a balance, says Mr. Read, between the two types. The idea of balance is essentially classical; it is also a *conscious* idea. Insofar as an over-extraverted artist was aware of his condition, there would be a possibility for him *consciously* to remedy it. In which sense Romanticism is a fallacy, which may be judged, and corrected.

Another point brought up by Mr. Read. "The artist is initially by tendency a neurotic, but in becoming an artist he as it were escapes the ultimate fate of his tendency and through art finds his way back to reality . . . Psycho-analysis finds in art a system of symbols, representing a hidden reality, and by analysis it can testify to the purposive genuineness of the symbols; it can also testify to the faithfulness, the richness, and the range of the mind behind the symbol." With the first part of this quotation I agree, as a statement of fact. But the second part seems to me largely untrue, and I think Mr. Read himself partly disagrees with it. If the qualities of genuineness, faithfulness, etc., mentioned, are not demonstrable to "general critical principles" (Mr. Read's own phrase, and in this reference) then they are not true of the work as literature. The supplementary testimony of psycho-analysis *cannot* affect the work as literature, as we began by saying; it can only affect the validity or dubiety of origins. The qualities mentioned belong to another realm than psychoanalysis altogether—the realm of morals, which is imaginative.

VI

This same opposition of extraversion and introversion may be applied to the discussion of wit and humour. The use of new words for old things accents the advantage, the latent power of precision; in that words long used lose their original shape and accrue to themselves much irrelevant colour and connotation:—so when the outline is obliterated, the meaning also passes or loses altogether its denoting limits. Thus many thanks should be given to Mr. Read for the following sentences.

"Humour differs from wit in the degree of action implied; or, to express the same idea psychologically, in the degree of introversion or extraversion expressed. The more the comic spirit resorts to activity or accident to gain its point, the more it tends to humour; and, in the contrary direction, the more the comic spirit seeks to achieve its effect in abstract or intellectual play, the better it merits the term wit. This distinction implies a no-man's-land where the categories overlap; and as a matter of fact it is in such a no-man's-land that some of the best English comedies, such as Wycherly's *Country Wife* and *Plain Dealer,* have their peculiar existence."

To make this idea more useful I would set it by the side of an idea outlined in one of George Santayana's *Soliloquies.* Santayana suggests that everything in existence is comic when seen in its flux as it passes in immediacy, tragic in conception or perspective, and lyric in its essence considered simply for itself detached equally from the hurly burly of its surroundings and its position in the fatal order. Here the interest is in the comic; and we might say, I am not sure how truly, that the comic spirit will attempt to set its subject, seen just as it *appears,* against the ideal or general view involved, but without in any way merging or identifying it with that ideal. The criterion and the impulse of comedy is the same as the substance of tragedy; hence the essential gravity of good comedy.

VII

Because in the nature of things it is a problem less subject to the criticism of
fact, the problem of the relation between morals and art has been aggravated
more than any other. As in most questions based on prejudice and feeling
deep in the soul and on facts only skin-deep, the points usually raised are artificial and are settled only by the contest of vehemence and the spring-board
of fanaticism. Yet how simple the question really is, what an easy probity and
good will are required to envisage it. Art deciphers all sensible things and
grants them almost the only meaning they may ever have for man. To perform this task the artist must be possessed of a deep-lying honesty and a true
conception of the values of things. It is almost an instinct the buried presence
or absence of which makes or unmakes the artist; for only when this instinct
is at work can the sensible world take form or assume a unity. Aestheticism
withers the vital roots as much as another fanaticism, and the arguments of
the bigot of any school ignore the principle that art is meant to understand
rather than to display profitable examples to imitate.

"We no longer expect (or even condone)," says Mr. Read, "the direct
moral purpose in art, but, if we have any critical principles of adequate reach,
we demand a quality in the mind of the artist which works out, in the end, as
the moral equivalent of this purpose." And Mr. Read quotes from Henry
James: "There is one point at which the moral sense and the artistic sense lie
very near together; that is in the light of the very obvious truth that the
deepest quality of a work of art will always be the quality of the mind of the
producer." And if I may be forgiven for quoting from Charlotte Brontë
something where the rhetoric a little overwhelms the statement, the artist
has to do with "what throbs fast and full, though hidden, what the blood
rushes through, what is the unseen seat of life and the sentient target of
death."

Mr. Read finds, and I think justly, that Marcel Proust and James Joyce lack
such a sense of values. The lack is illustrated by the absence of orderly intelligence, of discipline, in the major works of these writers. He adds in
reference to Joyce "But Ulysses does not altogether lack a sense of moral
values; it is even dictated by such a sense. But it does lack a sense of intellectual progress . . . It is an art deficient in aspiration; an art of the used and rejected remnants of life, a mortuary art."

Perhaps, most simply, morals in art are but the demeanour of the soul
before life, and imply an intelligent conception, upon whatever prejudice, of
life such as to produce a unity either of action or form.

VIII

Mr. Read never leaves aside his principles; rather they enliven and direct his thought. Which I do not mean as something obvious or a custom on general practice. There is a rare interrelation, in these essays, between principle and object such that the process of applying a principle to a particular field sharpens, or clarifies the principle itself. As a result the reader is supplied with a weapon for war and an attitude for contemplation in a very general sense, no less than a solution for a particular problem. That is, Mr. Read sets up and *grounds* an activity in the mind which will persist as useful so long as the problem it was meant to meet remains awake and important. This is the difference, or the chief one, between personal thought which can at best come to wayward insight, and disciplined abstract thought—that the latter, having the qualities just indicated, is susceptible to both correction and collaboration. The question of originality need never appear, but only the question of rightness. That part of Mr. Read's thought as a critic or a philosopher which we discount or explain away as personal will not much diminish the whole thought; only pare it cleaner, only make it the more ready for examination and judgment.

Mr. Read would have us begin with a critical attitude, fixed in character, which involves an attitude towards life itself. The tool of this attitude is the intelligence, the reason (the "widest evidence of the senses")—in short, the universal mind. Besides this, there must be a number of dogmas, articles of faith, applying to every form of experience, but construed in respect to literature. That is a moral and imaginative theory setting up a criterion of life as definite as possible: this based upon science and with a gesture towards St. Thomas which remains unilluminating.

"That is the final test of criticism: that its methods are perfected in science, but that the motives are spontaneous, impulsive—aspects of courage, constancy, and devotion. The real act is instantaneous, and the course of history is directed not so much by foresight as by insight."

The ideal is so august!

Politikon

The Young Man at Loss

The more he thought of it the less difference it seemed to make whether the Presidential Election that confronted him was that of 1868 or 1928. Neither in the perspective of history nor in the unseen focus of the present, so far as he had them in mind, was his heart ever at stake. The young man was saddened; his own indifference palled him, and he tried every facility of sophistry to make his negation seem a choice and his abstention from the polls the only possible exertion, for him, of political power.

There were the candidates. And there was the party system. Barring class preference to a certain extent, party and candidate were interchangeable: the platforms of the two nominating conventions witnessed that. The better to appeal to *all* the voters, conflicts had been ironed out, minimized to the degree of insipidity; whereas for the individual voter (as distinct from *all* the voters) it had seemed more attractive, had the conflict been organized as such, so that principle set against principle—even, for lack of principle, emotion against emotion. If the young man took the platforms at their face value, instead of finding, as he had been taught, all his personal prejudices flowing deep in that of his hereditary party, then the face value was nil, there were no parties, and he was left with a choice only of personalities.

Personalities were abhorrent; they obscured the character of government, which deals with expressions of power and continues to a considerable extent in spite of the personalities it enthrones. Parties were perhaps equally abhorrent, and for a similar reason; but they had the merit, at their best, of expressing principle in the form of action. No matter that the form was diluted. But American parties in 1928 were obviously not at their best; they were, taken literally, aside from certain men they contained, a rigid kind of anarchy. They furnished the prospect Jefferson must have seen when he remarked that if he had to go to heaven in a party he had rather not go at all.

There were doubtless still, however lost in oratory and the main chance, two really distinct ways of managing government under the American constitution. The one was perhaps interested in the consolidation of national sovereignty, and tended to the creation of a ruling class having political responsibility. Such a party would be Socratic in method, materialistic in philosophy, and classical in temper. The other doctrine tended to represent government as having a minimum sovereignty of its own, and as subservient, by an instinctive paradox, to individuals and states in themselves sovereign; it had a horror of a ruling class and left responsibility vaguely in the hands of the people: it thus acted on insight, thought idealistically, and felt romantically. Hamilton and Jefferson were the exponents; the Republican and Democratic parties presumably their residuary legatees. But no stretch of sophistry or good will could so define those parties to-day: the voter could not express his opinion, nor seek political salvation in the medium of either party. If by an accident of training and the lethargy of custom the young man found himself inclining to the party of Hamilton, he could hardly feel more than the slightest spur of loyalty to the pale ghost he was able to raise in Hamilton's image. Honest politics was no field for necromancy. What was needed was hardly a resurrection; rather, a reincarnation in a new body, with a new technique, of the old principle. And that, as he looked about, seemed to the young man impossible. The parties were not divided on political principles, or even political passions. Half of the Republican senators he knew of, had again and again, especially in the realm of foreign affairs, cast votes and made speeches contrary to the essential instinct of Republican principle. LaFollette, Lodge, Hiram Johnson, Borah, were all Republicans; Thomas and David Walsh, Wagner, Glass, Robinson, were all Democrats. How could these honourable members do anything but confute one another, severally, mutually, individually? A party vote, the young man felt, was the worst possible vote, since the parties could not be defined: it could be intelligent only by accident. It helped him not at all that he was able to trace the confusion of party back almost to the beginning. And it was small comfort that a contemporary historian could observe that, "Jefferson and Hamilton typified the two eternal spirits that contend for the government of all that men do or say; the spirit that creates and the spirit that denies; the hope that man can raise himself through the ages a little nearer God, and the mocking doubt that human nature can ever change its ways. But between the two parties that they organized there was not the same difference. . . . Both had something to give their country, and both were equally guilty of appealing to men's fears and appetites."

He had heard lately of very little but the fears and appetites; the articulation of which was from the seat of patronage and jobbery, the insatiable appetite for office. The only sincere voter was perhaps the office-holder, or the friend of the office-holder. Every other party vote was a vote thrown away.

As the young man neither held nor had any connection with any one who wished to hold office, he very much regretted that he could not, on that ground, vote for either candidate. But he was not yet, he felt, altogether lost. He had heard of the independent vote: the incalculable vote that now and then elected a Democratic president (for when it went Republican it merely increased the Democratic minority). By definition, in a presidential election, such a vote seemed practically useless: an expression of spleen. It was more satisfactory to stay at home and curse. But that was perhaps unfair.

According to his benighted theory, only the essential principles of government could persist and require loyalty. As an independent voter he might from time to time sustain measures in which his theory was interested: he would even belong to a party which was to his choice—a party without a name, without class boundaries, and with varying numbers of adherents. Opportunity should be easy to seize.

The essential problem of government was to make every power responsible and every expression of energy relevant to the general interest. In a society such as the present, where a majority of the doctrines of responsibility were limited to real property and the rights of individuals in real property, while the most obvious expressions of energy flowed from the irresponsible rights vested in intangible property, the young man felt sure that the opportunity for action must fairly snatch at the statesman's throat. The legal structure of society must be so altered that the real interest of the proprietors lay in the real interest of those who consumed, at a cost, the energies in question. In short, government should exert the same control over industrial society as traditional law enabled it to exert over agricultural society—there being no radical difference in inherent rights. In other words, government should consider that all persons can be treated politically as one class; and as its members act with political effect, so are they subject to government entirely and without sovereignty in themselves. Hence the quality of leadership would be predetermined and almost insusceptible of contention: intelligence, and the habit to a superlative degree of considering persons and events in their political sense alone. All that such a leader would need to catch the independent vote would be a particular program relating to a particular set of problems. Senator LaFollette had had, the young man thought, in 1924, some of the right problems, but with the wrong solutions. It was undoubtedly the wrong solutions which brought him a popluar vote of five million; but it was the right problems, as well as his personal power, which brought him the electoral vote of Wisconsin.

These considerations helped the young man very little as to what he should do in November, 1928. They brought him, chiefly, and as a practical expedient, back to what he had begun by abhorring—the personalities of the two candidates. But how could he judge between them? How could he conceive that he had the right data on which,—granting what was most unlikely; that he had the judicial talent—, to form a judgment? Must he presume, for example, that it was a case in equity, and that they both came to the bar with clean hands? Or could he be permitted to mould the private motives and secret engagements that might influence them? How much of their energy of character, for example, was the mere stamina of adulation? A presidential candidate must always appear something of a turkey-cock. The newspapers and campaign managers took care of that. But did the candidate strut in private, or smirk solemnly at the reflection, as he must see it, of his mind on the shining face of the people, in the dim mirror of destiny? And if he wished to know, who could answer him? Not the voters, not the newspapers, not the candidate's friends. All those who ought to know had either illusions or were prejudiced. And the young man suspected that even the most independent spirit, unless caught altogether unawares, would rush into the haven of instinctive prejudice before answering. The honesty of the million was the prejudice of the individual; and the presidency depended on the former in particular terms of the latter. There was no alternative. A public figure was also a private myth.

So the young man undid his bundle of prejudice, his spirits cheapened as well as chastened at the low necessity. He knew in the beginning Smith would come off better than Hoover; no quantity of thought could aggravate his instinct to choice; but he felt he must sophisticate his natural notions enough to make them seem facts.

The names of Hoover and Smith were both catchwords or indices to whole systems of feeling. Hoover represented something easy; Smith something difficult. Why, the young man had no idea; but there it was, and it was very important. Analysis of a desultory and imaginative sort suggested that Hoover was most at home with major political problems and forces when he felt most loyal to his party, when most tangled, when doing least. Hoover had not a talent for real initiative or real control. Where the end was not only in sight but without alternative, and had nothing to do with conflicting ideals and jarring interests, Hoover might concentrate every force to that end. He had a talent for pursuing given courses against any obstacles. But nothing was made so clear in his speech of acceptance as that, politically, he had no mind of his own. His experience in action had always tended to definition; in action he was free, bound only by necessity. In political thought he was not free, so far as the young man could see, because he lacked altogether the talent for abstraction. He needed control more than most figures of his dimensions. His character requiring movement and direction, and such not being naturally supplied to him in political matters, he was easily deceived, accepted with a discouraging whole-heartedness the myths of his party, and was thus peculiarly at the mercy of all sorts of obscure and irresponsible leadership. That his intentions were all to the contrary, was very little help. His personal integrity acted almost viciously with respect to his political integrity; was, indeed, such as to destroy the possibility of the latter. Personal honesty, personal sincerity—and with these the greatest vigour of being—were not enough; political integrity was the gift of a different god, it was an art, it was perhaps the quality of style; and its elements must be universal rather than personal. Surely Hoover had no style. His acceptance speech was stodgy; it tried to be clear from Hoover's point of view, but it failed altogether to clarify the emotions of the voters to whom it was directed. He had not the gift for the definition either of feelings or of principles. Worse than that, if the newspaper reports were correct, he could not bear criticism and gave himself away completely when he insisted on taking personally the adversity of opinion and confusion of effect as well as the party adulation which his speeches caused. Such a defect in character could not be remedied. And in some way it seemed to the young man that this defect was analogous to another on the more practical side of politics. His nomination had been secured by a skillful machine. Rush Holland and half the old Ohio gang had collected the Southern delegates, and Vare had delivered Pennsylvania, contrary to the probable intentions of Mellon. Hoover saw the taint in these men after the nomination and tried to get rid of them. He tried to get rid of Moses. He suddenly wanted an evangelist's bandwaggon. The young man felt that Hoover could neither play the game nor keep free of it; the candidate was constantly awaking to suspicious realities, but after the alliance had been formed, after his political integrity had been marred. The candidate lacked style and might be expected in the future as in the present to be quite unconsciously under the control of very vulgar styles indeed. The very strength of the candidate's personal character made the substitution of political styles the more dangerous; style is the control of great energies. In short, the young man felt that while Hoover might be the most open man in the world, in politics he would have no candour at all. He was not a politician; and in the politician's guise he must always seem a little undependable, a little irresponsible, because he must be unconscious of what forces he expressed. He could not vote for Hoover.

The objections to Al Smith were very different; were constituted largely of praise of a politics to which he objected on traditional principle. It was very difficult at some moments, for the young man not to find himself persuaded to vote for Smith. He had nearly everything Hoover had not on the personal side. Nobody knew, besides those concerned, how much of his style depended on the assistance of Moskowitz and Proskauer; but it mattered very little: he had for the general public a personal and a political style. He had dignity and address and sincerity. He had political integrity. He was a politician and he thought politically. If elected, he could be depended on to act politically. He was allied to no class and to no body of interests; very little, in fact to any political party. His original talents were all the young man could ask for: the only question was one of limits. The ordinary objections to Smith could be, so far as the young man saw, set aside as negligible to the independent voter in this particular instance. It was the triumph, in essence, of the individual over circumstance. The governor's associations with Tammany seemed only to have taught him to deal with an existing power of dubious character to very respectable purposes. Certainly the connection had in no way injured his personal honesty, the proof of which lay in his control of a legislature majority normally of the opposition party. He was not a party statesman. His Catholicism, in so far as he adhered to it, would, in American politics, make him more liberal. Sufficient publicity had been given to the possible subversive force of the Church in American society to compel the candidate to unnecessary extremities to nullify that force, real or imagined, in which, of course, the candidate did not himself believe. His wetness had the effect of freeing him from a national hypocrisy; and in the instance of his election might have the additional positive effect of bringing what was often treated as a moral, even a religious problem, to some extent back where it now belonged by an accident of history—, in the realm of politics. Tammany, religion, and prohibition might lose or gain votes among the fanatics and party contenders; but the governor's relation to these questions could never injure him at all in the eye of the independent voter. Al Smith was a professional politican; his training, which had been long and within its limits

thorough, fitted him to the business of government; and the young man had
no doubt whatever that as president he would be responsible to the people in
their capacity as a political class and as none other.

If there had been nothing more to consider, the young man could have
forgotten his political principles, paid attention to the flux of political opinion and fact for their own sake alone, and gone to the polls in November
convinced of the integrity of his own political action in crossing the ballot for
Smith. But there was much else he could not forget. His vote, were it successful, would help elect a party whose integral existence and real purpose he
denied; would continue the vitiating practice, no matter who was elected, of
devoting months and years of office to artificial problems which had so little
real existence that their solution must needs be partisan. The young man had
nothing, politically, to vote for except for one form or another of waste. And
that was the real horror in the young man's mind. Smith, no more than
Hoover, offered no signs of having witnessed contemporary American
society and contemporary international society as a whole. Both, by the fate
of their character and the data their talents furnished, would resort to a
politics of expedience: which meant in the long run the politics of a party
bent on keeping itself in power.

Prohibition had been much talked of, and though it was by no means the
most important issue, yet since it had been so much agitated, the young man
considered the attitude of the major parties and their candidates might be a
fair test of political capacity. The Republicans, being allied with the Anti-
Saloon League, were nominally dry. Hoover had therefore raised the long
windy howl of nullification in answer to Smith's plea for states-rights. The
young man had no idea what if any was the solution to the prohibition question; but he felt sure that neither the constitution nor states-rights were
involved in any relevant attitude in a preliminary consideration. They represented the most artificial aspects, and resulted, as in the matter of a political
tariff, in a manufactured problem, which made dealing with the real problem
impossible. So far as prohibition was concerned, it had struck him in the face
again and again that the real question it raised was this: Was there any wisdom in attempting to compel the people of New York, Philadelphia,
Chicago, Boston, to obey against their general will any sort of law whatever?
Could the real interest ever exist apart from real practice? Part of the answer
lay in the admitted corruption in the cities named. The nature and use of law
was at stake, if anything; because of the evident intrusion of legal practice
into a field where it could not apply. Neither candidate nor party seemed
able to pass further than the manufactured problem, in this case or any other.

This left the people to settle the matter by instinct and practice, if at all, so that politics bore a curious resemblance to academic philosophy, where technical problems received all the discussion and were resettled daily, while the real problems were left untouched in the soul.

The answer to his original question remained the same; if the young man voted at all, it would be either for fun or to commit political suicide, and in either case to be at rest from political obligations forever. But he hoped Hoover would get licked—on the ground of style.

A Postscript to Politikon

Understanding, in politics, is of things past: a futile necromancy; the rest is faulty instinct and the prophecy of prejudice. Either way the honest eye can see little as certain, and much only as ominous. If we understand the tone of the people as of November sixth as this or that, it is very like speculation about life in heaven or hell—a sense of the heart's ideal or the heart's hate. And if we take our speculation for fact, as the heart demands, there is little chance that the event will support it.

These reflections apply to victory almost better than to defeat. No man on earth ought to be more cynical of human motive and popular will than Herbert Hoover: he won the farm states and broke the solid south; took strength from the myth of prosperity and wrecked an institution by the force of religious animosity. Now that the thirst for office is quenched and the sick interim till March fourth keeps his active hands from the experiment of power, Mr. Hoover might rest, not on the laurels but on the thorns of the last two months' campaign.

There was William Allen White canting and recanting, mostly the former—the same jovial editor who not many months before had mentioned a fat capon when the nomination was still open to reason. Mr. White had a reputation for honesty and conviction, was commonly held to be the spotless, if unmanicured, right hand of Republican liberalism.

Mr. White began naturally a procession whose next member was the Reverend John Roach Straton, who interpreted and avenged the will of God on earth. Dr. Straton was the herald of the Hoover angels and the prophet of the Hooverized women. Bishop Cannon came next to mind. This angular iron soul had been evidently an excellent magnet in the back counties of the Carolinas, Kentucky, Florida, Virginia, and Tennessee. Except in South Carolina the magnetism had been overwhelming. Nothing, nothing whatsoever, had been able to keep Mabel Walker Willebrandt below stairs; she had had to come out in the open, speak where the enemy could hear, and get her speeches printed in the newspapers. It was to be said in this lady's favour that she was engaged in perfecting a noble experiment.

But what, it might be wondered, could be said of the hot stuff Senator Moses sent south from the bulrushes of New Hampshire? Had he been fooling his public all these years? Had he been himself an unhappy warrior, and at hearts-blood with Mrs. Willebrandt or Senator Glass?

Senator Heflin, the Ku Klux Klan, the Fellowship Forum, the Anti-Saloon League, the Protestant Book House had all either received or spent money, or both. The Anti-Saloon League had even threatened the public life of any man who publicly threatened the side of God; they had labeled Senator Norris' political candour a blasphemy. The Protestant Book House had gone further still; had asserted that they intended to distribute ten million copies of a pamphlet containing the following sentences: "She (the Roman Catholic Church) teaches that Protestants are heretics and may be killed without sin. At least more than fifty million souls faithful to Jesus and the Bible have been slain by Roman Catholics down the centuries." Some of the methods used: "Poured boiling lead in ears and throat; tore out women's breasts with an iron hand machine; stuffed and blown up by powder." If Smith was elected, these would follow: "High-handed drunkenness, lawlessness, robbery, murder, rapine . . . Bull fights Sunday—gambling dens of vice and iniquity—blacks and whites all together as in New York's underworld—Hell loose." The spectacle was entertaining, and its prophecy, judged by the results outside Massachusetts, useful in terms of votes. Had the contrary been true, Republicans would have been vociferously on the side of the angels.

Mr. Hoover, facing the record of this part of the campaign and observing the geographical distribution of his majority in the backward rural districts and small towns in the East and South, might feel certain that the perfect silence he had preserved proved, on his part, a miraculous political sagacity. If all you wanted was office, a political campaign was hardly necessary; you had, in 1928, only to find a wet Catholic for an opponent. What were evidently the natural instincts of the American people would do half the job.

For the rest there remained the everlasting gospel of Charles Evans Hughes, who rose, by his custom, rather late in the campaign, to say a few, dignified, final words. Much as he had done for sixteen years past, he renewed the Republican patent on prosperity, and found, as he had found

Taft, himself, Harding, and Coolidge, the only possible promoter of that patent to be Herbert Hoover. Issues did not count; if only the Republican ticket were elected, and prosperity guaranteed, the issues would settle themselves; or better still, issues might wait for that impossible emergency, a democratic administration. The Republican spellbinders who preceded and followed Mr. Hughes, including Mr. Hoover, did their best to emulate him. So the hustings were littered with manna and nineteen million votes rolled up.

What a far cry it must seem to Mr. Hoover to remember his own phrase of last August: We shall use words to make clear our meaning, not to hide it. And in that phrase, and the failure to keep its intention firm, lies the success of the Republican party and the collapse of the political character of the American people *as a whole*.

The proof of this statement is in the nature of Governor Smith's defeat. Smith behaved from beginning to end as a politician should. Even when he attacked the maligners of his religion, the tone of his remarks was political. Even his mistakes, his misinterpretations, were political. And to his politics he added only his own personality; where Mr. Hoover, having no politics and in the public sense no personality, transformed himself into a myth of expert good will. Waterpower occurred to Governor Smith as a political problem: the disposition of natural resources and the responsible control of wealth. Mr. Hoover, avoiding definite statement, may be regarded as having seen the problem as one in engineering: how to develop the most power out of the resources; and could never see that his view did not tinge the political complexion of the question at all. Similarly with farm-relief, Governor Smith engaged himself to a political principle, while Mr. Hoover appeared to suggest that the matter required only a business conference. It was perhaps this lack of political feeling that made Mr. Hoover again and again fail at candour in comparison to the Governor; he had no innate principles to sound, could only depend on party-hooey and a confused readiness for action. With prohibition the contrast is even more illuminating. It was part of the constitution and a noble experiment for him; hence it ought not to be considered as anything but sacred. To Governor Smith's more political sense the nobility of an experiment is no warrant of its relevance, and its essential constitutionality would depend on its viability and its general fitness to the general Amercian principle.

The American people, by the election, denied in effect the American principle. They resorted, not by Mr. Hoover's will, to bigotry, snobbism, race-hatred, and a general confusion of mind. Mr. Hoover's victory can not be assigned to party principles for two reasons: the breach in the South and the increase of several millions more or less over the last popular vote. What, from this refuge, was lost sight of was the instinct for political action as opposed to business action. From this point of view one of the most curious things about the election is the largely urban character of Governor Smith's fifteen odd million votes as compared to Mr. Hoover's rural plurality. It is a fact that would seem both to accent and diminish the intelligence of the Democratic vote. The articulate (independent) supporters of Governor Smith were able to maintain a constant intelligence, while this was not the case with Mr. Hoover's.

Such speculations cannot be verified. But what seems incontestable is that the conscious part of Mr. Hoover's vote (what brought him victory) was directed largely against Smith, not for Hoover. It was essentially a nonpolitical vote; it found its origin in the myth of prosperity and the abominations of prejudice. In short, it may be contended that Mr. Hoover does not politically represent the nation; he represents its occasional emotions. The tone of American politics is at odds, for a term, with its soul.

The result is a possible disruption and realignment of the two major parties. It also appears to have deprived American public life of its finest exponent. And that is the saddest thing.

—So it is a little mournful for us—the cold corpse of the election. We have hustled the dead thing underground without ceremony and with the utmost dismay. What died, died so young we had never the time to feel love for it—only a passionate hope. Now if we cry *Vive le Roi!* as good men should, the long, dead ringing in our mind's ear is not the echo of salutation, but the tone of the American people at the polls.

T. S. Eliot

Writing on the Tudor translations of Seneca,[1] Mr. Eliot observes that "They represent the transformation of the older form of versification into the new—consequently the transformation of language and sensibility as well. Few things that can happen to a nation are more important than the invention of a new form of verse." A few phrases and he adds this sentence: "But the Elizabethan mind, far more than the contemporary mind in any country, grew and matured through its verse rather than through its prose." It is the possibilities and implications of these statements in connexion with Eliot's own verse that this essay wishes to rehearse; and it is the attitude of mind inherent in these statements that will be examined in the discussion of Eliot's criticism.

A change in sensibility is equivalent to a change in identity, a change in soul. Sensibility is the faculty, the working habit, of the intelligence, and as such is the stress and qualification of experience. To assert, as is here intended of T. S. Eliot, that one man's poetry and criticism have been instrumental in modifying sensibility is to ascribe a very great importance to that man. A statement so dogmatic, of a man still living and writing, cannot perhaps be supported by any argument save that one which is both indefensible and immitigable—the testimony of individual experience.

But other arguments occur, of which Mr. Eliot's own critical essays is the chief. For in Mr. Eliot's work the relation of poetry to criticism is not, as so often, perfunctory; rather the effect of the one is involved in the other; because the two forms of expression spring from the same experience, differently formulated and with different adjudications.

In another part of the essay on Seneca quoted above, Mr. Eliot remarks that the critic really interested in his subject will always attempt to connect everything past with all that is contemporary; seeing everything as present.

And this statement is only another indication of the attitude suggested in the first quotation; the attitude from which poetry and its criticism are free and autonomous. And that autonomy may be defined as covering the whole territory of the intelligence; so that it is the peculiar business of poetry and the other arts to qualify with form and order so much of experience as can be made intelligible. It is notable that such an attitude establishes what poetry is not, more than it determines what it shall be. It is not thought, nor theology, nor science. What it is depends on the courage and genius of the practitioner, and on the nature of the sensibility which he creates or with which he is supplied. And what he creates will be largely in the collaboration which he compels on the past and on the present.

Our age decries the intelligence as it works in terms of poetry; giving all that is intelligible to science; and in some quarters even tries to force poetry to become scientific. Much of what we feel is in terms of what we vaguely call "science," and being *felt* in that realm persists in vagueness. Any effort towards defining those feelings in poetry—by the use of new forms, new manipulations of substance—is exceedingly important, and, if only the effort can be removed from the isolation of the very few, should have the enormous consequence of an adequate sensibility. This labour is Mr. Eliot's business; and there is none other so wholly devoted to it.

Poetry is various, like religion or philosophy; and all three claim a lien on reality. In the same sense that the validity of a philosophy or of a religion depends on its bias, the validity of poetry depends on the degree in which it lacks bias. That is, insomuch as the object is made present and *felt* in itself, the bias becomes negligible and disappears. It is the object more than the interpretation that counts; or in other words, by stretching language a little, the object is the interpretation: whatever, being perceived, is worked to a frame of words is at once object and interpretation. Hence poetry is either true or aside from the possibility of truth in the dialectic kind; which position is more tenable is a matter of temperament for poet as well as critic. Poetry makes no assertions about its contents; it is them. At the other extreme, poetry may not deal with intuitions in their simplest state, as essences; because it would then deny itself, losing the principles of order and freedom. By elimination, I have been saying that poetry is moved by the intelligence primarily; and by the intelligence within limits which guarantee the greater freedom and variety, the more rigidly they have been defined. It may tend, however, towards either intuition or intellect, and will employ both faculties when grounded in or associated with intelligence. Mr. Eliot's poems are an extreme illustration of the presence of intelligence making good poetry, when if the accent had been shifted towards the pure tone of specious intuition or towards the abstract schemes of the intellect, the same poems would have been bad poetry.

The *Waste Land* being presumably Eliot's most "ambitious" engine it is the most profitable example to analyze from this point of view. This is the point of view of the intelligence as it seizes the qualities of things—and thus something of their being—into an order and form which themselves so persist by the laws of contrast and context as to be, somehow, durable and sensible apart from their origins and apart from the poet who conceived them.

However clear the "structure," the scaffolding of this poem may have been in Eliot's mind, for us it need be only a vague presence, felt now and then as a pressure, poise, or a pointing finger. Take for example the Tarot pack of cards, which contain in microcosm the cycle of any life. One word of their history is enough;[2] and the reader will be able to catch something of the references to the various cards as they appear later in the poem. He must know that they were themselves a scheme to cover *any* life. But Mr. Eliot cannot content himself or his readers with giving the inference of an intellect or a certainty of the intuition. He presents a seance, Madame Sosostris, famous clairvoyante, had a wicked pack of cards, had a bad cold, was nevertheless the wisest woman in Europe. Madame speaks; it is true she speaks much less than one would like to hear, but enough to place her, to make her tangible, give her position as a myth: and the myth exerts, to the retentive mind, influence over the "structure" of the whole poem. But Madame is more than that; she is a compound of fraud, insight, and chicanery; she is a person; she is a contrast with Tiresias, and at once upholds him.

On the other hand, Tiresias does not at all depend on Madame Sosostris, or any one else, for the peculiar power of his being; he is the freest and most central figure in the poem. He is chosen primarily because the nature of his experience (which has left him "throbbing between two lives") makes him supremely the factor of intelligence, of consummate qualitative sensibility. He is the hero most appropriate to the spirit entered among the perilous experiments of the soul; which is precisely the spirit of this poem. Consider his attributes: he has the most intimate knowledge, by private comparison, of male and female love; he is blind; and he is that soothsayer with the fullest sanction of the gods. A man also who has walked among the lowest of the dead.

Leaving aside the possiblity of Mr. Eliot himself being the dramatis persona, it is reasonable to assume the mask of Tiresias being present at the doings of these verses and, by his presence as much as his comments upon them, holding them together. In other words, for the purposes of the poem, Eliot and Tiresias are identified, and are the sensibility of the poem.

There is a further, but subsidiary, analogue between Tiresias, the Fisher King, The Hanged God, and the (supposedly) drowned king in the quotations from the *Tempest*. By subsidiary I mean loose and obscure; something vaguely, nevertheless surely, apprehended—like the foreknowledge of rain, or dawn. Mr. Eliot, if I am not mistaken, has intentionally not distinguished too clearly between the disabled king, the wasteland, and the questing knight or hero of the Grail Legends, which he employs here; conceiving these perhaps as but analogues of the one soul. That is, the more the relation of the poem to the legend is considered, the more it appears that Mr. Eliot has purposely confused its elements; so that it becomes a constant ceremony of life and death, a "vegetation ritual"[3] of the soul in an agony of consciousness. The order is simultaneous in intention and only successive because of the exigencies of language. There is a constant attempt to heap everything up into one image, one feeling, one emotion, and sometimes one word.[4] The five parts into which the poem is enumerated are each the same thing essentially but with differing concrete forms. And each section separately subdivides itself into contrasted celebrations of the one theme.

This theme may be stated severally. Like the Tarot cards the poem is a mirror for any life; only it is a life posed dramatically in a series of events, not merely indicated in a scheme, either of cards or theology. The main idea, or attitude, is that found in the legend of the Holy Grail and in the story of Adonis. In a moment, a day, a season, or a generation, there is death and resurrection—for the spirit, the body and the world about us; each cycle is complete. And each event in a given cycle implies its accompaniment: each looks into the heart of light: the silence. The terms or events of each is known multitudinously; many have been described in poetry and religion.

The story of the Grail, as Miss Weston expounds it in *From Ritual to Romance,* is simply such a cycle. There is a wasteland ruled by a debilitated and impotent king. Either the illness of the king wasted the land, or drought and war, in wasting the land, have affected the king. The young hero, by asking the right questions and performing the right deeds, becomes himself king and rejuvenates the land. The legend also involves the young hero in three sorts of initiation—into the origins of life, or sex, into the horrors of physical death, and into the consummation of life which is the knowledge of god. The king in certain forms of the legend is called the fisher king; fish and the act of fishing are very common and very ancient life-symbols, so that the fisher king would be king of life, and in fact a god. But a god who dies, replacing himself with a new outward form. Like Adonis and Attis, of whom his myth is a later version, in his life, death, and reincarnation he repeats the drama of daily life and of the secret soul. He is especially important as a death-myth; hence his great usefulness in poetry. Death is the punctuation, perspective, and most excellent background for life: it is the most variously applicable myth, whether of a god or of the land, that man has made to set off and illustrate his thoughts and behavior. It has the merit that under the right persuasion it is the most immediate and inexplicable or, on the other hand, the most objective and intelligible of all frames for the movement of things. As we are sentient, we are rank with death's weeds.

In Mr. Eliot's *Waste Land*, as in the original, the fisher king has considerable significance, influence, and direction. He is not so vivid nor so great a figure as Tiresias, but his presence is nevertheless constantly felt; though it is hard to say always where, since according to the appended note, all the men and women in the poem are one. There is a danger in too much precision in these matters; for example, any statement as to how much of the first half of Part V refers to Christ would be, without the author's corroboration, subject to error. Christ is only one of the slain gods, and all the slain gods are in some sense one. As has already been said, the order of this poem is simultaneous in everything except fact.

Enough ought, in a vague way, to have been given of the kind of use to which Mr. Eliot has put anthropology and literature. He has imported figures from history and legend, has borrowed, giving them a new significance, many remarkable lines from older poetry: not to make a picture of history or an outline of literature but to give point and form to an individual "experiment of the soul." A line of poetry or a figure from history is chosen to enforce again in a new context the whole area of feeling and experience to which it was, for those already familiar, the key. And proceeding a little the poem itself seizes a situation, is itself a key—to what, depends on the reader's knowledge and temper.

Keeping these considerations in mind and remembering the last phrase of the epigraph: "I wish to die," the *Waste Land* has as much of an explanation as a poem may require: which is not an explanation at all, but the appropriate group of facts and feelings existing in the plane of "thought" most nearly parallel to the plane of the poem. You can set up a sensibility for poetry, and you can create poetry as the object of sensibility, but you can explain neither: for both poetry and sensibility are residua of qualities—a field where comparison may establish only the contrasting, and analysis isolate the individual; as in that other field we call real life. The rest, our fiction that we understand one another and one another's poetry, is convention; and convention when it is alive—that is to say, intelligent—is the most daring form the imagination takes.

It is worth repeating that the conventions of Mr. Eliot's poetry are extremely intelligent. The *Waste Land* is neither allegory nor metaphysics in verse, nor anything at all but poetry. There is hardly an "idea" in the poem; there are feelings and images, and there is the peculiar emotion produced by these. Mr. Eliot once wrote of Henry James in this reference that he had a mind so fine that no *idea* could penetrate it, and he has recently, in a paper on Ezra Pound, spoken of images which combined a maximum of concreteness with an almost infinite suggestion. These two phrases indicate, perhaps, how the mind acts as it is intent on poetry: it may employ any other faculties you choose to mention in different realms, but it is roughly limited in poetry to something covered by these two phrases. It is the action, to repeat, of the intelligence as opposed to the intellect and to simple intuition.

It is not at all meant to imply that the intelligence will not deal with the abstract or the immediate as its material; only that it will always put the immediate in order and qualify the abstract. Further these categories are not, for the purposes of poetry, entirely distinct; things normally, that is typically, abstract may by their occasion be wholly intelligible: as the abstract ideas of love in Crashaw's *Hymn to St. Teresa,* or Keats' *Nightingale*. At the other pole, phenomena as immediate as sunshine may have the *quality* of an eternal idea. It depends wholly upon the occasion and how the data are seized. The richness of a poet is measured by the variety of the material he makes vividly intelligible; is measured in other words by the degree in which his sensibility covers the material that interests him, the degree in which the poetry is equivalent to the material.

Let us take five of Mr. Eliot's poems; examining them from this angle: *What the Thunder Said (Waste Land V*); *Gerontion; Hollow Men; Whispers of Immortality;* and *Prufrock,* these being as different from one another as Mr. Eliot's poems ever are.

The section of the *Waste Land* is in a way the easiest to handle because it is the most complicated; has the most nameable parts, each involving or overlapping the other. There is no "story" in any of Eliot's work and here less than anywhere. That is to say: nothing happens: a position, an emotion is defined, as has been said several times, in terms of certain images. Some images are facts about things, some are feelings; others are possibilities of fact or soul. All are such as can exist nowhere but in poetry, in the particular poem being read.

What The Thunder Said opens with a set of images and feelings suggested by the crucifixion of Christ in the minds of two of His disciples setting off for Emmaus on the day of the resurrection. Observe that neither Jesus, his death, or promised resurrection, is once mentioned as such. Instead there is "the torchlight red on sweaty faces" and "reverberation of thunders of spring over distant mountains." Which phrases are intended to convey much more appropriate feelings and to result much more in the right emotion than at this late day would a literal recounting of names and events; so that a general emotion, which is vague, is escaped and a particular group of feelings, which may prove "universal," is defined. Not the experience is individual, for that would be incommunicable, but the medium of experience.

Christ had not previously appeared in the poem; hence to place him there is an immediate alignment or merging of his figure with the motif of "the freeing of the waters,"[5] or resurrection of the dead land, hitherto treated variously in the poem. The notion being that the freeing of the waters is analogous to the resurrection of Christ, and having the advantage also of being the oldest recorded ritual of rebirth vegetation. Here again the images introduced are particular, are "imaginative"; as witness:

> "But sound of water over a rock
> Where the hermit-thrush sings in the pine trees
> Drip drop drip drop drop drop drop."

After this appears the ghost, "the third who walks always beside you, gliding wrapt in a brown mantle, hooded." This is at once Christ, and presumably, Tiresias, and the Hanged God.

Next there is set up the image of a possible feeling; namely that of the cycle of cities, which is powerful because of its context, and because it covers a great stretch of time. The city over the mountains—perhaps the image of all possible cities—

> "Cracks and reforms and bursts in the violet air
> Falling towers
> Jerusalem Athens Alexandria
> Vienna London
> Unreal."

Similarly "unreal" is the woman in the following interlude who

> "drew her long black hair out tight
> And fiddled whisper music on those strings."

The woman is the same as in the first and second sections; she has also a likeness to the woman in *La Figlia che Piange*.

The passage about the Cemetery Perilous and the Chapel Perilous is again in the mountains; and after the reference to the initiation by death we have a "damp gust bringing rain." In this passage more than any other in the poem, the uninstructed reader would be at a loss. The atmosphere is not presented, except by a previous knowledge of the ceremony; nor, without such knowledge, does the passage fit into the poem. That the first and last lines form transition or connecting links is not enough. The symbolic possibilities of the chapel, the wind, the bones, and the cock are too various: they should have been more definite, not perhaps in themselves but by reinforcement, with the purpose of making them intelligible.

The remainder of the poem proper is Mr. Eliot's version of the fable of what the thunder said. Here there are no difficulties of apprehension, nor of reference, nor of context; only the inherent difficulty of the most excellent poetry. There is a sureness, a necessity, in these lines that make them the extreme articulation of the deepest honesty. Stripped of the "poetry" there remain only three simple statements about human life. What one gives or surrenders can never be returned. The mind creates the world it knows and is prisoned in it. Order and control are the principles of wisdom, or happiness, or success. These are familiar enough observations to be quite pointless. But because they are felt and situated and made wholly intelligible concrete instances of themselves—they present a personality in the terrors of contact and of isolation, and, alternatively, are graced by the dream of communion.[6] The feelings aroused and suggested by these lines form individual emotions which do not possess names or bounding lines as do the terms "love" and "hate" for example; but they have a symbolic quality which is, though not in any frame of words, far more definite. This is a very desirable quality in poetry; because it is only poetry—and the other arts—that may possess it; and because it is a quality come by only after so great labor that but few poets have ever understood what a privilege might be taken.

For the rest, Mr. Eliot heaps up eleven lines—images, feelings—each having a bearing on the entire poem, each a key to the whole, each the sum and articulation of much experience. The lines are disjunct, disparate, dissociate; and gain their power so. I quote the three having the most obvious meaning without their context.

> "Shall I at least set my lands in order?
> London Bridge is falling down, falling down, falling down
> These fragments I have shored against my ruins."

It may occur to some that much of what has been said here has very little to do with Eliot's poems and even less with the criticism of them; and none is more confused on this matter than myself. What seems important is—to expose sufficient of the data and methods of these poems to suggest, since it is impossible to define, the new way of feeling, the new forms for the combination of feelings of which Mr. Eliot is the creator. It is the question of sensibility which was raised in Mr. Eliot's own words in the first paragraph of this paper; and I think no one will disagree with me as to its importance; for a sensiblity may be a general as well as a private possession. Its construction is not the work of an individual; only its particular application and tone. Its use requires that it be understood and in a sense duplicated or incorporated in other minds. However fatal the essential character of a given sensibility may be, it is largely accidental so far as the consciousness is concerned. It is therefore liable to many failures at either of two extremes. It may be too personal, meeting the material too much in the private mind of the poet; or it may not control the material, may not qualify it personally enough.

The poem *Gerontion* is an example of an exceedingly interesting poem that fails in the issue of sensibility. Obviously exciting and pungent, it is not wholly intelligible. It may be that it needs the sort of key supplied by the notes to the *Waste Land;* but I think rather the failure is due to the fact that the material of the poem is intractable in the form chosen. There seem to be opposed two themes upon which it is intended that the body of the poem shall be hung, shall be manifested. One theme is continued in the very complex feeling about old age and the idea of old age as these are a condition of the spirit or temperament rather than strictly of the body. The title means the power of oldness, its essence. And the epigraph, taken from *Measure for Measure,* reads,

> "Thou hast nor youth nor age
> But as it were an after dinner sleep
> Dreaming of both;"

and continues in the play thus:

> "for all thy blessed youth
> Becomes as aged, and doth beg the alms
> of palsied eld."

This contrasted theme is given in the lines:

> "In the juvescence of the year
> Came Christ the tiger

> In depraved May, dogwood and chestnut, flowering judas,
> To be eaten, to be divided, to be drunk
> Among whispers."

And these two themes are the poles of consciousness in the mind of the "old man" of the poem—the old man who is at once an individual, a person, and "gerontion" itself. It is a kind of Tiresias again; only without the "wrinkled, female breasts." I mean he is an ideal figure self-seen, self-dramatised in a series of rapid, penetrating statements. Separately each statement is intelligible and sums a position in the drama. But the material *between* the statements is not always forced into being; and several times the reader finds his breath inexplicably cut short. There is verisimilitude, there are simulacra, because of the intensity, the ferocity, with which each statement is made, because of the verbal finish, the blank-verse finality of the phrasing.

> "I that was near your heart was removed therefrom
> To lose beauty in terror, terror in inquisition.
> I have lost my passion: why should I need to keep it
> Since what is kept must be adulterated?"

But there is another labor which has not been accomplished; and it is a formal labor. The intellectual structure of the poem, the scheme which can be formularized, is simple and clear: but the dramatic body is crippled. Emotional unity is not accomplished, not articulated. There is a feeling of a buried unity, and of a struggle for an apparent unity; but there is no complete apparition. It is not enough for the poem to end with the phrase:

> "Tenants of the house,
> Thoughts of a dry brain in a dry season."

The phrase should previously have been made good to an extent which would have made it superfluous and at most a fitting rhetorical gesture. The poem was an experiment on form as well as content; and the difficulty was experimental also: to find a dramatic form equivalent to the intellectual. This was not secured; and the ultimately fragmentary, disjunct character of the poem is due to the fact that in the transitions—not the transitions between lines but those between feelings—there is several times a lapse in dramatic form: so that there is material without—so far as this is possible—any form at all. And this is a failure of sensibility at one of the extremes mentioned before: that it does not control the material, does not qualify it personally enough.

The Hollow Men, on the other hand, is a complete success: and if some might complain it would be at the other extreme—that the experience is tempered too much to the author's intimate feelings. Understanding, that is, in this case may depend on instinctive sympathy—a matter which cannot be argued. The form of this poem is Mr. Eliot's own just as much as that of *Gerontion* or the *Waste Land;* technically is much more his than the other poems—the parallel phrase, the delayed rhyme, and the assonance are combined in a vocabulary of which the tone (not the words) is unusual and in itself startling. The symbolism of the poem is within the words themselves and needs only inspection. Words are so deposited, so poised, as to accelerate themselves; and in the rhymes of the second section very remarkably echo or carry over the *meanings* of the words to which the rhymes revert.

The technical structure of the *Hollow Men* is in itself complete and firm enough to be a fertile vehicle, as a model structure, for other poems. The structure here exhausts its given subject, but is by its very success an implication of infinite possibilities. Although the structure cannot be explained in words, it can, like its special content, be seized by the acute intelligence and the attentive ear; it alters and adds to the general body of poetry.

For the rest, each short line is loaded, by the process of imagination behind the words, with the extreme of palpable content. The lines are solid and are meant, like the phrases of the mass, to carry an immitigable potency. They are put together as a ritual to be rehearsed over and again. They are dramatic: they are feelings in action—not ever to be misunderstood as comment or history but to be conceived as the naked experience of the soul.

This effect depends on the convention of the verse used as much as on the matter the convention covers. The development of sensibility does not involve adherence to any particular form of verse; neither free verse, nor blank verse, nor rhymed verse, nor bastard verse, nor any sort of verse except in the particular poem. But, variously, the forms of verse employed are much more definite, much more conventionalized than they appear. Aside from the technical interest of the poet in virtuosity or experiment, a "form" of verse such as the sonnet or the heroic couplet, has this interest: that it often suggests and sometimes imposes the form of the content, the nature of the feelings, the character of the thought that makes it a poem. It is obvious, for example, that the Elizabethan sonnet and the Elizabethan tragedy were modes and orders for things as well as words; and once we have learned what these modes are we know what to expect they will contain. They become a quality of experience; and a quality which may be introduced into and modify the presentation of any new experience in poetry. It is in this sense that a form of verse is most important as a convention. Conventions of this order may be learned and are the intimate structure of the process of thinking with the feelings; and these are the terms in which emotion is defined.

So with Mr. Eliot's poems. Both the metrical and the dramatic forms of the verse he uses are a distinct qualification of his material. The Sweeney poems and *Whispers of Immortality* provide, among other things, a finished mode of feeling in poetry: a mode which can be adapted to the purposes of other poets. Even truer is this of *The Hollow Men,* and the recent *Salutation.*

It is equally true that these modes of feeling are not of an immaculate conception, but are to be construed with already existing intelligence, that is with the body of literature. The quatrains of the Sweeney poems have a relation to work of Marvell, Donne,[7] Dryden. The feeling in them has also a relation to the modes of feeling in the later Marlowe, in Webster, Dante, and Shakespeare. Readers of the *Jew of Malta,* the *Duchess of Malfi,* and the *Divine Comedy* will catch the incidence of image and contrast, and will understand their reasons for existence, better than those not so acquainted. Likewise, Tudor and Jacobean poetry in general will explain the kind of exaggeration, the kind of rhetorical stress, the kind of ferocious humor, and above all the kind of self-dramatisation in these poems. Also the "tough reasonableness" in *Gerontion, Prufrock,* and certain of the shorter poems can be found in the *The Coy Mistress* or in the *Poetaster.* Mr. Eliot's essays on Johnson, Marlowe, Marvell, Dryden should be read in this connection. The surface world of Jonson, the farce of Marlowe, the seriousness of Marvell, and the wit of Dryden as these phrases have meaning in the context of Mr. Eliot's essays suggest the nature of what Mr. Eliot does in his own poems; and this essay confesses a considerable debt to the points Mr. Eliot has made about others.

Consider *The Coy Mistress* over against *The Cooking Egg* or *Conversation Galante.* There is a slightness of surface, almost a frivolousness of image and conceit, in the poems of both authors which seems hardly sufficient to hold the feeling under the surface in its place. Hence certain lines acquire a kind of breathless density of texture. The feeling is made final but utterly precarious. The form lends a gaiety and rush to the movement; the form accents, sets off the material as well as molds it. This is wit at the height of seriousness; and what requires emphasis here is that the wit more than the metre is the form.

This sort of observation might be continued interminably: to include the uses to which Mr. Eliot has put the Neo-Platonists, the scholastics, and the works of certain contemporaries in anthropology, biology, psychology, and philosophy: and to but one purpose. Namely, to show Mr. Eliot at the business of unifying his sensibility. The idea of a poet being, among other things, the idea of an intelligent mind working freely over its experience, then his chief labor aside from his actual verses will be in the unification of the parts of that experience. We are aware of more kinds of facts and of more sets within the kinds than any past age; and the responsible poet will be anxious to consolidate the sense of all these kinds from the point of view of the intelligence. The weight of all his knowledge will be present in his poetry as an autonomous whole.

It may seem a far cry, but consider *Whispers of Immortality,* a poem which betrays a very complex mind assiduously devoted to just this labor of unifying the sensibility as it plays over the whole body of knowledge. By being concerned exclusively with the object—in this case a group of feelings about the way we know things, to put it very generally—an originality is obtained quite different from and superior, in kind, to the type of originality found say in Whitman; where this is so much ignorance on the poet's part that the object is never received—is rather lost in the rush of circumstance and sensation. Originality may not have a strong obvious connection with sensibility or various knowledge; but the more a poet knows of what can be known, of what "everyone" knows, the more original he will be. It might be posed as a sort of statistical law that the degree of interesting originality will depend on the degree in which the object under prehension is common, familiar, isolated, and in the degree in which the poet is not "personally" concerned in the object. Except *as poet,* the poet need not be individual or original; nor, except *as poetry* need be his object. If the process, which is the poet, and the frame, which is the verse, combine on the object—then the result will be as original and as individual as necessary. If the process, the frame in words, or the object, were unique, the poem would be wayward and pure solipsism. And as such it would be unapprehensible; or if by luck apprehensible—so only as perverse ingenuity. Yet the poem, if it is a good one, such as this one, must be itself unique; and will be so always, provided only that the sensibility and the frame employed are appropriate. These are appropriate when they incorporate the quality of the object in the total sensibility; they are inappropriate when they supply the deficiencies of the intelligence with loose or specious invention. Logic will not measure propriety, for the love of novelties is instinctive and incommensurate. Measurement and definition, as in morals and other modes of taste, require the whole intelligence; when it is autonomous.

Returning to the Sweeney poems, it is notable that each of these poems is made of two or more sets of contrasted images which are combined so as to produce something that was in neither. The contrast is in each case sharp or violent, and is yet by the force of the poem no contrast at all but a kind of identification. This identification, this startling image, as it appears in the reader's mind, is the poem. It is almost a formula: Sweeney and Agamemnon; Grishkin and Donne—all "expert beyond experience." But not quite; what remains outside the formula is the necessity of making the opposition itself, as well as the images opposed, intelligible; and I do not think there are any more particular words for this principle than those which indicate its existence:

> "Donne, I suppose, was such another
> Who found no substitute for sense;
> To seize and clutch and penetrate,
> Expert beyond experience,
>
> He knew the anguish of the marrow
> The ague of the skeleton;
> No contact possible to flesh
> Allayed the fever of the bone."

These lines with their subsequent accompaniment—Grishkin of the Russian eye, the friendly bust, and the feline smell in a drawing room—are not literary criticism and sociological comment; are not a contrast of types, or an expression of morbid moral fervour. They are a train of facts, the passage of which stirs up certain feelings. Or if you like they are conceits about facts of observation. They are almost concepts of facts, of an intrinsically abstract condition issuing in gestures of an abstract, conceptual character. And those gestures witness the last line of the epigraph.

> "Senza tema d'infamia ti rispondo."

And it is their reverberation that we hear as *The Love Song of J. Alfred Prufrock*. We are given considerable information about the odds and ends that make up Prufrock's life, and when enough of them have been put together, Prufrock makes a gesture. And every gesture except the last has a curious self-mockery which is peculiarly Mr. Eliot's own; it is the hero cheering himself down, so to speak. The uneasiness of the extremely honest soul facing a highly dramatised version of its fate is bound to be either caught in the grand manner, or else beholds itself with a mockery which itself creates a world. The grand manner is not for us; except as a trick, a convention consciously distorted into something else. Our grand manner is the simple statement—such as the whole plaintive and delicate poem—*La Figlia che Piange;* or such as these lines from the *Hollow Men*:

> "Is it like this
> In death's other kingdom
> Waking alone
> At the hour when we are
> Trembling with tenderness
> Lips that would kiss
> Form prayers to broken stone."

or these, from the *Waste Land:*

> "My friend, blood shaking my heart,
> The awful daring of a moment's surrender
> Which an age of prudence can never retract."

But the "cynicism," the self-mockery of poems such as *Prufrock* is equally notable. It is more difficult to isolate for quotation; it is more in the tone, in the intense levity of feeling (a phrase Eliot once applied to Catullus) which suffuses the poem.

> I should have been a pair of ragged claws
> Scuttling across the floors of silent seas.
> _____
> I have measured out my life with coffee spoons;
> _____
> But though I have wept and fasted, wept and prayed,
> Though I have seen my head (grown slightly bald)
>   brought in upon a platter,
> I am no prophet—and here's no great matter;
> I have seen the moment of my greatness flicker,
> And I have seen the eternal Footman hold my coat,
>   and snicker,
> And in short, I was afraid.
> _____
> I grow old . . . . . I grow old . . . . .
> I shall wear the bottoms of my trousers rolled.

Almost immediately after which last comes, as a very lovely and astonishing surprise, the well-known passage about the mermaids. And half its loveliness depends, perhaps, upon its quality of surprise. The reality of each sort of verse is mutually guaranteed. To explain the success of either is difficult; but consider the associations of the words *footman* and *mermaids*.

These associations and others of a similar kind as they rise from the conceits, positions, and gestures with which Prufrock supplies us measure and define the emotion which is the poem. But this, like all the emotions of art, cannot be re-defined in logical language. When a work has a plot or revolves upon a particular series of events, and we describe these, we sometimes think we have defined the emotion. We have really been indicative only of numerous possible emotions, and have touched nothing of the substance of the work. The more articulate that substance is made, the more indefinable, except by analogy, it becomes; because it is the more individual, the more qualified—the more it is *itself*. If we persist in further definition, we are either killing death, or defining something different from the object, an abstract or schematic illustration of it.

T. S. Eliot occupies a position in the body of poetry which may be the more limited the more his relations are observed, but which will not be diminished, nor be well lost sight of. The taste for his poetry may be rare; but it is perennial—from moment to moment, and no doubt from age to age.

Great subtlety of feeling and bottomless honesty of insight into feeling may make a remarkable philosopher or a true poet, depending on the terms in which experience informs the intelligence. In either case, finally, the merit, and the truth, is the same. Mr. Eliot is a poet; and to describe his poetry there is a good phrase in Santayana. Life seen in immediacy is comedy, in perspective is tragedy, and in essence is lyric. The great feat and peculiar quality of these poems is that they present certain perspectives of the soul with the comic force of the immediate. That is why his levity is intense and his ritual dramatic.[8]

But this would not be true were it not for another quality which his poems possess—that is their astonishing purity—their extreme fidelity to poetry and intelligence. The reason Mr. Eliot leaves aside English poetry since the Restoration is that its inspiration is impure, and its movement in a sense undirected and wayward; its emotions not founded on the facts of feeling exclusively. The pure intelligence went, in letters, to the novel, and elsewhere to science.

That Mr. Eliot is a "classical" poet is obvious. The extraneous, the irrelevant—all the fraud of false invention—these are lacking. The limits have been designed perfectly for each poem, and are not the limits of competence but of mastery. And this is what limits Eliot himself; he has perhaps not risked failure enough. He has devised too economical a perfection, set himself limits too much within his means, and has never yet stretched his sensibility to its utmost. It is no apology for Eliot but an indictment of the times, to insist this may well be the fault of an age which leaves almost all the work to the poet. There is nothing rarer than the kind of intelligence to which Mr.

Eliot continually testifies, and its full testimony would require only a set of conventions already existing to hold the qualities of things when they were discovered. And that this age does not provide.

> "Faun's flesh is not to us,
> Nor the saint's vision;
> We have the press for wafer,
> The franchise for circumcision.

II

"Eriger en lois ses impressions personelles, c'est le grand effort d'un homme s'il est sincère."—So runs the epigraph to the first essay in *The Sacred Wood,* which is called, very much to our present purpose, *The Perfect Critic.* If we knew what laws were, and could all agree as to their validity and application—or if our ignorance of these matters was total—we might describe the criticism of Mr. Eliot or of any other critic in a paragraph, add a period of commendation, and have done. But our knowledge is only interrupted by our ignorance; and there is no set of theories more contentious, no principles existing in such wayward isolation, as those of literary criticism. With the result that if the critic does not jade us he supplies us with stimulation and excitement, with almost anything, surely, but criticism. We have thus a necessity beyond the criticism of literature; we are ramified entirely in the criticism of critics, and end, each of us, where we began—in kissing, without zest, our favourite cow. We can show no more contempt—or possibly, sympathy— for the judgment of others by repeating Mr. Beerbohm's Greek: "ὅστις τοῖα ἔχει ἐν ἡδονῇ ἔχει ἐν ἡδονῇ τοῖα"*—each looking, meanwhile, at his neighbor's heifer.

No critic but confesses somewhere to his impotence in this respect. Even Mr. Eliot can step aside in mid-career and say, with an air of incorrigible seriousness, "Our valuation of poetry, in short, depends upon several considerations, upon the permanent and upon the mutable and upon the transitory. When we try to isolate the essentially poetic, we bring our pursuit in the end to something insignificant; our standards vary with every poet whom we consider. All we can hope to do, in the attempt to introduce some order into our preferences, is to clarify our reasons for finding pleasure in the poetry that we like."

---

*"For people who like that sort of thing, that is the sort of thing they like."

Mr. Eliot indicates, I think, the only exit when four pages further in the same essay (that on Dryden) he discloses these observations. "The poet who attempts to achieve a play by the single force of the word provokes comparison, however strictly he confine himself to his capacity, with poets of other gifts. Corneille and Racine do not attain their triumphs by magnificence of this sort; they have concentration also, and, in the midst of their phrases, an undisturbed attention to the human soul as they knew it." This resolution consists in, or at least involves, the discovery of morals, of representative significance, in the values assignable to literature.

Art is ethics in action and has all the intimacy of going off to sleep; it is the action of the soul. . . . It is enough here to indicate the existence of this idea; later, it will furnish the main dish of this essay.

The quality which makes Mr. Eliot almost unique as a critic is the purity of his interest in literature as literature—as art autonomous and complete. Hence the power and penetration of his essays—the fullness of his point of view—the disciplined (and thus limited) fertility of his ideas. Personal taste has its influence but is not paramount. He may or may not suffer from a romantic morality; may adhere to the tory principle in politics, and the catholic regimen in religion—or be both whig and protestant: these connexions are private and cannot much prejudice his business as a critic. This separation of interests is accomplished not by an arbitrary divorce of forms but by an honest recognition of limits. Mr. Eliot's purity of interest has been the chief taint on his reputation as both critic and poet; the accusation of sterility is common, and his very lively, even agonised mind is sometimes described as without interest in human life; whereas the right indictment will be more technical, that his choice of limits has been a little imprudent, that his essential virtue has been pushed a little beyond the extreme verge of the appropriate. Literature the most sophisticated, the most refined is yet very much in the raw: the most intimate because the most controlled contact with the feelings and emotions other than those personal to us: and every critic, in his criticism, must needs save himself from submersion. Some critics make a new work of art; some are psychologists; some mystics; some politicians and reformers; a few philosophers and a few literary critics altogether. It is possible to write about art from all these attitudes, but only the last two produce anything properly called criticism; criticism, that is, without a vitiating bias away from the subject in hand. The bastard kinds of criticism can have only a morphological and statistical relation to literature: as the chemistry of ivory to a game of chess.

Mr. Eliot has chosen to be a critic, and because the profession is unpopular and scantily membered, has used much of his time in emphasizing the limits of his task and in setting up a handful of principles and definitions suitable to the control of his material. Naturally, everything depends on the general problem of order and structure. Most of his principles are ideals of form (and a given form is only a manifest order). Most of his definitions are of distinctions and contrasts of the modifications of form. The approach is invariably technical; I mean the matters touched on are always to some degree generalised characteristics of the work in hand. No overt attack is made on the "contents" of the work directly; the marvel and permanent value of the technical method is that, when prudently and fully applied, it results in a criticism which, if its implications are taken up, provides a real and often immaculate judgment on those "contents."

Possibly a special sense of the word "technique" is here understood. A little has already been said on the subject in the earlier section of this essay. The real technique of an art is in the modes of registering feelings and creating emotions. It is not the possession of any one man but the affect of a more or less general sensibility. We judge a poet by the intensity with which he expresses the emotions cognate to the sensibility of his time—not the intensity of the emotions, which matters only to the individual, but the intensity of the artistic process. Upon which M. Ramon Fernandez comments: "It follows that the parts of a work should not be related to such or such feeling of the author's, but to the totality of the work, and the work itself to the totality of works in its order." M. Fernandez further comments apropos Eliot's general ideas on the method of the poet that he has an "anxiety to transpose the integral experience of man," and a "conception of the hierarchy which brings him to instaurate what others suppress or forget."

Again if the following phrases taken from Eliot's paper on Marvell are considered as an attempt to expand the theory of technique, they will have an explicit force and use denied to them in their capacity as mere general observations. "We can say that wit is not erudition; it is something stifled by erudition, as in much of Milton. It is not cynicism, though it has a kind of toughness which may be confused with cynicism by the tender-minded. It is confused with erudition because it belongs to an educated mind, rich in generations of experience; and it is confused with cynicism because it implies a constant inspection and criticism of experience. It involves, probably, a recognition, implicit in the expression of every experience, of other kinds of experience which are possible."

Byron's misanthropy was part of his technique, not of his "philosophy" so far as we are concerned. Similarly with Keats' view of the Greeks, or Swinburne's sweets of sin. Swifts' Houyhnhnms and yahoos increase their savage contrast if they be considered as *technical* devices for the definition of emotion. In Shakespeare certain of the characters exist as part of the technique, as witness the character of Enobarbus and the astonishing emotion defined with it.

On another plane, such things as the dying speeches in Elizabethan drama, the nature-effects in poets such as Cowley or Gray or Rossetti, the five-o'clock feeling in Mr. Cummings and certain of the Georgians, are conventions of the most technically useful order. What cannot be conventional (and allow the appearance of poetry) are the feelings which warrant the particular instance of the convention: and this is the sure test for false feeling in poetry.

Another sort of technique lies in the state of language at a given time and the relation of language to the feelings which it denotes, and its equivalence or disproportion as the case may be to the sensibility then current. Hence Mr. Eliot observes the great importance of the fact that in the year 1600 French prose was already mature—an exact equivalence had been obtained; and that English prose was not. Montaigne could not have written in English, but he could be translated.

Music and painting are ordinarily free of "ideas" and the correlations of science; and these matters can be more firmly established in those arts by a little inspection. It is easy to see, to take an obvious example, how the paintings of G. F. Watts fail by the substitution of a literary idea for the original feeling which that artist never possessed. It is not so easy to compare Thackeray and Flaubert and to prove that Thackeray's lesser stature is due to an analogous failure. Flaubert possessed what Thackeray to a large extent did not, a fresh feeling for language—a feeling at once for the precision and the indefinable suggestive qualities of words as they take hold of and signify things. It is the difference between conventions which are inspired continuously and with each use by a particular experience, and conventions which, inspired only by themselves, become empty simulacra, effective only by the fictions of intercourse. Art is not much concerned with intercourse but with intelligence; it is prone to no exigence but that of the facts. And as for proof of the artist's allegiance we do not need Sterne's letters to show his agonised fidelity to his feelings, nor Eliot's essays to show his: we need only read the *Sentimental Journey* and the *Waste Land*.

It will be observed that technical criticism of this order has the merit of being altogether literary. Every other consideration is subordinated; and being subordinated takes its appropriate place. It does not cheapen intelligence, it heightens it, to limit its field; its penetration is increased by the diminution of opportunities. The essays on Jonson, Marlowe, Blake, and Dante in *The Sacred Wood* are essays of this order. But a full estimate of Marlowe is implied, is even logically articulated, by the consideration of the tone and tempo of the blank verse of *Tamburlaine* and *The Jew of Malta*. Some of this estimate is worked out by the introduction of a theory of ferocious farce and the isolation of the quality of feeling, the quality of distortion, belonging to it. Some of the estimate is left *in parvo,* for the imagination of the reader familiar with Marlowe to supply; but the imagination is directed.

Mr. Eliot's essays are never without point to present problems in style or feeling; which is always the mark of the good critic, that the past is alive as it bears on and exists in the present. This quality arises only from the critic whose angle is technical and whose material is the facts in the work under consideration as they are relevant to literature as such—and not the same facts or others contorted to the interests of psychology, philosophy, or general good will.

Mr. Eliot has made his choice as a literary critic out of what one supposes were the necessities of his mind, of any well ordered mind. Yet he is practically alone not only today but in the past. A fragment of Arnold, a little Coleridge, a little Dryden, and now and then Dr. Johnson; and of these perhaps only Dryden's interest was serene and whole. From the rest, as they are valuable in this connexion, we have less than fragments. Hence the occasional superstition that Mr. Eliot is essentially sterile, that he is out of touch with human life.

Mr. Francis Fergusson, in an essay published in the *American Caravan* dealing with Eliot's impersonal theory of art, makes the accusation very plain. I extract a few sentences from their context. "The only significant thing in the world for Mr. Eliot is art; no wonder his theme can only be the struggle to create, and that he presents the spectacle of a man doomed by sterility in the effort to make art out of art . . . The kernel of Mr. Eliot's position is his inability to see man the free being which is in all humanly significant figures . . . By preferring a literary tradition to a human background he has limited himself to form . . . Deprived of any sympathetic connecton with the world outside poetry, he can only mount to an ever narrower and less significant field of thought."

So far as this is metaphysics, one sits somewhat in another corner; so far as it describes Mr. Eliot, it is, if one thinks of it, impossible in a literal sense and can be a valid description only of intentions and emphases in Eliot's mind.

What is a "literary tradition" but a more definite "human background"? As for "man the free being" there are those who believe that the only freedom consists in the recognition of necessities and the submission to control. And so on. But the general indictment while not found true has yet a taint of cause. It is not, however, a cause which Mr. Fergusson mentions. It is this, that just as Eliot attacks literature proper from a technical angle, so the frame of his theory is made as abstract as possible; and for the same reason— to make it more supple, to make it *inherently* imply more. Interest in and connexion with human life were thereby increased, granted, even, something of the purity of the abstractions themselves.

Take for example the essay to which Mr. Fergusson resorts, *Tradition and the Individual Talent*. Eliot is a classicist and this essay is simply his own most abstract statement of the classical dogma. Recourse to dogma, when the dogma is critically held, is not the sign of an opinionated or sterile mind but of an active intelligence in need of a principle of control; it may be the sign of a realistic mind, a mind interested in its object without wishing to be lost in it, a mind which neither identifies the universe with the self nor the self with the universe, but distinguishes the difference as well as the connexion between the two.

The inveterate tightness and concision of the style of Mr. Eliot's essay make it almost necessary—to give the cogent strength of its argument—to quote it entire. I leave the burden of cogency to the individual reader and detach a few ideas and phrases.

If we approach a poet without prejudice for what is individual to him, "we shall often find that not only the best, but the most individual parts of his work may be those in which the dead poets, his ancestors, assert their immortality most vigorously." This suggests the sort of tradition in which Mr. Eliot is interested. But tradition "cannot be inherited, and if you want it you must obtain it by great labour." It involves the historical sense, which "compels a man to write not merely with his own generation in his bones, but with a feeling that the whole of the literature of Europe . . . has a simultaneous existence and composes a simultaneous order. This historical sense, which is a sense of the timeless as well as of the temporal and of the timeless and of the temporal together, is what makes a writer traditional. And it is at the same time what makes a writer most acutely conscious of his place in time, of his contemporaneity." The necessity that the poet "shall conform, that he shall cohere, is not one-sided . . . The existing monuments form an ideal order among themselves, which is modified by the introduction of the new (the really new) work of art among them . . . For order to persist after the supervention of novelty, the *whole* existing order must be, if ever so slighty, altered; and so the relations, proportions, values of each work of art toward the whole are readjusted; and this is conformity between the old and the new."

This is a fragmentary formulation of Mr. Eliot's dogma of tradition. The relation of the individual poet to such a tradition is a necessary result and concomitant of the attitude which recognizes the tradition. The main principle is this: that art demands more from the artist than the artist, *as an individual,* exacts from his art. Precisely as the poem is not able to exist aside from its connexion with other poetry, so the poet must continually surrender himself "as he is at the moment to something which is more valuable . . . The poet has, not a 'personality' to express, but a particular medium, which is only a medium and not a personality, in which impressions and experience combine in peculiar and unexpected ways. . . . It is not in his personal emotions, the emotions provoked by particular events in his life, that the poet is in any way remarkable or interesting. His particular emotions may be simple, or crude, or flat. The emotion in his poetry will be a very complex thing, but not with the complexity of the emotions of the people who have very complex or unusual emotions in life. . . . The business of the poet is not to find new emotions, but to use the ordinary ones and, in working them into poetry, to express feelings which are not in actual emotions at all. . . . Poetry is not a turning loose of emotion, but an escape from emotion; it is not the expression of personality, but an escape from personality." We wish to find expressions of "significant emotion, emotion which has its life in the poet and not in the history of the poet." And, if I may quote again what so many have quoted before me, "It is not the 'greatness,' the intensity, of the emotions, the components, but the intensity of the artistic process, the pressure, so to speak, under which the fusion takes place that counts. . . . The difference between art and the event is always absolute."

Properly understood, these dogmas of an impersonal and traditional art, far from divorcing poetry and life, ought rather permanently to establish the only connexion possible between them;—to make both in a high sense more germane to the mind—which is not, after all, except diminutively and pejoratively, either poetry or life.

Other dogmas might permit mature poetry; but these guarantee to exclude the immature. By the adoption of such dogmas we lose the right, as we think it, to a great deal of loose "self-expression." We lose our natural talent for being ravished by every stray emotion and each successive dream. But we permit ourselves these great losses only because of the depth and delicacy of our interest in emotions. We discover that our poetry has, because we do not leave it in the anarchy of the flux, a far more direct contact with the emotions, the passions, and the person. If we look for the individual in any field, we shall not find it in the specious alone; what is specious is undefined and incoherent, is inchoate by necessity; to discern the individual requires the presence of an order, a direction, something very like a purpose, to which all the data subscribe, and in relation to which they shall be defined. In art this is an emotional unity for the given work; and is an intellectual unity, a tradition, for the body of works of a given kind. The business of the critic will be to preserve contact between the emotional unity of the individual poem or picture and the sum of the tradition. Whatever dogmas he may erect will be in the interest of these unities. If he is a philosopher also, he will take the matter of "self-expression" for granted and apply himself to the consideration of art as a measure, a judgment, and a definition of experience.

When we wish to define we do not wish (except ideally) an exact tautology, an entire identity; because we should then possess a duplication which in the degree of its success would leave us where we began. We wish a symbol, some sort of general formulation of significance. An apple does not define an apple except to itself. In art, the definition of an apple would be an arrangement of its qualities as they entered our feelings and were adjusted by already existing feelings of a relevant variety: what we would end with would be an emotion about that apple, of a highly qualified order, which yet did not inhere in the apple itself. It would be an emotion appropriate to art and not to produce-dealers. But it is originally and incorrigibly important that the particular apple should have been directly felt, perceived; not as free sensation, which is impossible, nor with an idea of action, which is irrelevant, but for the sake of its being and meaning. The artist's native talent will be for perceiving apples, and everything else, in this way: his equipment will be the technique of transmuting his perceptions, his feelings, his experience, into a kind of objective emotion. Only in this sense does art create the object it contemplates. Otherwise, in every rhetoric of reality, the eye is on the object *in the beginning*. The object may not be recognisable as such when it comes out in a poem or a picture; but it will be something much more important—a definition, in the terms of art (of feeling and emotion) of that object. Your romanticist thinks he can do without objects, or use only strange objects, and persist on novelty alone. Or to the contrary he believes that the objects can take care of themselves, and his poem will be comfortable and prosperous if he stuffs it up with the first objects that come to hand. He is an adept at sensation and intuition but he knows nothing about experience. Your mature artist is distinguished by his adherence to experience, as it is conceived apart from its flux and seen in perspective and in order.

To quote the last sentences of Santayana's essay on Goethe's *Faust:* "To be miscellaneous, to be indefinite, to be unfinished, is essential to the romantic life. May we not say that it is essential to all life, in its immediacy; and that only in reference to what is not life—to objects, ideals and unanimities that cannot be experienced but may only be conceived—can life become rational and truly progressive? Herein we may see the radical and inalienable excellence of romanticism; its sincerity, freedom, richness, and infinity. Herein, too, we may see its limitations, in that it cannot fix or trust any of its ideals, and blindly believes the universe to be as wayward as itself, so that nature and art are always slipping through its fingers. It is obstinately empirical, and will never learn anything from experience."

Mr. Eliot's great deficiency, according to Mr. Fergusson, is that, in his present position, "he can only mount to an ever narrower and less significant field of thought." He is "deprived from any sympathetic connection with the world outside poetry." And so on. If the interpretation I have made of Mr. Eliot's dogmas is correct the essence of Fergusson's indictment is false. Those dogmas rather insist on a connexion, whether sympathetic or not, with the world, a connexion all the more thorough for refusing to be lost in it. Only by insisting that art is not life can art express life.

The difficulty with Mr. Eliot's ideas is that they have been put rather one-sidedly. We have on one side a rigid and exquisitely formulated doctrine of method. We have a thoroughly satisfactory conception of the artist as a responsible technician, and we are told what that technique should control. But the account is always on the technical aspect of the feelings and emotions of which art is made; very little is said directly as to standards for the judgment of these feelings and emotions. "Art-for-Art's sake" seems just around the corner, an awkward ghost. Awkward because inherently out of place in this regimen. But if the present examination of Mr. Eliot's dogmas bears up I think they will be found to have stated, though indirectly, a very satisfactory scheme of values. A talent for significant experience is a prime prerequisite for any intensity in the process of expression. The earlier part of this essay attempted to show Mr. Eliot as a poet putting his sensibility to work and to establish as a working principle for the construction and judgment of poetry the standard of the intelligence. Such a standard involves the closest possible contact with experience consonant with significance and value.

But what is important here is to show that Mr. Eliot's critical work in some measure sets up and supports such a standard. Mr. Eliot has, in other words—

and this is what some of his critics deny—aligned his method of technical approach with the moral world. The effort in this direction has been more articulated since than previous to the publication of *The Sacred Wood,* but it was to be found even in that volume, and especially in the essay on Massinger, which will be employed as my chief example. Only, a recent shift of emphasis makes the effort easier to distinguish.

The general position of a critic, or of any mind aware of its responsibilities, is liable to change when the impetus of thought is altered in mode or intensity; but the change, in an interested mind, will usually occur along a line the chart of which only ignorance prevents us from predicting. The past will not be destroyed nor its sense often confuted; but understood with a different emphasis, reproportioned by the present interest so as to maintain its usefulness. If the change turns out well we call it growth, and say it represents an increase in the depths of personality, the dimensions of sensibility.

In a review of Herbert Read's *Reason and Romanticism* and Ramon Fernandez' *Messages,* published in the *Criterion* for October, 1926, Mr. Eliot articulated such a change of position. The articulation was accomplished with an energy so dense that it has not yet been exhausted; when it began a controversy even now intermittently proceeding, which has included Fernandez, Middleton Murry, Father D'Arcy, Charles Mauron, and T. Sturge Moore as participants. The matter in dispute is the opposition of intelligence and intuition; Mr. Eliot being, as against Mr. Murry, on the side of the intelligence. Mr. Eliot makes these observations of his two authors. "Both, instead of taking for granted the place and function of literature—and therefore taking for granted a whole universe—are occupied with the inquiry into this function, and therefore with the inquiry into the whole moral world, fundamentally, with entities and values." Mr. Read and M. Fernandez reject in consequence of this inquiry the work of Marcel Proust because of *l'absence de l'élément moral chez Proust.* Such a judgment, says Mr. Eliot, is "a point of demarcation between a generation for whom the dissolution of value had in itself a positive value, and the generation for which the recognition of value is of utmost importance, a generation which is beginning to turn its attention to an athleticism, a *training,* of the soul as severe and ascetic as the training of the body of a runner." Mr. Eliot then proceeds to distinguish between the generation (our own) which accepts moral problems and that which accepted only aesthetic or economic or psychological problems," and outlines the divergent attitudes towards moral problems expressed by Mr. Read, the metaphysician, and M. Fernandez, the ontological psychologist. The reader is referred to the works of these gentlemen.

We are not here interested in Mr. Eliot's dialectic; but in the assertion of an ideal, and in the connexion of that ideal to the body of literary criticism. Hence the sentences quoted require an alignment, which the author does not make, with other essays. They require even an interpretation.

In an earlier essay on *The Function of Criticism* these sentences occur: "I do not deny that art may be affirmed to serve ends beyond itself; but art is not required to be aware of these ends, and indeed performs its function, whatever that may be, according to various theories of value, much better by indifference to them. Criticism, on the other hand, must always profess an end in view, which, roughly speaking, appears to be the elucidation of works of art and the correction of taste."

To perform the complete transition between the ideas embedded in these last sentences with the idea that this generation accepts moral (as opposed to *merely* aesthetic or psychological) problems would be to confront the chief dilemma of the artist and his critics with something very like a solution. This is the dilemma variously construed as the relation of art to morals, of the individual experience to the total judgment, of the content of art to that which in "reality" it does (or does not) represent. It is also the question of the possibility of a dogma of external authority which the artist is so much concerned, not to obey, but to discover; and to which he everlastingly feels the necessity to adhere—and feels, as a rule, and at this time, in vain.

Mr. Eliot is in the process of making such a transition and is perfectly competent to distinguish the implications of his own thought. But he does not always aid his readers, and of late he tends rather to take up his implications outside the field of literature altogether and lingers rather in religion. But it is not difficult to re-import such of his ideas as we need into the realm of our own interest.

Thus, the semblance of an attitude, at least a tentative solution for our dilemma, will be provided if we place beside the sentences quoted above a third set chosen from the essay on *Shakespeare and the Stoicism of Seneca*. Mr. Eliot is quarreling with Wyndham Lewis over that gentleman's statement that Chapman and Shakespeare are the only *thinkers* among the Elizabethan dramatists. "It is this general notion of 'thinking' that I would challenge. . . . We say, in a vague way, that Shakespeare, or Dante, or Lucretius, is a poet who thinks, and that Swinburne is a poet who does not think, even that Tennyson is a poet who does not think. But what we really mean is not a difference in quality of thought, but a difference in quality of emotion. The poet who 'thinks' is merely the poet who can express the emotional equivalent of thought. But he is not interested in the thought itself. We talk as if thought was precise and emotion was vague. In reality there is precise emotion and there is vague emotion. To express precise emotion requires as great intellectual power as to express precise thought." To which should be added this from the essay in *The Sacred Wood* on Dante: "Dante's is the most comprehensive, and the most *ordered* presentation of emotions that has ever been made."

The distinctions expressed in these quotations and the ideal of practice implied in the last, form Mr. Eliot's most important contribution to literary criticism. Their literal truth need not concern us—though I think it could be provisionally established. What is the pressing *energy* here is the attitude towards the nature of poetry and its responsibilities.

It is an attitude (and a theory emerging from the attitude) which attacks chiefly the facts about the contents of art in their most concrete terms. For Mr. Eliot this array of facts has evidently generalized itself, and has enabled him to perform judgment as to the *moral value* of Massinger's plays, for example; and to determine, besides, for his private self, precisely what constitutes moral value in a work of art.

If we examine the essay on Massinger with such of the ideas quoted above as can be kept in mind, we may be able to account for his judgment and discover the principles on which that judgment can be formulated.

Mr. Eliot's essay was evidently prompted by the appearance of a scholarly work on Massinger by Cruickshank. He quotes Mr. Cruickshank to the effect that Massinger was "typical of an age which had much culture, but which, without being exactly corrupt, lacked moral fibre," and announces this quotation as his text: and sets out to find cogent reasons, or facts, to support the judgment.

The facts which Mr. Eliot presents almost all have to do with the use and abuse of sensibility—with the modes of perception, the modes of expressing perception, and the substitution, by Massinger, of something other than his own perception.

"One of the surest tests," says Mr. Eliot, "is the way in which a poet borrows. Immature poets imitate; mature poets steal; bad poets deface what they take, and good poets make it into something better, or at least something different. The good poet welds his thefts into a whole of feeling which is unique, utterly different from that from which it was torn; the bad poet throws it into something which has no cohesion." Mr. Eliot then places next one another passages from Massinger and their "originals" in Shakespeare and Webster. As a result of these comparisons he finds cause for observations such as the following: "Massinger's is a general rhetorical question. Shakespeare's has a particular significance. . . . A condensation of meaning frequent in Shakespeare, but rare in Massinger . . . Massinger gives the general statement, Shakespeare the particular image . . . Massinger's phrase only the ghost of a metaphor." And so on. "We may conclude directly from these quotations," he adds "that Massinger's feeling for language had outstripped his feelings for things." The language of Middleton, Webster, Tourneur, had a talent "for combining, for fusing into a single phrase two or more diverse impressions" where "the metaphor identifies itself with what suggests it . . . With the end of Chapman, Middleton, Webster, Tourneur, Donne, we end a period when the intellect was immediately at the tips of the senses. Sensation became word and the word was sensation. . . . It is not that the word becomes less exact. The decay of the senses is not inconsistent with a greater sophistication of language. But every vital development in language is a development of feeling as well." Massinger's verse "is not a development based on, or resulting from, a new way of feeling. On the contrary, it seems to lead us away from feeling altogether." So much for the "technical" defects of Massinger.

The judgment of Massinger's moral fibre is similar, in fact the analogue is startling. "What may be considered corrupt or decadent in the morals of Massinger is not an alteration or diminution in morals; it is simply the disappearance of all the personal and real emotions which this morality supported and into which it introduced a kind of order. As soon as the emotions disappear the morality which ordered it appears hideous . . . Massinger dealt not with emotions so much as with the social abstractions of emotions, more generalized and therefore more quickly and easily interchangeable within the confines of a single action. He was not guided by direct communications through the nerves . . . Marlowe's and Jonson's comedies were a view of life; they were, as great literature is, the transformation of a personality into a personal work of art. Massinger is not simply a smaller personality; his personality hardly exists." . . . He "looked at life through the eyes of his predecessors, and only at manners through his own."

Comparisons are indeed odious. Consider Mr. Galsworthy's latest novels and plays under the light of these observations on Massinger. Compare the *language* of, say, Herman Melville and George Eliot with an eye to discovering in which was "the intellect immediately at the tips of the senses." Apply the whole judgment to the works of W. D. Howells, Edith Wharton, and Henry James: James increases his eminence, and his extraordinary moral value, precisely because his talent for *feeling* was so thoroughly developed; Howells and Mrs. Wharton sink just because their moral codes very often prohibited feeling, made whole classes of feeling impossible. In making these observations you have performed moral judgments on literature on grounds which are altogether literary. A great confusion is gotten rid of: in the arts, moral values have nothing to do with the preoccupations of professional moralists, but concern, first, a technique of language, and, second, a technique of feelings which combine in a sensibility adequate to a view of life.

Whether Mr. Eliot's observations on Massinger can be made to contain the basis of a general theory supplemental to and modifying the theory of tradition and the individual talent, is at least highly interesting. Consider again with these observations the quotations drawn from the essay on Shakespeare and the review of Read and Fernandez.

These notes present themselves very tentatively as being in the direction of such a general formulation. We are looking for a method of criticism whose approach shall be technical, in the terms and in the interests of literature as an art—not as an exercise in science of dialectic. Only so shall we be free of preoccupation and prejudices. Only so shall we reach the moral values where our last interest lies.

We take Mr. Eliot's distinction between thought and feeling in poetry. We do not wish "thought" in poetry unless it is "felt" thought, unless it is not thought at all. The distinction is arbitrary. Thought defines relationships as formulae and makes a shorthand, a blueprint of its subject matter. The definition of an emotion establishes a very different sort of unity; it places or condenses perceptions of quality (including the *quality* of thought) together so as to form an emotion. Both have a unity of structure. The structure of thought is schematic, dialectic; the structure of an emotion is felt; is organic. The definition of an emotion, for the purpose of art, will have nothing to do with its origins in the glands but will concern its origins in associated feelings. The definition will be in the most concrete form possible to the medium— which is language when words are taken as surds of feeling.

Interest does not lie in free sensations, but in perceptions, in feelings which have been adjusted to other feelings and made intelligible. Here the problem of representation enters. What is represented is not the object in physical reality (if any) but the object in the imagination; the object as conceived for its qualities and significance and moulded with other objects. The object is emotion. Emotions in art are never reproductions of experience, but its result. Art judges as well as expresses its field. Representation is ideal, but the ideal must have a "real" reference; must be *of* something.

Art is itself experience. It is a transmutation of ordinary experience into so precise a form that it cannot be redefined qualitatively, and must be understood as the expression of sensibility. An adequate sensibility conforms to ordinary experience as its only original source and inspiration. But it modifies ordinary experience in so far as it is conventional (that is, makes general symbols), traditional, and impersonal. Its particular experience is individual but the general frame is the result of collaboration. Emotions continue under the same names and specious characters, but the feelings which produce their specific instances are unique. Else convention substitutes for emotion instead of being filled by it. In poetry the difficulty is to maintain the proper equivalence between the feeling for words and the feeling for things; when the unity of emotion will take care of itself. To establish such an equivalence implies an adequate sensibility.

Sensibility makes all that is intelligible to it germane to the spirit in the sense that it forces its own terms on experience and gives it a concrete and significant character.

Moral value in art will then depend on the degree in which the sensibility is truly adequate to its subject, and, precisely as much, on the degree in which the sensibility is kept fully on the stretch to dispose the material which experience supplies to it. Poverty of experience would prohibit value and ensure sterility after the first initiation; as in love. Sensibility, if it is to establish values, must not exceed its object. Any object is appropriate to art provided only it is made sufficiently intelligible;—if it is sufficiently allied to the intelligence to give it actual significance. It is at this point that the "intensity of the artistic process" (as that is differentiated from the mere intensity of the emotional object) becomes important. Technical superiority when real, and directed upon the real world, involves moral judgment, because it establishes value upon the object of necessity.

The failure of ordinary systematic moralities could be shown in their inadequacy to judge such works as *King Lear;* where it is the intensity of the fusion of the emotional elements that makes the play intelligible and *valuable*. It follows, almost logically, that any conflict, any triumph, defeat, despair, or glory, any *movement* of man as he is conscious of himself and his environment is a good subject for art; and if that chosen movement is made intelligible in the terms of art it will possess moral value—because it represents the most concrete fate and character in an ideal form in itself ultimate.

The necessity for great art is the necessity of completeness, the necessity of a complete attitude towards life. A philosophy is not necessary—as in Shakespeare; or if present is not used as a philosophy—as in Dante. But a view of life cannot be absent. It will depend, in the artist, on the presence of real

emotions and a unity between them. Every system of morality is equally excellent, if it is alive; if all feelings are permitted under it, and all are valid to
their objects. Hence the necessity of change; for moralities are the briefest of
conventions and live at the ends of the nerves. The intellect must be kept
always "at the tips of the senses." In art all values are eternal for their time;
but the times are always way ahead of our thoughts.

There is no more a *stare decisis* in the judging of literature than in judgments
at law. The learned court is, presumably, in possession of all the facts as they
concern the case under consideration; whereby he is enabled to apply, and
modify to the necessity of the moment, the full body of precedent. He sees
the case before him as isolated, but to be fitted into an existing system. On
the other hand, the critic of literature, no matter how learned, is never in
possession of all the facts; because those facts are such as to be insusceptible to
a frame of logic—they concern the feelings and amount to an emotion, and
can be seized only by the imagination. The case exists not only isolated but in
a sense complete; and the problem is not to fit the case into the rigid body of
precedent, but to mould the already existing *corpus* and the individual case
together, so as to form a fluid and coherent whole. It is a problem of order.
Law tempers its formal excesses with mercy and sometimes wisdom; literary
criticism can only depend upon insight to govern the rigidities of its prejudice
and the extravagance of its rules. All this difficulty comes because the critic
cannot temporise, must aim at the facts, and is compelled to a thorough going
honesty. With *insight* the mode of first contact as well as last resort, and with
only the principles of taste between, how can a literary judgment be anything
but the most daring—the judgment of a soul? and the most uncertain—the
judgment of a moment? We should say, perhaps, that literature is its own
judge; that we have, as critics, only to recognize and to elucidate—to expose
and arrange; and so let judgment come of itself. But to judge is a necessity of
the spirit as it touches the world, and one of its finest triumphs; and it is better, surely, since judge we must, to educate and bring thoroughly into consciousness the insights with which we judge. This is to make a structure of the
intelligence, to acquaint our intuitions with their neighbors and predecessors,
and to instruct the absent minded intellect, on every occasion, in the doings
of the senses. We shall need great genius—that incalculable constant, intelligence at its utmost.

Hence most great criticism occurs in the mind of the artist at the moment
of creation; hence the merit of Mr. Eliot's remark to the effect that Shakespeare had a very extraordinary *critical* mind; and hence the fact that there is
almost no *permanent* judgment to be found in any criticism other than that em-

bedded in works of art. For the rest we can make statements about works of art and invent theories to govern their arrangement; and if the critic has a good eye for facts, has the insight to connect them, and the intellect to arrange them, the kind of judgment we desiderate will sometimes be implied, as it were, under his words, if not expressed. Something very like ideal law would then be articulate in the back of the mind; a kind of consensus of, and prophetic instinct for experience; so that if we could not make eternal judgments, still we should know what they would be like if they did appear.

Mr. Eliot is, on his own plane, very much such a critic; both as a practising poet and in his consideration of other poets. He has a very highly developed sense for the facts pertinent to his obligations. A talent which would have made him an admirable scholar, had he not also been given the rarer faculty for finding his facts taking their place in a scheme much more important than the sum of those facts. His most remarkable criticism and his most trivial equally carry that mysterious weight of authority—which is really only the weight of intelligence. For the intelligence is powerful just to the extent that it discerns and submits to the authority of facts, and its work is permanent just to the extent that it is able to conceive an authority beyond the facts and independent of the self. Such a discipline may prevent an easy tranquillity and certainly increases the labour of the mind; but it has this advantage, that the criticism which it produces assigns values other than the personal, and gives the reader, not the experience alone of sharing Mr. Eliot's experience of poetry, but of examining the poetry itself. The rarity of such a mind will be observed in the degree that the reader is familiar with English and American criticism. Mr. Eliot's labours in the restoration of interest in literature as opposed to the interest in opinion and psychology deserve all our gratitude; his work on the theory of literature requires all our collabration; his criticism of individual poets makes some of us feel that criticism had hardly ever been consistently written before.

It might be advanced as one of the strongest proofs of the validity of the doctrine that the whole of poetry has a simultaneous existence, that Mr. Eliot's criticism of the poetry of the sixteenth and seventeenth centuries has had a wide and notable influence on the poetry of many men writing today. It is also notable that with the exception of an early pamphlet and a late review on Ezra Pound, a paper on Henry James, and a note on Paul Valéry, Eliot has made nothing but the slightest remarks on contemporary poets. His investigations have been limited to the Elizabethans and their successors with the addition of Dante, Blake and Swinburne. Whenever this interest becomes modern it turns to the works of other critics, which is excellent; or to the ramifications of the Thomist movement and its analogues—and these are not, as M. Fernandez points out, quite to the spiritual baking of our generation. Yet, says Mr. Eliot himself, we criticize the past only in order to understand the present. So far, he has performed only half his job; he has made a present possible, but he has not yet put it in order.

To conclude this essentially random discussion with even a provisionally formal estimate of Eliot as a critic would be both unnecessary and ridiculous. It is easy, and no doubt irrelevant, to say that his chief contribution so far has been the nebula of doctrine around his concrete observations. To define those doctrines closely would be another matter, not as easy; there are the essays themselves. I have accented the purity of his interest in literature; I have perhaps distorted his idea of the definition of emotion and its imputation of value; I have made intelligence the criterion of possibly much more than there is warrant for in his assertion that he "is on the side of intelligence." All this because I feel that at the moment these are the most important parts of his work. Other views are possible. No attention, for example, has been given to the validity of his express judgments of *Hamlet,* of *The Jew of Malta,* etc., or of his implied judgment of Milton or of the nineteenth century. The skill of the technical approach, the insertion of the the small wedge, the fertility of the compressed observations, have hardly been indicated. Nor has much been said of the excessive limitations of this particular method of criticism—of which the most considerable is that through its use it is almost impossible to touch what we call the *content* of a work of art except by implication, or indirectly and as if with an ulterior purpose. Mr. Eliot has been very careful to *imply* as much as possible; the method is inexhaustible, and it represents an extreme mode of criticism, but it is not the only mode. The other extreme, from a similar point of view, is in the essays of Ramon Fernandez. Herbert Read occupies an intermediary position—where the attitude is accented more on the dogmatic side. The general point of view, which is what is important, is that of this generation—which accepts moral problems and judges them by the intelligence. A consultation of the various books of these gentlemen should present opportunities to the collaborator, even to the disciple, but none to the secretary.

NOTES

1. Seneca. His Tenne Tragedies Translated into English. Edited by Thomas Newton, anno 1581. With an Introduction by T. S. Eliot. London and New York, 1927. The reference is to pp. XLIX and L.

2. The Tarot cards are a considerable mystery—both as to their history and significance. They have a triple utility—as a game of chance, as a system of fortune telling among European gypsies, and as the outward index or set of emblems of a secret mystical philosophy of life. Mr. Eliot professes ignorance on these matters and uses them as a dramatic convenience. As to their interpretation, Mr. S. Foster Damon insists that all tests must be taken with a grain of salt. A complete pack consists of four suits and twenty-two trumps; and it is in the trumps only that the initiate finds the secret of life, the other cards being added for some games. The card that Mr. Eliot makes most use of is the twelfth trump, the hanged man, which is the most interesting of all. Mr. Damon says "He is hanging by one foot upside-down from a cross (his body forms a cross above a triangle); and this was a favorite symbolic posture of Blake's throughout his work." Mr. A. E. Waite in his *Pictorial Key to the Tarot* (London, 1911, p. 116), furnishes the following description: "The gallows from which he is suspended forms a Tau cross, while the figure—from the position of the legs—forms a fylfot cross. There is a nimbus about the head of the seeming martyr. It should be noted (1) that the tree of sacrifice is living wood, with leaves thereon; (2) that the face expresses deep enchantment; (3) that the figure, as a whole, suggests life in suspension, but life and not death." Mr. Eliot's Fool, trump zero. Those interested should consult Mr. Waite's book as above; Papus—*The Tarot of the Bohemians*, London, 1892, which has these italics on the title-page: *For the exclusive use of initiates; and Les Cartes à Jouer du XIV au XX siècle*, by d'Allemagne, Paris, 1906. All these have plentiful illustrations of the Tarot cards.

3. Objection has been made to the kind of anthropological material used in this poem, on the ground that the particular data employed is becoming rapidly "dated" and, therefore, vapid. To which the retort is that April will always be the cruelest month, Tiresias will always have forsuffered all; that the process of birth and life and death will always equip itself with ceremony and issue in symbol and ritual.

4. As for example in lines 20-30, the image of the shadow under the red rock, and its company of death's rhetoric. It may be added in this reference that during the Aurignacian culture, kings were always buried under red rock, or lacking rock, *red clay*. Red was a general life-symbol (for which gold was a later analogue); so that its association with death is especially significant. See G. Elliot Smith's book on gold.

5. See J. L. Weston: *Ritual and Romance*: Chapter on Freeing of the Waters.

6. Another translation or interpretation of this passage would put the matter thus. God speaks in the thunder: "Da Datta." And the rest is man's answer to God. The line "What have we given?" becomes then a rhetorical question, even an "irony." God is given back His thunder with vengeance.

7. On Eliot's relations to Donne there is an interesting paper, to which I am indebted for some part of the following observations, by George Williamson, called *The Talent of T. S Eliot*, and published in the *Sewanee Review*. I am unable to give the exact date.

8. Mr. Eliot published in two numbers of *The New Criterion* portions of a play, or Agon, which carry this quality further towards the serious farce than do any of his poems. One is reminded of the remarks in his essay on Marlowe relative to the vir-

tues of farce. Not much can be said of the fragments except that they are highly interesting and intensely amusing. The versification is colloquial, hard-boiled, and the lines issue from a definite formal paraphernalia very much Eliot's own. The verse construction is easy and simple to catch, and ought to fit a variety of subjects. But there is not yet enough to judge.

The Discipline of Humanism

Humanism is supposed to be a discipline, based upon the law of measure and upon the dualism of the higher and lower natures, which is applicable to every kind of life and art. "Humanism,"—says Norman Foerster— "Humanism does wish to emphasize discipline, whenever, as to-day, it needs to be emphasized. . . . It does desire to show that the quality of all life is higher or lower according as our power of vital restraint is exercised." Etc. I think it will be agreed that all fifteen contributors to *Humanism and America* subscribe to this intention; and I hope that none of them will object if some uninvited but willing guests cooperate with them a little in their great labor.

It is so great a labor—this matter of achieving a discipline—and they have so far begun it, that we should take from them our inspiration. Since, unfortunately, none of the Humanists achieves his discipline in terms of creative art, or in original work of any kind, all are bound at this time to express the notion of discipline only as it affects the work of others—in the criticism of the arts, philosophy, and science. So we must, on our part, observe what discipline they recognize and what lapses from it they condemn. Then we may understand, perhaps, something of that mysterious discipline they draw from the higher will, which gives them their courage to write and their ardor to judge.

The evidence in *Humanism and America*, and elsewhere so far as Humanism has dealt with contemporary art and thought, is peculiarly unsatisfactory; it is made up almost entirely of adverse criticism of various literary works. This adverse criticism never refers to the kind of discipline in which the artist is interested—the discipline of his subject-matter—but chiefly examines that discipline which involves a view of life or the apprehension of the higher will; discipline, that is, in which the artist need not be directly concerned at all. Humanism has refrained, and no doubt this is an admirable instance of vital restraint, from all that a novelist or poet would mean by literary criticism. There was nothing to compel it to refrain, so that it must have been an act of choice; either Humanism is not interested in the content of literature and the problems surrounding it, or it has had no experience therein. Or, positively, it may be that Humanism intends to deal, and has enabled itself to deal, only with that one significance of the arts which may be transformed to the Humanist ideal. Certainly the bundle of Humanist tracts contains many stray sentences which suggest as much. For instance, there is Mr. Foerster's comparative condemnation of Shakespeare (in his *American Criticism*) because he only mirrored life rather than Humanistically transcended it.

But before we decide among these interpretations,—thus deciding upon the actual value of the Humanist discipline as the standard of criticism—we should, lest haste mistake us for Humanists, examine in a general way some of the particular judgments the Humanists have made. Mr. Babbitt, Mr. P. E. More, and Mr. G. R. Elliott condemn modern literature wholesale on the grounds that it is naturistic, realistic, mechanistic, monistic, and romantic; also because it is pessimistic—a ground which I separate from the others, since I think it is only because the Humanists misunderstand themselves and their position that they include it. What these gentlemen mean by the application of such adjectives is this. In the novels and poems which they have scanned, certain ideas and certain points of view, some actually present in the works and others only present by strenuous implication, have struck them as violently antipathetic to their own scheme of an ordered society. A similar prejudice led Plato to banish the poets from his Republic; and I suspect that if they were "historically minded" enough, the Humanists would agree with Plato in his judgment of the Greek poets. And that would save our ears from many a gratuitously enobled reference to Sophocles.

This is the judgment of the masters. The younger men—younger at least in Humanism—are more naive; they risk immediate contact with particular persons and works. They apply with the disingenuous frenzy of converts the principles of their elders. Mr. Thompson sets up a theory of tragedy in the word admiration, a theory of which the chief virtue is that it lets Shakespeare in. He then proceeds to show that because of our naturalism we have lost the talent for admiration. Hence, every nine-pin topples almost before it stands: Hugo, Rostand, Ibsen, and O'Neill being prominent among the pins. In relation to O'Neill, Mr. Thompson makes the following remarks: "Indeed, he seems to find no man whom he can whole-heartedly admire; he can exalt no character or cause, and thus does not gain the elevation of heroic tragedy. He finds life a muddle; he leaves it a muddle." Mr. Thompson appears to believe that modern art fails because of its naturalism. "So long as he (an author) thinks of man as in no way superior to the outer world, or different from it, he is subject to the naturalistic point of view." To the Humanist, he says, it seems that art must deal with ethical laws. "Romantic art as recreation is a blessing to jaded mortals; and naturalistic art at its best is, within limits, penetrating. But to the Humanist it seems that both types of art have failed in dealing with ethical laws." Since Mr. Thompson has himself pointed out that O'Neill presents in his plays the problems of extreme conduct, it must be merely that he is not satisfied with O'Neill's philosophy, or lack of it. That is, the plays do not come to Humanist conclusions.

Mr. Shafer, in order to explain Dreiser's mind, uses ten pages to sneer at that novelist's life and loves. With the sneer to prompt him, he pronounces Roberta Alden, in *An Amercian Tragedy,* to be without importance. Her grievous distress, he observes, takes on "the same significance as the squirm-ing of an angle-worm, impaled by some mischievous boy—no less, but cerainly no more." As to the book as a whole, I select two sentences. "Eight hundred and forty pages devoted to the unconscionable prolongation of a mere sensational newspaper story! . . . The more successful he is, the more insignificant his work becomes." Between these two sentences appear reference to Aeschylus, Sophocles, and the Moral Law (the capitals are Mr. Shafer's). We observe that Mr. Shafer grants Dreiser neither his life, his sub-ject, his knowledge, nor his treatment of these; because he fails apparently to observe Mr. Shafer's Christian notion of the Greek Moral Law in Sophocles' plays.

In Mr. Clark's resumé of American fiction, I find this highly indicative hiatus. "Let us skip the realism of the later nineteenth century, most of which is essentially arid, and approach such a figure as Floyd Dell." Mr. Clark pro-poses to skip Stephen Crane, which is his own loss, although it amounts to skipping a heartbeat. Mr. Clark proposes to skip Henry James. That is, for the sake of making his Arcadian monstrosity perfect, he skips, as essentially arid, the most dignified, the most disciplined, and, I should have supposed, the most humanistic of American masters. Let us see where his skipping and hooping leads him. He is looking for a literature which, "ministering to all the higher needs of the mind and spirit, yields the greatest delight and the greatest beauty." The one example, presumably the best he knows, which he can bring himself to name, is Dorothy Canfield's able but vacuous novel, *The Brimming Cup.* There he finds the higher will, the will to refrain from experi-ence, with a vengeance; he also finds an "exalted human happiness." He does not find such matters in Hawthorne, Melville, and Mark Twain; they have not an Emersonian aspiration, and hence are evidently not the right sort of writers.

Thinking of T. S. Eliot, Mr. Chase releases the following summary of contemporary poetry. "Lovemaking carried on with an accompanying sense of its futility and ridiculousness, an acquaintance with art and poetry which serves only to confirm misgivings as to their relevancy for us to-day, the employment of religious symbols to arouse a poor mirthless mockery—in such experiences our young intellectuals find mirrored the age and body of their time." Mr. Chase's paper is called "Dionysus in Dismay," but I think it is Mr. Chase who is unconsciously dismayed; like many a more learned man, he is bluffing without knowing it. There are an insufferable patronizing reluctance, a dullness of sense, a weak weariness about his disapprovals, which are worse than the immoderate ecstasies of Babbitt, More, and Shafer. It is possible that Mr. Chase is really a humanitarian in villainous disguise, and not a Humanist at all.

Mr. Munson does not here cry Mahabharata, nor even Mahabracadabra; he is perforce restrained, since he is dealing with critics, to the less stringent vocables, Babbitt! More! and a final, ghostly Arnold! Arnold! . . . with perhaps as a prevalent echo of equivalence the faint "susurrus of his subjective hosannah." He combines misjudgment of and insight into certain living critics, and omits all mention of the half-dozen men, aside from T. S. Eliot, now actively engaged in literary criticism; he comes finally to the conclusion that nobody writes like Babbitt or More, and that we ought to write like Arnold. It is difficult to take a serious view of the sensibility of a man who asserts that, "Objectively considered, literature may be found to have been in decline, not just for a century and a half or just for six hundred years but almost from its classical sources and from the Scriptures of ancient lands." Mr. Munson is, just now, a freelance Humanist; I do not think a real one needs so great an antiquity to promote his arrogance.

The passages elected for quotation and comment should make plain in themselves what sort of discipline the Humanists exercise; every one of these gentlemen is working to suppress, to prohibit, to censor such literature as does not fulfill, in the most obvious manner, the notion of a Humanist society. And in view of the fact that all the evidence here collected of disciplined judgment is drawn from the essays of teachers of literature, there is something profoundly sad about Mr. Richard Lindley Brown, a last year's senior at Bowdoin. Mr. Brown believes that, "The teacher of literature may well turn out, in the end, to be the sole means by which society and literature can be raised from their present depression." The sadness lies not in the truth or falsity of his faith, but in its objects. There is no choice between natural depression and elevated vacuity.

Oh, well, we have seen the drama, the novel, and poetry go by the board, and if Mr. Mather has his way, and a hundred Humanists be born to-morrow, we shall see the arts of the future similarly disciplined before they bud; providing the Humanists have their way. But we may be grateful to the Humanists that by their own principles we may save ourselves. Not one of the judgments quoted above but can be set aside. Not one of these judgments stands firmly upon its own feet, not one of them is imposed through such a discipline as the Humanists profess. In fact, we may begin to imagine that the Humanists have no discipline at all, and further that they do not know what it is; that they are possessed by principles they have not the knowledge, the subtlety, the life, to apply to an actual instance. They have only the fanatic's notion of moderation, an arrogant love of the golden mean; and without moderation no principle can be intelligently acted upon: discipline becomes merely a pejorative, a censorship, or a prohibition.

II

Here is a deep distinction, among many, between Humanism as it is and Humanism as it intends to be. The contributors to *Humanism and America* undoubtedly intended to discipline their contemporaries. They have succeeded in writing as if they were censors, and the tone they have taken towards present-day literature is very similar to the tone of the supporters of prohibition, another example of *frein vital*. It is to be assumed that all authority, all light and truth, is on their side: Human nature must be as they assert: any difference is wishful thinking, or the illusion of disillusionment; and further, every difference must be ruled out, so that what remains will be right and healthy, even if what remains is infinitesimal.

Their writings, and their decorum, would have been very different had they honestly bent their attention to their chosen task. An intellectual discipline, their avowed instrument, is that routine of thought, that activity of mind, whose principles so fit the subject-matter in hand as to promote the clearest understanding, or the finest expression, as the case may be, of that subject-matter. An emotional discipline, likewise, is a routine or faculty for the delicate recognition or expression of feelings in oneself or elsewhere so as to permit their finest adjustment to the subject-matter. Great knowledge, obtained by great labor, of the particular subject is necessary. Discipline inherited or already acquired, is an aid to the particular discipline only when the necessary knowledge is had and the labor performed. Any application of discipline in general, or discipline *per se,* can result only in some form of censorship—a decidedly malicious and far from equivalent substitute. It is in a connection like this that T. S. Eliot's converse of the biblical maxim is most apt: "The spirit killeth; the letter giveth life."

Put the other way round, the censorship which I think the Humanists so often inadvertently substitute for discipline, is the judgment of a mind whose principles do not fit the subject matter, because they were gained *a priori,* accepted as a rigid body of arbitrary doctrine without reference to the material they were intended to judge. It is a distinction between form and formalism, between experience, raised in the individual mind to principle, and principle taken whole as a pill or purgative, and intended to substitute for experience. Principle of this second order, when absolute or formalized, is invariably heretical; that is it may not pronounce truth without vital exaggeration or distortion. So I think that the principles of Humanism, as they are held, cannot avoid heresy; they do not arise out of individuals—out of a sensibility, a civilization, a religion, or a generalized experience of any sort—but only from the notions of these. It is obvious that such principles prevent what they aim at: deep penetration and right judgment of human nature and art. They cannot penetrate, they cannot judge, because they must exist and move without data—that is without experience of the work in hand.

Another way of getting at this same difficulty between discipline and censorship is to import, fairly loosely, an analogue from the courts. In the common law there is a broad distinction between *malum in se* and *malum prohibitum,* the first being an act inherently evil, and the second an act evil only by custom or regulation. The law deals with these different kinds of evil differently—*malum prohibitum* being always subject to extenuation, *malum in se* only circumstantially or conditionally so. We see the Humanists listing the errors to which man is subject, confusing the two, and more often than not treating every activity of the mind and of the feelings which they disapprove as action evil in itself. A notorious example is their general, thorough-going condemnation of every act, thought, or desire which springs from or ends in expansive emotion. As Edmund Wilson has pointed out, the need of most of us to-day is just these expansive, easy emotions; and their condemnation is an excellent case of *malum prohibitum* assuming the absolutism of *malum in se.* It is a case which arises whenever the leaders of a community become afflicted with the legalistic spirit to the detriment of intimate knowledge and sympathy. In the instance of Humanism, such legislation and such judgment occur when the law of measure and the interpretation of the higher will, to mention two main tenets, are strictly applied to the contemporary scene in terms of some other scene. We have the condemnation of Dreiser, O'Neill, *et al.,* and the elevation of Dorothy Canfield, noted above, *and in the language and for the reasons there given.* And we have Babbitt making a gigantic and exhaustive study of nineteenth-century romanticism, and then proceeding to castigate what he calls the naturalism of the twentieth century as if the evil were in both cases the same. Though there may be a superficial resemblance in effect, the experience, the feelings, which produce it are very different. The fact is that the notion of measure and the law of higher will cannot be treated as if they were rules of conduct, rigid in nature and inevitable in application, but must, to be useful, be understood as convenient myths, susceptible only to such application as the times demand. As for Babbitt, we shall be able neither to understand nor to answer, if that be necessary, his judgment of modern literature, until he shows us something comparable in length, care, and knowledge to his study of Rousseau or Pascal. At present he but preaches, and his prophecies hang in the thin air of inspiration, a pretty pyrotechnic.

III

Now, I think it is worth inquiring how a movement so genial, so broad in inspiration and history, could come in our day to seem so arrogant and narrow. There are two explanations: first, the solitude in which that social creature, Humanism, is confined; and, second, the great stress it lays on its dualism as an active principle of practice.

When I say solitude, I should perhaps rather say isolation, in the vacuum of formalism, from every immediate perception of life and art; for such an isolation seems the positive condition of every effort witnessed by the Humanist symposium. Who could say, for example (except some weaker Humanist), that Mr. G. R. Elliott's essay, "The Pride of Modernity," has touched at any critical point the modern sensibility? Mr. Elliott would have us believe that among the failures of contemporary literature is its failure to express the tragedy of pride, its inability to conceive some driving force in human character approximate to the Greek *hubris.* One example of just such an expression, just such a conception of human nature, worked out with as much pity and terror and honesty as most of us can stand, is James Joyce's *Ulysses.* Ample proof of this is found in two recent essays, those of S. Foster Damon and Edmund Wilson; but that Stephen Dedalus is struck down by an overweening pride should catch an earnest reader by the throat. Another example could be shown in a four-volume novel of which I think Mr. Elliott must have heard, Ford Madox Ford's tetralogy about Tietjens. Something of the sort is at least implicitly present in the works of that anathema of Humanists, Dreiser, and in O'Neill's *Strange Interlude*. Mr. Elliott's difficulty is that he has taken his principles so much to heart that he can understand only Greek and Christian pride, which it appears that he and all Humanists who deal in pride have unwarrantably confused. Our ethos is neither Greek nor Christian, but only our ethics—and this is but the thinnest formal superficies to the feelings and events which are the substance of both life and letters.

Mr. Elliott is not alone in isolation; his brother symposiasts share it. What they have done, with the exceptions of T. S. Eliot and Bernard Bandler II, the first of whom undermines and the second modifies Humanism, is very simple and very stultifying. They have taken principles and notions once embodied in Greek civilization, medieval Christianity, and perhaps the French seventeenth century, and made them their own without embodying them in the civilization of to-day. They have conceived a tradition which cannot move except by imitating itself, by remaining static and duplicative—which is not, therefore, and cannot be, a living tradition at all, but merely the dry intellectual shell of once vivid sense. They have so equipped themselves with these principles and this tradition, that they can admire only Sophocles, Dante, and Racine—and them only in a Humanistic way; so that when they come to deal with moderns they cannot get inside them; they have no discipline in their minds suitable to their substance, but rather a foreign and irrelevant discipline which acts in the way of a censorship. It is not objected that they admire Racine, but that they condemn Dos Passos and Dreiser because they do not do what Racine did; and that they prevent themselves in advance from reading Dos Passos and Dreiser. And it is not only in dealing with their contemporaries that the Humanists fail. Mr. Babbitt's marvelously exhaustive condemnation of the Romantics succeeds largely because he separated what cannot be separated without decimation, the ideas from the poetry which alone permits the ideas to flourish.

What is there in American Humanism which seems to compel its isolation from its own subject matter? I think it is that higher will on which it claims to depend. Certainly, to an ordinary mind, the distinctive intonation with which all American Humanists rehearse their ritual is that of their dualism. It is an article of faith, this assertion of a higher will characteristic of man and foreign to the rest of creation; and since it is an article of faith, the mystery of its nature and workings may not be questioned; it requires merely the complete assent of the individual. By this higher will he is governed. With it as a standard he will criticize the arts and actions of this world. Both for the individual and for society as a whole it is the source of discipline and the end of life. Here is Mr. Babbitt's latest definition: "Positively one may define it as the higher immediacy that is known in relation to the lower immediacy—the merely temperamental man with his impressions and emotions and expansive desires—as a power of vital control (*frein vital*)."

This would take a good deal of consultation and stretching and private interpretation to make it intelligible; so we had better leave it what it is, a cathedral statement, and assume that it means something explicit. But there are some points that may be indicated as descriptive of any will superior to that will which expresses, in relation to mundane and passionate affairs, a continuous intense intention, the opposite extreme to velleity. Higher will has usually been associated with religion, and in Christian terms has been usually known as the will of God; its professors have been saints or mystics. We may notice that in the degree that the saints or mystics kept their knowledge of the will of God on good terms with their general body of doctrine and feeling, it was intelligible and useful; and to the contrary, that in the degree to which their notions escaped the terms of general faith, they became unintelligible excrescences. The Humanist is not a saint; and for him the higher will may be a useful hypothesis, whatever character he may assign it, only when it is connected at every point with the infinite area of common experience. Then it may suggest a sound poetic report of human nature in terms of the hypostatic imagination; and its character will vary with the flexibility of its object—the needs of man at the time. The great difficulty is to prevent that which the Humanist does not prevent but rather proclaims, the transformation of the higher will from sound myth into a set of principles. It has little to do with any type of conduct except as an ideal reference. Certainly it has nothing to do with either the making or meaning of art in general; and it cannot be a source of discipline upon worldly things of any kind. It is avowedly either supernatural or ideal. If it is ideal we must admit that every object and every life expresses it differently. If it is supernatural, it is a mystery we can only recognize, not expound. It is the last weapon we should use in criticism or judgment.

The Humanists themselves show us very clearly what happens when an inconstruable mystery is adopted as an instrument of understanding, order, and discipline. It promotes a dualism which is merely a kind of double life in the mind: such a double life as that of a shadow successfully pretending to substance. For that is what dualism does; it divides life into the material and spiritual, the lower and the higher wills, and asserts that the spiritual, the higher will, is the meaning of the material. The Humanists, lacking either the dogma of Christianity or the body of Greek civilization to infuse the spiritual with the nourishment of earth, tend to divorce their higher will from experience altogether, and to employ it, so divorced, as a standard by which to judge others' experience. It is no wonder, then, that what the humanists call their insight, their imagination, their discipline, should seem to us their arrogance, their blindness, and their censorious ignorance.

Psyche in the South

> There is a tireless and deafening vehemence about these sceptical prophets; it betrays the poor old human Psyche labouring desperately within them in the shipwreck of her native hopes, and refusing to die. Her sacrifice, she believes, will be her salvation, and she passionately identifies what remains to her with all she has lost and by an audacious falsehood persuades herself she has lost nothing.
>
> George Santayana.

> If I could not go to heaven but with a party, I would not go there at all.
>
> Thomas Jefferson (in 1789).

The most interesting period in a social revolution is neither in its beginning nor in its end but in that middle period which has the double character of prolonged depression and recurrent convulsion. Then counsel is divided, desperate, heroic, and blind. Single and relative goods are everywhere exaggerated until each seems, to those who suffer for the lack of it, the whole and absolute good of society. The heat of the distraught or of the violently depressed imagination makes every expedient seem a panacea. That is how it falls out in America today: interests are sharply divided and deeply confused; and the one thing that may be said of them all is that by choosing the wrong enemies, even more than by choosing the wrong friends, they seem bent on defeating themselves.

Society seems, in short, suddenly to have revealed its separate parts; and the sections which are exhibited are economic as well as political, cultural as well as social, nation-wide as well as provincial in the geographical sense, and are sometimes a confusion of all these. We have farmers who wish to secede from the nation, farmers who wish to control it, and still others who want national benefits without national responsibilities. Similarly the New England and Middle Atlantic states sometimes think themselves a section independent of the west and south; sometimes on the contrary, this section believes that national security can only be maintained by its own essentially irresponsible industrial supremacy. There are also, on the social and cultural side, a number of groups with equally pronounced sectional views. There are those who believe that art is only produced by home talent in specifically provincial localities: we have California, South Western, and Middle Western poets, as we used to have New England poets; and there are those who retreat upon New York as godhead. We have artists who insist on being proletarians and those who persist in being snobs. They are all of a piece in that they stand committed to the same principles, each exaggerating a different aspect and a different interpretation. The most impure, because the most unconsciously and vaguely held, form of sectionalism is that of the national government, where we see such contradictions as a monetary policy intended to restore foreign trade and an economic policy of which one effect is to destroy it. The purest form of sectionalism, if we except communism which is numerically weak and geographically scattered, and the banking interest which is undertaking the impurity of reform,—the purest form is the sectionalism of the new South. The South has a body of dogma, a program, and a collective voice of increasing volume, and it believes it has the double advantage of historic unity and a definite geographical extent.

Presented with such a view, of society sick with depression to the point of convulsions, the observer who wishes to provide himself with unacceptable alternatives (in order, of course, to make necessary the resumption of intelligence and common sense) is justified in predicting at worst the unreason of civil war or at best an impasse which could terminate only in coma. It is the purpose of this essay to take the pure and articulated Sectionalism of the South as a typical example and so to analyse it that its attitudes towards society—especially its attitudes towards politics and the arts—will be seen as mistaken and based on a false reading of the history that guaranteed it. So far as the essay argues successfully the rudiments of other forms of sectionalism will transpire by implication. For all heresies have this in common, by exaggerating their particular insights in the same way, they lead to the same sort of blindness. If, for example, we find the Southern agrarians objecting to the achieved fact of the highly centralised industrial community, we may expect to find the industrialists unwilling to accept their responsibility for the agrarian community over which the fact of centralisation enables them to exert power. Similarly, if we find that an antiquated notion of property persists in both communities, we should not be surprised that the abuses to which it is put are inimical to the interests of both: as when, in foreign trade (whether between sections or nations), a permanent money balance is held superior to the balance of complete exchange which alone can maintain the life of trade free of exploitation.

Mr. Donald Davidson's essay, "Sectionalism in America," which appeared in the The Hound & Horn for Summer 1933, brings the southern dogma to the point of crisis. The quest, the demand, the argument—and, I think, the pious prayer—which twelve southerners had made in their testament of 1930, I'll Take My Stand, demanded only the sympathy and indifferent good will the mind ought always to afford the labors of the uncertain human Psyche for order and peace and self-expression in the outward forms of her life. The southern Psyche knew and declared passionately what she wanted; and she knew even better and attacked bitterly what she did not want. She wanted an agrarian economy, a Jeffersonian politics, and an authoritative or aristocratic culture; and she wanted to be left alone. Her exaggeration of goods and distortion of evils seemed but the prompting of warm blood and the conviction of integrated character. This Psyche stood, by her own account, in desperate need, and was driven to cry out at length. To the outsider her plea was won on eloquence alone. Let her use victory as she could. If her rhetoric fell short of or overshot her target, she was free to find in experiment correction for her mistakes.

Three more years of depression have spoiled her freedom, and as a cure for despair, she has made her provisional wisdom absolute. Mr. Davidson's essay is an absolute heresy of the distracted imagination; and in retrospect, or I should say not in retrospect but in the change of time, the twelve essays and especially the dogmatic Statement of Principles that precede them in I'll Take My Stand, today make together the declaration of an heretical creed, of which the heresy is the more nearly absolute as it pretends to catholicity and asserts the right of tradition.

For the outsider even more than for the initiate, what is absolute and heretical has its attractiveness; the attractiveness of a chosen tragic fate, an envisaged death; but the tragedy is more ominous and instructive than it is admirable: its dead will not spring to life in the purged imagination. That is why the outsider—that most characteristic creature of our times—must needs resist the attraction with all his will, preferring even the bewildered tragedy of his isolation, since it is not absolute and therefore not ending in death, to the clearest and most passionately pursued extinction. But independence— even that of the outsider—is perilously held; the contingencies of life, both material and spiritual, are everywhere urgent, and nowhere more insistently than in the guise of human absolutisms—since they predict while they mar so many human fates. Criticism seems expedient, counsel advisable, and the temptation to set up a counter-absolutism (on the ground that like must be fought with like) almost insurmountable. To that temptation I hope only provisionally to succumb; as one succumbs to instinct only where knowledge is in abeyance.

The core or root of such a heresy is naturally sound and wise; it is at the periphery of action and perception that it is suicidally mistaken. It is sound to love history and to feel it concretely in your loins and houses; but it is misleading in action not constantly to remember that history is never done and that, above all the aspects of substance, it is the concrete which is most subject to change. It is sound to love tradition of all sorts and especially the traditions of manners and wisdom and human relationships; but traditions which are alive are thereby constantly being modified and given new shapes by the hands that transmit them. It is sound to love the land and to choose its tillage as the basis of a profound way of life, but like history and tradition, not our regard for the land but our social way of using it is subject to change.

Geographical Sectionalism was conceived in terms of an Industrial Revolution that had already occurred. What is called the rationalisation of the machine, mass production, straight-line production, has, in its intensification of the earlier, amounted to a second Industrial Revolution. It is the character of this second revolution that it does not recognise geographical barriers; its power, like that of the finance that directs it, is none the less real for being intangible; and the attempt to resist it along geographical lines is tantamount to unconditional surrender.

This surrender, it is true, and fortunately for the human spirit, is only ideologically secured; and we can see this elsewhere, how in spite of itself the severest absolutism nourishes the spirit unawares, for the spirit has its seat or instance in the body, and the body, not being reasonable, cannot be guilty of the heresies of reason. Communism and Humanism, for example, under the head of their single insights, attempt to hypothecate absolute disciplines which if effective would destroy the very spirit which animated them; whereas their actual success is only to impoverish spirit by restricting its field. As long as the body survives so, too, will the spirit. Unfortunately, ideologies are the prompts and guides of action, and action may destroy the body, and with it all else. The single interest, the single insight, are never enough; the clarity of vision they afford is specious, their rigidity deeply irrational. True insight and true reason are plastic like the life they are meant to sound and control, and their forms, if they are adequate, change with experience, and are always, like any form of understanding, on the edge of bewilderment. The problem is always, with any absolutism, to make it plastic again, to make it resume consciousness of its initially provisional, tentative character.

It is not by accident that the heresy of Sectionalism should resemble in its ideological structure both Humanism and Communism, and it is natural that, resembling, it should disagree with them. Absolutes are self-contained and if they spring from similar origins must seem, in their relative perfections, all the more deeply in conflict; since each from its special angle insists on handling the whole human field. The discipline of Humanism is moral and grounded in the will; the discipline of Communism rises sharply from a materialistic view of the class-struggle under Capitalism and cites the economic life as the measure of value. Both disciplines pretend, like good Catholics, that their special dogma implies the whole of life. So, in their own way, and somewhat more humanely, do the Sectionalists; they look for their source and day-spring in morals and economics to a limited field of local history (and if I exaggerate their position it is not only for the sake of the argument, but with great warrant in their writings): they look to the history of the South before the Civil War.

The avowed agrarian economic principles of the Sectionalist, at which the various essays in *I'll Take My Stand* intermittently arrive, already represent the confusion. They look to history for their principles, and are mistaken. If they looked further, into the social intent to which their historical principles were ancillary, and saw that they were really not principles at all, but tools, they could, seizing their history still intact, inspire new tools for the new conditions. As we clarify, by describing, the confusion into which the Sectionalist have fallen, the character of the new tools required may be indicated.

A purely agrarian society, such as the Sectionalists envisage for the South, might, by hypothesis, exist alongside of a purely industrial society. But America does not instance such an hypothesis. The real opposition does not contain the word industrial but is the opposition of Agrarian and Urban, and the problem is one in government before it is a problem in economics: the problem of setting up a responsible control of a political character over common interests.

The common interest is, in economics, security of life, and, to a varying extent, equitable distribution of wealth and the management of power as it takes the form of wealth. It is the problem of a society that has at once two characters—centralized and diffuse, urban and agrarian. It is no use assigning to either, even in its own territory, theoretic supremacy; then the one struggles to make the other responsible with the wrong tools, an effort which when successful results in injustice to both parties, sometimes the omnivorous injustice of civil war. We have, inherited and embedded in our state and national constitutions, legal and other institutions which sprang from a predominantly agrarian mode of life, and which were thus able to control, to make responsible, only a form of society which retained that characteristic predominance. The point is, that a surviving fragment of the old society, such as the South believes itself to be, cannot, without the predominance, use the old tools for its protection.

In the old days that the South remembers so well, the momentum of American society within its orbit was not initially great, nor for a long time; and therefore could not be conceived of as requiring a heavy governor to hold it steady. The technical requirements, too, were thought to be simple, and those who had power by land or other wealth, or who could seize it by a natural aptitude for oratory, were considered, no doubt justly, competent technicians. It was taken as granted that the extraordinary man, by whatever reason or in whatever degree, not only knew what the interests of society were but also knew how to secure them. Some, in theory, granted the same ability to the ordinary man by birthright. Without ever giving it deliberate form, American society felt it was a good principle to check knowledge with the weight of common ignorance.

And so long as the gap between the knowledge and the ignorance was not great the principle was sound. But today, when the gap is widened, it seems futile to delegate every two years a Congress of representative ignorance. American society is no longer simple and the good will of ignorance is not enough; for ignorance under the enormous pressure of complexity, becomes obstinate and insists on using the old tools. That is to say, because instinct thinks itself right because it is real, it refuses to see that the best it can do in new conditions is to tinker, and that it may by insisting on an ax where a wrench is in order wreck the dynamo altogether. The persistence of the ancient Southern view of State's Rights is a political example; the Scottsboro case a social example.

Both these views, political and social, flow, I think from the persistence of an antiquated concept of property. The evils of which the Sectionalists complain and the illusory character of the goods they envisage arise to a considerable extent from their dependence upon a concept which has the suicidal virtue of seeming fundamental when it is only instinctive. I refer particularly to that way—the American way and especially the Sectionalist way—of thinking about property, which insists that if you preserve the old rights of ownership you will have secured the new responsibilities, or put the other way round, if you preserve the old responsibilities you will have secured the new rights. Neither proposition is correct for the simple reason that the fundamental balance between rights and responsibilities has been altered; so that if you recognise that one has been changed you must recognise that the other has changed also. Failure of such recognition amounts to abdication of control.

The specific change which escapes the attention of the Sectionalist is the change in what, politically, should be regarded as private and what public property; what changes have taken place, that is, in the public and private aspects of all property. When the character of society was diffuse and agrarian the character of property was concrete and control could be most responsibly vested in individual ownership. Now that society is enormously more centralised or complex, property tends to assume abstract forms and to require a more public control in order to secure the same degree of responsibility envisaged under the old society.

Since our society preserves as much as it can of the theories of the old society, we now see the concept of property breeding incompetence and irresponsibility everywhere in its field. The need is certainly not to abolish property or to vest it wholly in the state, but only to construct a more adequate concept of it. The power of property at the present time remains the power of expropriation—as Proudhon said, theft. That is what the agrarians the country over are really complaining of, that while they are sometimes left the name they are being deprived of the wealth of their property. This is because the character of the most important kinds of property—the kinds which control the others—has changed.

When our concept of property was set up, even in the late form it takes in our Constitution and in the Common Law, the important kinds of property were either land itself or were based on the land and were in the terms of the institution responsibly held. Such property involved rights to be defended, and protected by the state from public encroachment as well as from private trespass, so long as the responsibility was maintained. Nor was such property in any socially dangerous degree theft during the greater part of the century; the gospel and the fact of free lands both breached (speculation, greed, and exhaustion rediminished the rigor of responsibility) and made its sources at that time insignificant. In short, the spread of property was great and the conditions of society—its unrestricted movement westward, for example— facilitated its greater spread. Furthermore, and far more important, so long as property was predominantly in land, control—both of use and earning—was comparatively synonymous with title. Thus property was seen as a right with a genuinely social character, and the duties implicit in the right were largely observed as a matter of course within the terms of the concept under which it was held. The essential thing is: these terms were enough, not only to control the tenure of land, but also to make society stable.

To-day the same concept and the same terms, as they remain paramount in our institutions and frivolous in our actual conditions, not only fail to control the tenure of property generally and the tenure of land in particular, they also promote social instability and social decay, because they guarantee as legal rights to new forms of property a private control socially valid only with the old forms. That is to say, we require of Corporate, Investment, Labour, and Utility property what is, by and large, the same order and degree of responsibility that we required of the farmer and his farm, the merchant and his fleet. We proceed not by analogue nor from principle but by precedent. And when the effort is made to control an obvious evil by precedent, failure is sharp and immediate, though sometimes misunderstood.

In other words, the concept of property adhering in fact to the individual and determining his concrete life is not an appropriate concept of property where ownership, as in the great common stock companies and all banks, has very little to do with control. Worse—and especially worse for the Southern Sectionalists—a centralised society, of which concentrations of irresponsible power is the idiosyncrasy, cannot fail to control with a surpassing irresponsibility the agrarian system upon which it is superimposed and upon which it depends; and this irresponsible control is not only legal, it is almost a formal desideratum, so long as the old property concept persists.

There is no panacea for any society, no end to the ruin and damnation of man. But the agrarian fraction of society cannot withdraw from the urban society of which it is an integral part as well as the prop. The agrarian fraction implies the integer; likewise the urban fraction. Nor will either fraction prosper on principles proper only to a purely agrarian society; we have Australia as an example of failure; and the attempt to do so will only hasten ruin. Spiritual retreat is more fruitless than physical (except for a few individuals), because it is, actually, no retreat at all, but only a wilful blindness; the body will continue to suffer unawares and will eventually blight the spirit it gives a home. It does no good, as the Sectionalists do, to call the land the great vocation of man, if the land may soon cease to support them; nor will it long conceal losses to follow the advice of Andrew Nelson Lytle: refuse to keep books and insist on bad roads. The educational obscurantism of John Gould Fletcher when he pleads for a definitely "useless" education for a chosen few; the historical obscurantism of Frank Lawrence Owsley—I mean his persistent galvanic revitalisation of the historic Civil War; the political obscurantism of

John Crowe Ransom, when he puts hope in the existing Democratic party; the religion of the whole horse and the short view adumbrated by Allen Tate; the social pietism of Stark Young when he reflects on manners and morals and smell of chivalry and honour: none of these sentiments, admirable and profound as they may be to minds committed, as they think, by history, to a departed mode of life, none of these sentiments will afford the sight of salvation to the Southern spirit; they accelerate, rather, and accent, because they leave it defenceless, the damnation of that spirit. And the damnation is the more intolerable because—or so it seems to an outsider—she brings it on herself by holding to the very notions of economy and government which, when used against her by her enemies, she calls Leviathan and vicious.

Mr. Tate's whole horse—the horse of all good Southerners—has bolted, almost as if it were real, as indeed he must have expected, or he would not have introduced into his conclusion a phrase so strong, sudden, and inexplicable, that any horse would shy at it. Mr. Tate has been writing about religious conviction of which he says that economy—our present subject—is the secular image, and he asks—"How may the Southerner take hold of his Tradition?" And then, in a separate paragraph, he says, "The answer is, by violence." Here, again, is the heresy of the absolute; and the truth of the heresy is, as always, counter to the intent expressed. The violence is suicidal and final, and exemplifies as the absolute must, being the condition of the dead, the defeat of every expectation and every memory that led to it. Except life, you cannot take much by violence; and certainly you cannot take what does not exist, and in the effort to do so your violence, having no other real object, will most likely turn back on your self.

No man can counsel another, not knowing the nature of his imperfection, to the perfection of suicide. But it is possible to point out even to the proud Psyche of the South that her desperation, so far as it is economic, springs from having assigned a false solution to a mistaken problem; to point out that Mr. Tate's secular image is a false idol, and cannot be propitiated even by the sacrifice of suicide.

Economics is not an idol at all, nor an image, nor a science. It is a description of the structure of property and the methods of distributing commodities; it has principles, not laws, and these are political and human, not objective or religious, in origin. Thus every economy is provisional and should be subject to revision by the changing conditions which it must meet. The great political principles are negative and admonitory. A regimen conceived for one set of conditions will apply to similar parts, only, of another set of conditions, and, second, no government is strong enough to govern until it is implemented to control in the public interest all the forms of power which it meets.

Under this view the Southern Sectionalists are clearly wrong *prima facie*, in their retreat upon the detail of classical economy and Jeffersonian politics as such, that is, in their received forms. We need—I mean both the agrarian and urban sections of the country together—the exact opposite of the received forms in order to accomplish the object of those forms at their inception: namely, an orderly society based on free institutions. We need a powerful Federal government controlling a non-competitive economy. What we have now is actually what the Sectionalists think they want, a weak government fostering a competitive economy, a government completely at the mercy of all those powers it was not initially designed to control: the powers of intangible, concentrated wealth. To repeat, you cannot control a society which expresses itself in the fiction of national corporations by the laws and customs of a society which expressed itself principally in the 18th century farm; nor, in the presence of the corporations, can you any longer control the farm on the old theory—it is no longer the same farm.

The difference, however, in actual economy, between an urban society and an agrarian is no greater than that between an enthusiastic pioneer society and the stable agrarian society of the old South. Likewise the assumption of national sovereignty necessary to make our present economy responsible is hardly greater than that made by Jefferson in consummating the Louisiana Purchase. Our principle is that as the uses of land are within the domain of the public interest however title may be assigned, so too should be the use of every other form of wealth, and if we need Leviathan to make them so, let us have Leviathan: he will be ours, and seem no more domineering than he is now in the Reclamation Service, the Forestry Service, the Coast Guard, the Post Office, or the Weather Bureau.

"Reaction," says Mr. Tate, "is the most radical of programs; it aims at cutting away the overgrowth and getting back to the roots. A forward-looking radicalism is a contradiction; it aims at re-arranging the foliage." That is the reaction of which I am in favour; it is the reaction, the response to our political predicament, which I have just been suggesting. But it is a getting in, or down, to the roots, which is necessary, not a getting back. The conception is delicate and a quibble can control it.

If we take our history correctly, as Mr. Tate wants us to, I think my point may be made clear. The quarrel between the Jeffersonian Democrats and the Federalists of 1800 was not so much a quarrel between a theory of weak or minimum government and a theory of a strong or maximum government, as a quarrel between a government strong enough to control the whole of the then existing society and a government with an added power designed to secure the domination of a limited creditor and/or commercial class. Had the Federalists won, a government actually far weaker than Jefferson's would have taken office; in losing, their strongest feature—an independent judiciary—was secured. Whatever the philosophy they thought guided them, Jefferson, Madison, Monroe, and J. Q. Adams were practitioners of strong government, a balanced and responsible government. When Jackson destroyed the dynasty in the interests of the debtor class he destroyed the tradition of balanced, responsible government; at least we have had none since 1828. That is, government itself has never since then been dominant; individuals, parties, interests, classes, rather, have dominated government; particularly, perhaps, in Whig and Republican administrations, but hardly less so in Democratic, and mainly less only because the sin of the Democracy was more usually of omission rather than of commission.

The present-day Republican party, so far as it celebrates the ritual of strong government at all, does so only to enable itself to surrender properly governmental powers to special interests; it reserves to itself, and this is what I suppose Mr. Shaw meant in his address to America in the spring of 1933, the power to use the Constitution to charter private anarchy. Its characteristic slogans are unimpeachable witness: rugged individualism; keep the government out of business; and stop bureaucracy.

Mr. Roosevelt's Democracy is thus far a soup in the cooking and has not reached the point of savour. Himself a man with inclinations rather than intentions, eloquence rather than style, talent rather than insight; his cabinet and establishment a medley of irresolvable contrasts rather than a harmony of interests; the Congress confronting him a confusion of ignorance, vanity, desperation, smugness, and fanatical ability, cut theoretically by party lines but actually by the outlines, curiously fantastic and unreasonable, of blocs;—it is diffcult to see how such a mixture can produce anything but that species of compromise which amounts to inertia.

But all this was predictable and was to have been expected as the expressive consequence of our system. It is a testimony to the complexity of urban society and a proof, perhaps, of the necessary degeneration, under the impact of such a society, of a two-party parliamentary system. The Jeffersonian formula is not, however, at fault—and here the Southern Sectionalists may take whatever heart they have left. The weakness of Mr. Roosevelt's government is not the Jeffersonian weakness, which was apparent only, and was really a great strength—the strength of control over adequately balanced institutions; it is, rather, by inadvertence, the complement of Republican weakness—that weakness of intellect which holds compromise to be the equivalent of control.

How, then, shall the Sectionalists choose? or rather, what, in his own interest, must he choose? and still hold fast, for his heart's sake, all that is dear to him in the history of the republic. In 1800 Jefferson and his friends could consider that the Revolution had removed America from an unwilling membership in an irresponsible Colonial System, and could, looking around them, see a stable society possible in terms of agrarian institutions alone; these institutions were sufficient to control the commercial and infant industrial systems from the domination of which in their larger English forms they had just divorced themselves by violence; society had, it seemed, a moment of autonomy. In 1934, looking for an analogous autonomy, the inheritors of Jefferson must see, and on Jefferson's principles, that autonomy—that is, the maximum freedom within a discipline—can only be gained under the institutions of a social service state.*

If I may, I should like to quote Mr. Tate again; his powerful mind has, it seems to me, quite aside from his intention, expressed the matter exactly. "The Southerner," he says, "is faced with the paradox: He must use an instrument, which is political, and so unrealistic and pretentious that he cannot believe in it, to re-establish a private, self-contained, and essentially spiritual life."

These remarks might well have been made by a sympathetic critic of Jefferson; so that I feel the less guilt at having twisted them, by excising them from their context, against Mr. Tate, who is an avowed legatee of Jefferson. Very good, then. The Southerner, in order to be self-contained, to be himself autonomous, must seize on a political form which still seems to most Americans a formula for regimenting the individual out of existence. That is part of the paradox; no man can feel free—except in the fatal freedom of a thief—without first imposing on himself the bond and limit of responsibility. The aim of a social service state is not to regiment the individual, but, after defining them, to control the social acts of individuals, and, where collections of acts have a predominantly public character, to assume the function as well

---

*I have intentionally used the loose phrase, and without capitals, "a social service state" because, first, I do not want to commit any body or thing to any of the proffered socialist leaderships, and, secondly, because it is easier in a loose phrase than in an indoctrinated label to preserve in the mind the real business of government, which was, in Disraeli's tautology, to govern.

as the control. The rule for determining character is the same which determined a national post office and national army: the public convenience.

Whether such a state can be secured under our present parliamentary system is questionable. The success of our Congress, and of our state legislatures, depends on the parties which compose them being in *fundamental* agreement both as to the character and the general line of the solution of the problems which confront them. The chief hope in America lies in the condition, which at present seems vicious, that party lines are always broken on major issues and are consolidated only for superficial and mechanical reasons, such as gaining office or organising the House. This is a fact of which the Sectionalists may take advantage, so soon as their measures assume political form. Such elections as those of Roosevelt and Harding were accomplished in spite of the party system: by the sudden preponderance of representative, if misguided, emotion. The increasing emergence of blocs in both houses suggests that Congressional as well as Presidential elections may be accomplished in spite of as well as through the use of local party organisations.

The hope is slight but it must be pursued, that in not too great a time we shall have a Congress able to recognise the revolution that has already taken place. The hope must be pursued because the alternatives are violence or the resumption of the Dark Ages, more likely violence, and not quite the violence Mr. Tate had in mind. A cumbersome and perhaps only vestigially functioning Congress is better than either the great encumbrance of blood or the evolution of a vestigial society. We can wait, not vaguely letting things go, but definitely, laboriously, until the amount of ruin in the country, of which there remains a good deal, is about to be used up. When a society has reached that proximal point it no longer has any need to wait; it will have been replaced, or it will be dead.

That is the end of *laissez-faire* in an accelerating society; and though there be a kind of absolute autonomy in either oblivion or death, I think it is hardly the kind of autonomy for which the Agrarian South, seizing on the paradox of politics, is looking. (The paradox of politics is this, that definite interests can neither be conceived nor secured except by compromise.) The Southerner, the American agrarian anywhere, cannot find autonomy alone; that is a further paradox, not in significance but in action; he must, to succeed, ally himself conscientiously and laboriously with those whom he mistakes for the enemies of his way of life. He must, I think, ally himself with the urban worker and the urban intelligentsia. If the common destiny of the two classes is not manifest—your Southerner thinks manifest destiny smacks of empire and progress—it is at least a sore thumb. And since the Southerner loves history, the reasons for the alliance may be found analogous to those which in 1776 secured the alliance between the Virginia planter and the infant commerce of Massachusetts against the irresponsible and usurious Colonial system.

The Southerner must, I repeat, ally himself politically with the urban worker; the evils from which they suffer are expressed with different accents but their origins are identical and some require the same words to define them. For the agrarian there has been a persistent and cumulative depression of prices below the subsistence level; for the urban there has been increasing permanent unemployment; these evils are fundamentally the same, in the one case the accent is upon the class as a whole, in the other upon a part. Both evils express themselves identically in mortgage foreclosures; only, perhaps on account of our geographical politics as well as because of the mere acute incidence of our money economy, the farm-mortgage burden is politically better known. Actually the burdens of farm mortgage and urban mortgage are equally heavy, and the two are inextricably involved. The origin of these evils is not, as some Sectionalists and all Capitalists believe, in original sin; nor is it in the inefficient distribution of goods alone; it is in the extravagant cost of uncontrollable institutions.

Nor must the agrarian deceive himself that he can be cured alone. However successful the Administration's farm relief might be for the moment, the disease remains contagious and re-infection is certain. The cure must be radical, and neither of the suffering classes is strong enough or clear-sighted enough, to accomplish it alone. There are, however, a number of collaborative acts that may be taken up, as it were, separately, and there is one ready-made at the moment for the Southern Agrarian. If he will support the Tennessee Valley Authority, he will strike at the very root, because he strikes at money, of one of the most vicious financial structures in America.

The problem is national; if you like, international; that is the idiosyncrasy of centralised society; its complexity while it aggravates the desire prevents the possibility of independent political action. The charter of right Sectionalism is this, to combine with cognate sections in order to recover the only autonomy worth having, that which is co-extensive with the society that actually exists. The point is that these cognate sections are political and not geographical in character. And if the Sectionalists want a phrase, a cry, a device upon their banner, both conservative and radical, I offer them the proud boast of the Popes, that they may be *Servi Servorum Dei*.

Anything else is retreat or a confession of futility; both of which are impossible in politics. But politics is not all. A sensitive soul—and the Southern

Sectionalist, like any Sectionalist, like any heretic, is sensitive to the point of pride—may well be reminded that only life itself is immortal, that its forms, and the more so as they reach the condition of clear ideas, carry always within them, to prove their futility, the seed of their death. Such a soul may choose to refrain from politics and clear ideas alike. Some of the Southerners, at their most excited moments, seem to have made that choice. These call their refuge the cultured life of a leisured, aristocratic, provincial society; and they speak as if there were a private salvation, only waiting to be tapped, in Sectionalist literature. I think it may be demonstrated that this is an artifact rather than an ideal; a dream of escape rather than an object envisaged.

Certainly this notion, this view which ascribes a provincial source and character to the arts and to that part of social life which may be dealt with as an art, has both the absoluteness and the contradictoriness commonly found in dreams. The contradiction is this, that a limited, provincial habitat is assigned to a culture avowedly catholic, and this assignment is made particularly for the present day America.

It is striking and instructive—and it is what makes discussion necessary and valuable—that the Sectionalist theory of art should preserve in the structure of its dogma and the nature of its appeal a complete counterpart of its political theory. A mind which had a knack for transposing symbols from one plane of reference to another would require only a hint and a push to find the criticism of Sectionalist art already perfected in the criticism of Sectionalist politics. But this fact, unfortunately, is no witness of integrity, or balance, or adequacy. As in politics passionate adherence to an historical agrarian economy, so in art the passionate insistence upon a single group of social and natural conditions limited by such an economy leads with equal fatality to the fragmentary, the disproportionate, and the irrelevant. If in politics a received view of history makes action upon existing conditions impossible, in art the consequence is that subjects are either misconstrued or altogether missed. The effect, the opposite of that intended, is due partly to a misconception of the social aspect of art, and partly to a misconception of the society which it must today particularly interpret; and both misconceptions rise from a single insight—namely the insight of a limited agrarian life—so exaggerated that balance is impossible. By seizing on one good to the exclusion of others you invariably surrender, defenceless, to the evil aspect of the goods you excluded.

The argument is roughly this (it may be found in Mr. Davidson's two essays, "A Mirror for Artists" in *I'll Take my Stand* and "Sectionalism in America" in the *Hound & Horn* for Summer, 1933):—The final subject of art is nature. An agrarian society reveals art to the artist as nature. The best art of the past is associated with agrarian societies. In America agrarian society is found in the sections of the South and West, and the artist had better either be born agrarian or become so.

That is the positive side of the argument. As in the realm of politics, it is the negative side of the argument that is more important. Because of industrialism art has been going down the hill of romanticism for a hundred and fifty years. Industrialism permits only a romantic, protestant, personal art. Art cannot be industrialised, and under industrialism it cannot be made at home. Good art, in the industrial, homeless communities of America is becoming more and more nearly impossible altogether. It is therefore necessary in art, as in politics, to overcome the sick and sterile culture of industrialism by the restoration of the agrarian culture. And in any case, the artist must, for the present, put his art in second place. "He must enter the common arena and become a citizen. Whether he chooses, as citizen-person, to be a farmer or to run for Congress is a matter of individual choice; but in that general direction his duty lies."

With the positive side of the argument, taken as provisional and appropriate to one of several views of art, it is possible to be in agreement. The artist in America or elsewhere needs a locality for knowledge, a home for stability, and a vantage, more or less remote from at least some of his interests, for vision. He can perhaps best secure all three by going into the country. As for the revelation of nature as inspiration and subject-matter, taken literally the Sectionalist dogma is good for one sort of art and one sort of nature. Nature permeates and finally gushes forth from every disguise men put upon her, whether in city or country or in their own hearts. And as for nature in her purity, nature is much more herself, more sublime and more ominous, in the mountains or at sea, than on a farm; and even in the city, for those who are attentive, there is often the sky overhead. Taken figuratively, as I imagine Mr. Davidson meant us to, nature as the subject of art is neither agrarian nor urban. Shakespeare, Dante, and Racine were urban men, and so is Thomas Mann today, and of these, three at least make liberal use of nature in all her forms; nor are any of them the less great artists for being primarily concerned with that complex human nature developed only in cities.

And this fact or this attitude toward a fact is the key to the fallacy in the negative side of Mr. Davidson's argument for a Sectionalist art in America today. Industrialism in economics is a real enough force, but in the arts as in politics, it is only a bogey. The real opposition is between agrarian and urban, localised (or diffuse), and centralised power and culture, and what is wanted in the conflict between them is not victory but balance, control, and assent. With assent so conditioned goes mastery; and mastery, over industrialism, over the machine, over society, does not, as Mr. Davidson says (specifically of the machine) imply contempt, any more than assent implies submission. The artist's mastery, like the politician's, implies understanding.

Let us say first, that America is irretrievably committed to an urban society; a society, that is, which centres itself in cities. It is a plain fact, and there is nothing but confusion to be gained by denying it. Greece, Rome, and Egypt were similarly committed, in their hey-day as well as in their decline. The Italian Renaissance flourished in specifically city states where the impact of war, starvation, disease, and an usurious economy were as constant and at least as repressive as the impact of industrialism is today. History will multiply instances, and no doubt exceptions for the asking. All that is important here is the obvious fact that while the societies depended upon the land for food and on its farmers for soldiers, and no doubt, too, for the soil of their arts, yet their greatest art flowered in their cities. There is hardly an analogue in history for the belief that an urban society is in itself inimical to art. Even in the arts of living, aside from the peasant arts, society has drawn at least as much from the city as the country. The capital (this perhaps is spiritual capitalism) was always both the seat of culture and a source of it.

The question remains, is there a specific character to urban society in America today which is inimical to art? I think, rather, that there is a specious misunderstanding and a series of superficial irritations, and not any essential fault in character. The evidence generally taken is the prevalence of bad art, and, specifically by the Sectionalists and the Humanists, that so much of the good art fails to be either classical or objective and is merely romantic protest or romantic escape or romantic defence.

As to the prevalence of bad art, I doubt if, relatively, we are any worse off than other eras, or that the bad art in America is much more prevalent than bad art in other countries even in predominantly agrarian countries such as Greece, Bulgaria, Canada, or Australia. There is always bad art, even in the great periods; and since art is both our most casual and our deepest form of expression, both casual and deep people are always asking it to be either better or worse than it is. But for examples:—There are acres of bad Renaissance painting, and there is an enormous mass of bad Elizabethan poetry. Good art is only partly predicated by general conditions; it depends as largely upon the accident of the right individual at the right time. Economic stability seems to have very little to do with the goodness of art, except insofar as the artist has more or less difficulty in securing his leisure. Shakespeare had great difficulty, Racine little, Proust none, and the Renaissance painter about the amount that was good for him.

Our real interest is not in bad art at all, but in good art; and in that field the notion of Sectionalism is sound or unsound depending on the definition you put upon it. It is certainly unsound in the light of the remarks above if it means that the urban community, industrial or otherwise, cannot produce both great art and folk art. The very nature—I use the word advisedly and invidiously—of urban life has only to be observed in its terrifying complexity, its sophistication and its stupidity, its endless yet predictable variety of needs; and it cries out for expression at every plane of art, from the game to the epic. Where the artist is likely to fail, when he comes to exist, is in the technical difficulty of imposing a form upon the diversity of his material; the forms of society tend to change faster than the forms of art. The material is there, however, and is in itself no more formless and inchoate than the artist's material always is.

One thing it is necessary to remember, that we may cancel before-time improper expectations: the major art of this age cannot employ the major forms of another age, and if the attempt is made the material is most likely impoverished and is certainly partly out of control: an instance where art and politics resemble each other. We need not expect tragedy in either the Greek or Shakespearean form any more than we expect to see the modern novel resemble the work of Cervantes or Fielding. It is, furthermore, possible that contemporary society is incapable of producing major forms or major artists; but if that is our case no amount of retreating upon the land will help us. A wilfully naive agrarian art could hardly interpret an urban society.

So much for the Sectionalist view that industrialism prevents art. If, on the other hand, the core of the Sectionalist theory is that a most interesting subject for art is the agrarian life, and that agrarian life is propitious for the appearance of the artist, then the Sectionalist insight is, if not taken too literally, sound and beyond argument. There is an art that springs from the land—its being, its tradition, and its history—which is certainly a deep art and sometimes a great art in cumulative effect.

But this theory must not be taken too literally, even in a given Section and for temporary purposes; because a theory about what the arts must portray and with what bias of sentiment, can never rightly be more than provisional and wishful. You can plant the seed of a subject in the artist's mind, or the individual artist may choose the seed you want him to; but that is the end of certainty. The rest, I think—the problem of growth and maturation—is beyond conscious control. The necessary contingence of circumstances may or may not come. The artist can suggest, prod, and try to fit what comes into the forms of which he is master; and that is all. The problem is the same for any art, whether it is specifically Sectionalist in the Southern sense, generally agrarian, or otherwise.

The real or at least the insistent problem of art for contemporary American society, and especially as it impinges on the Southern Sectionalist, may be indicated in much the same terms as we applied to the political problem. It is the exact opposite of what they think it is. Instead of defying, fighting, or ignoring—with the great load of the land on their backs—the existing urban society, the Sectionalists ought, to preserve their own good, to ally themselves with it. As the meaning of the cotton crop and the mortgage is bound up with the factory and the slum, so the meaning of the land and of provincial society is conditioned by the meaning of the metropolis. Similarly the provincial society of a great city can no more express than it can control itself without a deep awareness of the land from which it sprang and with which it is interdependent. Awareness does not mean detailed intimacy; acknowledgement is perhaps enough to set the necessary interaction in motion. The point is this and a paradox, like that of politics. The Sectionalist of whatever description cannot, in a centralised, complex society, achieve integrity in his own art unless he also pursues and seizes some image of national integrity. He is, otherwise, in some sense, no matter how small his chosen terrain, inadequate in relation to his own subject.

It is because the Sectionalists like the Communists refuse to construe the terms of existing society that they fail to realise the substantial unpredictability of art. Mr. Davidson's exhortation to the artist that he must descend into the arena and either turn farmer or run for Congress, is not very different in spirit from the Communist insistence that the only subject for art at present is the class-struggle in its Marxian terms. Both pleas are from the heart, both are absolute and both are heresies. I do not need to show the Sectionalist the heresy of the Communists; I almost wish it were necessary; nor do I think that the Sectionalist will listen to the Communist. But both heresies are plain enough, and both would end not only by denying art but also by denying their own objects. If they must use art for propaganda, let them use bad art; good art is always more and always less than propaganda— its honesty is personal and universal, never public and particular. As for the rest, it is probable that if poets became farmers and congressmen we would have more sensitive farmers and more naturally intelligent congressmen, but fewer poets.

It would have been perhaps useless or a mere game to have employed so many words and so much argument upon the particular dogmas of the Southern Sectionalists—who make a minority even in their own country—if they were alone or were isolated exceptions. But they are not. They exemplify more eloquently and more articulately than any other, the heresies—which may conveniently be termed the forms of sectionalism—to which America has been driven by economic despair. The politics of Mr. Borah or of the American Legion, of the so-far abortive fascist groups or of the American Bankers' Association, the art of the Marxists or of the Minnesotans, the poetry of Mr. Jeffers or that of Mr. MacLeish—to mention only a few examples—may certainly be described and ought necessarily to be attacked along the same lines. Above all, the sectionalism of the national government—its striving away from balance and its surrender of integrating power—must be attacked. Otherwise we put ourselves collectively at the mercy of the worst of all tyrants—our exaggerated selves.

The heresy is that poetry gets put in second place from its own point of view, and that is the form heresy generally takes in protestant absolutisms. The various images of God get put in second place, with the pretence, and the belief, that they are being put where they belong. Thus the images lose their objective validity, and instead of remaining ideals of natural life, where they create meaning for the spirit and define purpose for the Psyche, or impetus, that carries us forward, they become mere artifacts without meaning or reference in the real world. The guide for action is lost, and since we must act willy-nilly we act at loss; and all from a sincere desire and a sound insight. If I may repeat once more—and it has seemed necessary to fill this essay with repetitions—the Sectionalist, if because of his historical insight he insists on feeling himself one, must combine with what he feels to be other sections in order to recover the only autonomy worth having, that which is co-extensive with the society that exists. And this is as true on the artistic or interpretive side of life as it is on the political or enacted side.

If he wants to find his all in history, let him choose the moment in it that seems altogether good. But history is living, let him look therefore for the seed from which his history sprang rather than to its faded flower, because only the seed contains the possibility of life. Only with that knowledge can he nurture and control the history that is being related to-day. Otherwise he puts history in second place, with a dead flower stuck upright in its grave. So in his arts, his education, his politics, his necessary relations with those who do not resemble him, so with the precious intangibles that make up his way of life; with all these particularly, as well as with the sum of them, he must look for the seed, the vital, persistent principle, and not at the provisional, almost casual, and necessarily imperfect rendering that was its specious bloom. As the social soil is different, run down or enriched, and as the political climate has changed, the new bloom will have a different freshness and even a new colour, and it will in time create a different nostalgia. He must do all this and not be surprised at the result. If he will not do it, then with his history he has put its contents, of which he has made himself the most singular example, in second place.

Chaos Is Come Again

The proceedings which here prostrate themselves for comment were held on Patriot's Day as it is generally called, or, more specifically (in the neighborhood of Boston), the anniversary of the Battle of Lexington. The American Philosophical Society was in tune to the day; the proceedings quite generally kept up the holiday spirit. There was a good deal of good-natured self-applause, a kindly smugness, a righteous motion towards panacea, and an almost perfect avoidance of serious statement, which together pretty well covered up, or at least blurred one's vision for that genuine analogue for patriotism which was the announced subject of the day: Characteristics of American Culture and its Place in General Culture. It may be observed as indicative of the commemorative spirit that in the discussions recorded between the set pieces no one was willing actually to object to anything any one else had said; and, it may be added, no one seemed to notice the inconsistency, the incongruity, or the inadequacy of the various points of view there compromised. A vast aura of the unsaid and the unthought hangs over the printed pages and no doubt thickened the air of the hall at Philadelphia. The two forces which could have clarified contest and excited the audience to judgment were almost ignored both on the program and in fact. With one exception, neither religion nor philosophy was used at the proceedings. No doubt some tariff barrier of the American cultural system made them ruinous to import, and the home-products lacked recognition. This may well be the prone idiosyncrasy of American culture, that in it philosophy and religion lie low and when taken at all are taken for granted and at a discount.

But they are present, at work nonetheless, and may rise—by implication even in these comments. Meanwhile let us estimate the rates of discount they fetch from place to place in these papers and these discussions. The heaviest discount is appropriately that of the first paper, which is Mr. Frederick Lewis Allen's, under the heading, *Today*. Mr. Allen is frank. He begins by quoting a little book on *Standards* published by W. C. Brownell in 1917. Brownell, according to the quoted phrases and Mr. Allen's interpretation of them, was much depressed by the popularization of education, and foresaw, with everybody reading, not the best which took pains to read as it took pains to write, but what everybody wrote regardless, that the cultural domain would become "an absolutely unenclosed domain—the common of civilization, so to say, whose weedy aspects and worn places and rubbish heaps are as legitimate details as its cultivated area. Ought not," asked Mr. Brownell, "ought not access to this territory to be made more difficult, as difficult as possible?" Brownell's book is not fresh in my mind, but as I remember his primary concern was with the operation of taste without standards and education without aims, a concern which, if not annual and in the foreground, is at any rate perennial and in the background of all critical work in a democratic society. Mr. Allen does not look at it in that way; for him Brownell was a "backward looker," and he quoted him because "he described so well what *has not happened.*" He believes, rather, "that this country is making cultural progress in a new and exciting way, and, I may add, in a way which Benjamin Franklin would have appreciated and welcomed." Mr. Franklin was concerned with the founding of the American Philosophical Society with the purpose of promoting useful knowledge, and had rather a knack for discerning standards and envisaging aims, though it is true that he was deficient in taste and could sometimes be deceived. He was at any rate a philosopher and submitted his prejudices to reason.

Mr. Allen does not; he is frank to the point of disarming himself in accepting at far more than its face value the mass evidence of activity which confronts him. We can only recite it. Four and a half million people hear Toscanini, ten million the Metropolitan; there are thirty to thirty-five thousand school orchestras; the best-sellers of today are better than those of a generation ago; there are now twenty-six magazines with a circulation over a million, of which thirteen have over two million, and five over two and a half million; 99,503 people saw the Picasso show in fifty-one days, and in seventy-three days 277,794 people saw the Italian masters; and, lastly in this recitation, that "if there is in Pennsylvania or Georgia or South Dakota a boy of genius, he will be found out and aided to bring his gifts to fruition." Mr. Allen goes on to celebrate the new arts of movies and radio and parkways and bridges and dams and color lighting at the World's Fair, and reaches the conclusion that at last we have grown up and are building for ourselves, and proceeds to say that he will not estimate either the absolute or relative values of what is built.

I submit that Mr. Allen is right on the prospect and wrong on the evidence and blinkered in his point of view. If, as Mr. Allen and I agree, the arts in America are more mature than they were a generation ago—that is, there is more of a better grade of work produced now than formerly—it is precisely because, willy-nilly, some American artists have begun, through feeling the force of the standards appropriate to their arts, to work through the difficulties of their crafts rather than against the difficulties of their society. The point is that the artists have made their progress towards maturity without aid from the leaders of society—and among leaders I include the editors of commercially successful magazines and publishing houses—and particularly without aid from our educational systems. Indeed, they have been compelled to work against the program of the more successful leaders; which is the program of undifferentiated popularization—precisely Mr. Allen's program. In fact, mass appreciation of the kind that Mr. Allen approves represents the constant danger to the artist of any serious sort: the danger of popularization *before* creation. Those who are in any sort serious writers or painters will understand immediately what I mean when I ask Mr. Allen to consider the dreadful vitiating pressure of popularization which Mr. Steinbeck, Mr. Hemingway, Mr. J. S. Curry, and Mr. Grant Wood must feel when they confront their *next* work; they will understand because that pressure is in some sense upon us all, inescapably. The difference between great art and popular art is relatively small; but the difference between either and popularized art is radical and absolute. Popular art is topical and natural, great art is deliberate and thematic. What can be popularized in either is only what can be sold. Mr. Allen, at the moment, together with many, is confusing all three to the detriment of all but the last. He is avowedly bent on selling American art and letters in quantity, as is, and without regard to quality or significance; a scheme which requires the constant replacement of shoddy goods. He does not mean to avow this; he no doubt means the contrary; but there it is. Until American or any other society is educated either up to the level or educated *back* to the level of art with standards, whether popular or great, it can be sold nothing but art without standards; and if the attempt is made notwithstanding what happens is that only the popularizeable aspect of the art is actually sold and consumed. Mr. Allen's real business, the real business of the American Philosophical Society in this quarter, is still to promote useful knowledge, which is an educational pursuit: the promotion precisely of standards of taste and the sense of aim in achievement to that level where they may be useful in what we call roughly the enjoy-

ment of art—an enjoyment which in this context may better be called the discovery of those elements in art which cannot be popularized: the vital elements.

Lastly, it may be remarked that insofar as Mr. Allen's evidence is relevant,
W. C. Brownell was right. Indiscrimination is the discount Mr. Allen sought
(for that is the equivalent of general consent), and the penalty is lack of
awareness even of that to which he assents. This is perhaps a virtue in commercial publishing; certainly it is a characteristic long endured by those outside the fold; but the point here is that no mind in the least tainted by a
religious or a philosophical point of view could tolerate it for a moment.

It is perhaps with some such opinion in mind that we turn with pleasure to
Mr. Alfred V. Kidder, whose subject was *Looking Backward,* far back of the
backward-looking Brownell, so far back indeed that had he not been
forewarned Mr. Kidder might have come on Mr. Allen instinctively assenting
to the first significant scratchings in that age when even man came into the
world "endowed with all, or very nearly all, the knowledge required to carry
on [his] individual existence." But Mr. Kidder is on a different track; he puts
philosophy at a discount only by inadvertence—because he does not happen
to tackle it; and you have the feeling in reading him that if only someone had
reminded him of it in his early days—when his education was formed—he
would have used it all through his paper. For certainly there is a philosophical
notion—even a pious notion—at the heart of what he says. "The world's
worst troubles," he says, "have in the past been, are now, and will continue
to be due to a single underlying cause; and that is to man's inability to cope at
certain critical periods with the cultural machine he has built." We shall
return later to this notion in dealing with Mr. Mumford and Mr. Compton,
for it presents in a practicable form the cultural problems which these gentlemen raise. It is quoted here primarily to suggest the vast area of human
ability which is unavailable when the power of discrimination—the evaluat-
ing, the judging power—is deliberately discarded by Mr. Allen in his
capacity of man on the street; secondarily it is brought up to show with what
justice and appropriateness Mr. Kidder would bring the study of anthropology to bear on the study of our own society; and finally it is singled out so
that it may be seen to press on Mr. Kidder's own final question: Is the evolution of intelligence still going on? "Are we equipped with better mental
tools, are we innately more intelligent than we were one, or five or fifty
thousand years ago? Or have we come to be so thoroughly dependent upon
culture that we have left it to do our evolving for us? If so, God help us, for
our culture, like Frankenstein's monster, is a soulless thing."

What Mr. Kidder is saying, or what we can legitimately make him say for
our purpose, is that as Western culture has evolved it has gradually more and

more completely dispensed with the continuing background of philosophy and religion; that is what he must mean by calling it soulless. To him, within this paper, this is a fact to be dealt with, but not, for he cries God help us! as he deals with other facts by the laboratory and historical means at our disposal, but rather in desperation emotionally, which is to say with religion, and through a "greater knowledge of man" which means, if it means anything, through philosophy. It is therefore regrettable that we see Mr. Kidder resort to what must have been desperately inadequate even for him and at the moment that he made it, a plea for more and better archaeologists. The plea is but to cheer oneself up in the dark; is in fact but to obscure the central clarity of his vision of our problem.

Before we look forward with Mr. Mumford and as it were sideways with Mr. Compton and sidelong with Mr. Brooks, let us first pose that problem in the sharpest words that come to hand. It is borne in on us every day, that problem; it is superficial, quotidian, cuts into the mere cuticle, which is why it is so irritating and so controversial and costs so much in temper; but it is also profound, affecting our respect for what we inherit (our culture) and predicting our relations to the major actions we take or do not take as a society. It is the problem of getting along without conviction and without faith as we are used, as humans, to enjoy these. At best, we enjoy an intelligence that is deprived and a faith that is undermined and a spirit without refuge; and this is true I think even of those who still have conviction and faith, for the actuality runs faster for the sensibility than for the mind, just as it lags behind the imagination that would overcome it. We are committed, in short, to the experiment of a society without access to a supernatural order; and it is no solution to the problem of that experiment either to assert that it will fail, as those Christians who see the problem at all assert, or to insist, as some that are merely hopeful do, that at the right time the old conviction and the old faith will live again. The first of these notions is merely panacea in reverse and the second is merely the absolutist notion that the Kingdom of God is at hand. We must deal, if we deal at all, with present damnation and the commonwealth of man. We are condemned—if we value our heritage at all, we must think of ourselves as condemned—to act, for the first time in history, out of the strength and weakness of the human imagination alone. It is not the imagination that is different, but our relation to it: that we know it to be unreservedly human, immitigably worldly, utterly subject to our own control. We know its smallness.

What is at once both worst and best about this position is that we suddenly know that man has never occupied any other position; he has always been on his own but has never previously been successfully able to avow it collectively, and never able to avow it at all individually. It is the collective avowal that gives us our new vantage, and the fresh sense of the individual's continuing inability to avow it that marks the lonely privation of the single minds that must think and speak and lead and make up the collective imagination to the point of action and judgment. To do deliberately, to choose voluntarily, what had hitherto been done by necessity and decided to heaven, these are the penalties imposed upon the imagination by the stage of culture which we may fear has overwhelmed us. I say specifically that these penalties are suffered by the imagination as differentiated from what is usually meant by the reason; for the reason alone is too small to cope with them. Reason is a little fellow and when driven or scared runs straight into the arms of God in the guise of absolute authority, or human nature, or statistical patterns of material behaviour; reason is only good, as I think Bertrand Russell said, like instinct, in familiar circumstances. In other words, we see that it was faith which kept reason flexible; *fides quaerens intellectus;* it was only under the pressure of faith that reason could be made to fit experience into forms that could be handled and interpreted. Thus we have now as the chief critical task of imagination the labor of making reason flexible by rational means alone. A frankly provisional, avowedly conventional imagination is the only superrational authority we can muster. Muster is here the right word in that it represents an extreme and continuous effort; once you let up on your effort you give in to inertia; which is what Mr. Kidder was saying in his language, and which is what we can see, even more clearly, in the present war. To give in to inertia is, humanly, to give in to the adventitious; and to accept the adventitious is to acknowledge the inadequacy of the human mind to cope with the social and material energies it has released.

On this nexus we reach Mr. Mumford, whom we find in this symposium *Looking Forward,* who has recently published a book called *A Faith for Living,* and who generally and all round refuses to accept inertia; and after Mr. Mumford we reach Mr. Arthur Compton, who finds *Science Shaping American Culture:* who in other words does tend, as we shall see, willingly, wilfully, and gladly, to give in to all of inertia the human mind can engorge. Two men the products of the same culture in the same country and at the same time, could hardly be further apart. What they have in common is what, in these papers, they ignore—a history, a circumstance, and a fate; a history of what Mr. Mumford calls "the weaknesses and disintegrations that were inherent in" the culture that made them, a circumstance of clear present crisis, and a fate which depends upon their ability, as representative men, to solve that crisis. As the Greeks called character fate, we may for this context call ability character. It is an access of stature seen as ability that is wanted; an ability flowing out of an increasing imaginative responsibility to our knowledge of the world; an ability, in Mr. Mumford's words, to establish Western society "upon a broader human base than the conquistador, the militarist, and the industrialist of the past thought wise or necessary." To rephrase once more our problem of faith in a merely human world, how shall we erect an authority at the same time competent and acceptable, strong enough and flexible enough, to resume control over those energies which, though we developed them ourselves, have gotten away from us?

Mr. Mumford does not answer that question because he has not permitted himself to ask it. But by keeping the question in mind and the necessity for an answer as it were just round the corner of vision, the questions he does raise and does answer become both richer and more immediate. He begins by stating that American culture—whatever it is that we live in—is the result of the great expansionist movements, geographical, mechanical, energetic, and anti-imaginative, which began in the fifteenth century; and that that culture "is universal but not uniform." That is, it is universal in having a common general shape, pattern, and stress, common general possessions, but is eclectic in its local emphases and endearments, its motions towards piety and prejudice; but that it is predominantly material and quantitative, as opposed to imaginative and qualitative. Being, at the same time, everywhere expansionist, it has tended naturally and briskly towards submitting to control by inertia, or naked power, rather than towards the assertion of control by political or philosophical intelligence—responsible power. This language is mine, not Mr. Mumford's, but I do not think it is inconsistent with his language, and especially with the development which it at once takes up: namely the inexorable closing of every frontier upon an expansionist impulse which had not run out. He recites the familiar tale; the land frontier, the machine frontier, the population frontier (with the spread of contraception) are all closed. Mr. Mumford sees in this closure, this constriction, this stoppage—again, the words are mine not his—the first possibility since the Middle Ages of a genuine human culture, a culture both stabilized and diversified, qualitative instead of quantitative in its values, in which "once more every life becomes precious: not merely at the moment of birth and through infancy, but at every subsequent phase of life, not to be used frivolously, not to be deprived of its great heritage." The end he has in sight is "man's development and perfection as a social being, and society's development and perfection as a vehicle for personality."

Before proceeding with Mr. Mumford's implementation of his ideal, two or three preliminary considerations need to be given tongue. The first is sprung from the notion of closing frontiers. Not all are closed; there is Mr. Mumford's own chosen frontier which if it is not open will abort his ideal, and that is the frontier of the imagination, a qualification I am sure Mr. Mumford would insist on; and there is also a sort of inner frontier, far from exhausted and probably inexhaustible which may abort the ideal regardless, namely the frontier of violence—suicidal, naive, direct violence from within. The expansionist impulse has not run out, merely the optimal forms in which it hitherto expressed itself; and it is that unused impulse which we see express itself in the wars today. We have then a conflict between the forces of intelligence and the forces of violence; a conflict during which intelligence must surrender to the means of violence in order not to surrender to violence itself. We have indeed a deeply implicated kind of internecine war where if either side kills itself the other is murdered. Victory by the intelligence will require that both frontiers be kept open, with control conceived of as a balance of forces. (A better word for balance would be *homeostasis*, which may be found in W. B. Cannon's *Wisdom of the Body*, where it is shown to mean the critical maintenance of precarious body states.)

A second consideration which needs to be brought into focus is, like the consideration of frontiers, again double, but may be stated more briefly. The conception of the development of man as a perfect social being and of society as a perfect vehicle for personality, is almost directly contrary to the central conception of Christianity, in which the aim of the good life is seen as salvation, and where neither man nor his society is seen as possible of perfection. The practical merit of the Christian conception was that a good human life fitted you, up to a point, for heavenly life; but its real attractive force lay in the fact that the Christian aim was infinitely larger than the mere worldly means. The question is whether a similar disproportion between aim and mere means is not necessary before an aspiration can be made generally operative in any actual world; and it is a question which needs particularly to be asked of Mr. Mumford, for his aspiration is towards perfection in this world. On the face of it he is discarding what has been one of the most powerful practical motives towards the good life, the dogma of the radical imperfectibility of man. The point I should like to emphasize is double: that despite our loss of access to a supernatural order there is no need to assume man as perfectible, and that, secondly, to make such an assumption makes for too close a dependence on unmitigated reason and therefore tends towards inflexibility of intellectual demeanor: which is to say towards a kind of totalitarianism of the imagination, the very thing Mr. Mumford is most bitterly against. It would seem more rational in the great sense to take a position in which the means were thought of as perfectible with relation to the end, the end itself beyond perfectibility.

Now to return directly to Mr. Mumford's implementation, what he has to say directly about what we may call the impasse in looking forward, the taking-off place for action. We find him at once asserting an ambiguity and underwriting an ambivalence; which is all to the good because it undermines, at the beginning, planned perfectibility. "Our health and our safety," he says, "consist in living more deeply as members of a regional community, and living more widely, as members of a world community." That the emphases are verbal and interchangeable is clear if we transpose Mr. Mumford's adjectives, so that we would live more *widely* in the regional community and more *deeply* in the world community. The transposition does not invalidate his statement, it adds to its ambivalence and therefore to its availability when he puts it at the level of putative prescription. "Our best regional products are always a contribution to humanity's common store; and our culture in America will live or die by reason of the skill with which it establishes local conditions that can be universalized throughout the planet, and creates universal conditions that aid, instead of hampering and discouraging local life." The transposition enables us at once to assent to Mr. Mumford's emphasis on the primary place of regionalism, and at the same time to regard the home community, the region, as merely the locus, the focus, the *actual expression* of universal society.

That emphasis made, Mr. Mumford sums his necessities in the single word balance, and opposes to it the idea of cultural isolationism. In the sense that St. Augustine thought that the love of God was best expressed in knowledge of his works on earth, we may make Mr. Mumford say that the macrocosm can only be apprehended in terms of the microcosm; which is to say, in long practice though not in short, that the two must be united in the act of apprehension, because only in terms of the one is the other either possible or worth having. It is because Mr. Mumford feels something like this that, despite his rejection of uniformitarianism, he cannot help asserting in his last sentences both the logical *and* the providential unity of the Western world, indeed the whole world, in language which at least implies the necessity of universal, or central, authority. "If the Dark Ages return in Europe and Asia," he feels, "there will be no dawn in America." I will not say he is right, but if he is right, then there is no escape from his impasse except through both philosophy which puts man wisely at the center of his life (which Mr. Mumford does) *and* through religion which is that super-rational (no longer super-natural) order which sees man not as the center of life only but also as one aspiration or the target of judgment. I do not see how in this context we can define our desideration of a rational faith better than in the old language: Faith is the substance of things hoped for. I cannot suggest to Mr. Mumford how he may reach that substance, except negatively, that it is not by the desperate, merely rational assertion that we have it that he makes in his *Faith for Living*. I suspect that the route is *both* poetic and philosophic, a kind of knowledge both provisional and absolute, actual and ideal, but these are intimations and no better than Mr. Mumford's own, and rather than insist upon them I would turn to Mr. Kidder's archaeologists, or better still to the merely immediate picture, which comes after Mr. Mumford's drawn by Mr. Van Wyck Brooks.

Mr. Brooks quoted Henry Adams in a letter of 1862, when Adams was twenty-four, that what we need "is a national set of young men like ourselves or better, to start new influences, not only in politics, but in literature, in law, in society, and throughout the whole social organism of the country—a national school of our own generation. And that is what America has no power to create." Mr. Brooks thinks that while in the eighteenth century Franklin had succeeded in forming such a school, by Adams' time "all hopes of this kind went by the board." But now, he thinks, there is again a community of "ingenious minds," and ends with this sentence: "We do not forget that Franklin was the first of American writers to see the value of this community of minds; and how good it is that on this spot we writers should be brought into closer relations with workers in all the other intellectual realms." I hope Mr. Brooks is right about the writers, and I wish I could feel from these papers that he was right about the rest; but I shall finish with Mr. Brooks by applying to him certain phrases which Henry Adams once wrote about a quite different figure in a quite different time; it applies to this paper and to all Mr. Brooks' work no less. "Sometimes bitter, often genial, always intelligent—Brooks had the singular merit of being interesting. The usual writers flocked in swarms like crows, black and monotonous. Brooks' plumage was varied, and, like his flight, harked back to race. He betrayed the consciousness that he and his people had a past, if they but dared avow it, and might have a future, if they could but divine it."

Mr. Francis Taylor of the Metropolitan Museum and Mr. Otto Luening of the Bennington Music Department present a number of encouraging bits of evidence about the increased popularization of their respective arts. Mr. Taylor, in particular, seems vastly pleased with the increasing use of the art museums and with the widespread base of mediocrity from which, sometime, genius will spring. Mr. Luening is sharper; more directly concerned with the problems of living composers and performers in relation to a critically conceived culture. But neither raises any cultural problem.

It is rather a pity that Mr. Arthur Compton is not similarly encouraging on a practical level about his own specialty, which is physical science. But he is not encouraging; he only thinks he is encouraging. Actually, from a cultural or philosophical or religious point of view, the prospect he holds up—that of *Science Shaping American Culture*—is singularly depressing to the point of devitalized terror and bottom dismay. He is all this, not by will, not by interpretation, but merely because he may be irretrievably right on the facts which he presents. There may be no energy in this or another society to combat them, only enough to receive their impress—I will not say their embrace, which would involve consent. And if that is the case, there will soon be no human energy at all.

Mr. Compton's general position is most easily and fairly seen in a series of quotations and paraphrases. He begins with the assertion that no country has ever been so greatly influenced by science as our own: in means of living, thought, amusement, art, and religion. Item: "With the help of science, labor and capital are efficient, the government co-ordinates the activities of a widely spread people, and our continent has become a national community." Item: "A survey of current literature can leave no doubt but that in American society most of our creative thinking is in the field of science." Item: "In art . . . the American certainly does not excel the Greek nor hardly even the prehistoric European. . . . Those aspects of our culture which have been developing owe their growth primarily to the advance of scientific knowledge . . . If this claim is valid, it means that the society in which scientific knowledge is most rapidly growing is the spear-point of man's advancing culture." Item, speaking of the development of communications: "Thus even the non-mechanical inventions have found their most effective application through the aid of scientific developments." Item: as a result of recent science "our life differs from that of two generations ago more than American life of that day differed from the civilized life at dawn of written history." The next item is a telescoping of history to fifty years of a man's life, so that he lived all but a week to find Galileo, and only this minute could he read by fluorescent light. At this point Mr. Compton begins to draw conclusions under the heading that *American culture is that of a changing society,* by which he means that it is necessarily an incomplete, imbalanced, almost wayward culture, and must remain so for many generations, until, like the Greeks, we can adapt our habits to our knowledge. "In course of time," he says, "though it may require centuries, we may expect the development of science to approach a new plateau of knowledge and invention. Then we may hope again to refine our mode of living to fit precisely the conditions of our greater world." Meanwhile, like Daedalus, we are bound not "to make man happy, but to make him great."

Mr. Compton's description of the present pause in the parade to greatness is worth quoting almost entire. We "see science replacing the human interests present in literature, art and music with technological developments in which the human factor becomes less and less significant. The most fundamental values of morality and religion are ruthlessly shaken, with the implication that their value is negligible. It is just because so many scientific men seem blind to these human difficulties that one feels the greater concern lest in following science mankind may lose its soul." Mr. Compton's own comment on this is as bright as any, though not his interpretation. In the *Phaedo*, he says, Socrates describes how he gave up the study of physics because it failed "to account for the important things in life." He then ascribes Socrates' willingness to take the hemlock to honor not science, and goes on: "Such moral forces as honor were not to be explained by science; yet it is these forces that shape men's acts. Since it did not meet their human needs, the followers of Socrates and Plato abandoned science, and the study of the truths of nature was forgotten for a thousand years." Coming to our own day, Mr. Compton believes that "science is a source of enormous strength . . . The world's leadership must go to those who are served by science and technology. That we shall live with science is thus decreed by the immutable laws of evolution."

I think we had better call a halt for an intermediate review of Mr. Compton's parade before it gets to be such a crowd that it passes all at once. Let us assume that all his facts are true and pertinent about what science does—or would do if permitted—to human society up to the point where he states the radical novelty in human history of the last two generations. The assumption is inescapable anyway, but it can be made with better grace deliberately than negatively; and it is that grace which gives us the strength to disavow the radical novelty and the courage to insist that the major aspects of man's emotional, intellectual, and personal habits and needs remain unaltered since at least the days of classic culture and probably long before. That he thinks otherwise is Mr. Compton's major delusion. The new age differs only in technics and in the failure to realize that that *is* the difference. The true advantage of modern technics is that properly understood they should permit the realization of our ideal policy towards an identical world, a policy which if we have it, we *inherit* almost unaltered. It is Mr. Mumford's problem all over again from the opposite angle. It is, too, the problem that troubled Henry Adams on the political level: the question whether or not man as a political animal could develop mental powers equal to the energies newly released by technics or science. It is the unifying power of the imagination that is sought; a power not dependent on technics, but which must control them by using them as implements. To drag in an old word again, still vaguely understood, the unity achieved by imagination was felt as reality and called God: energy incarnate, force seen as significant because seen as manipulated. The irresponsible routine administration of inertia (which is energy seen with a reality less than God) is very different from the responsible control of energy. To get back to Mr. Compton's level, which is the level of immediate impasse, the same men cannot make and administer policy. We have the men in the power houses. Our problem is to control them, neither to give in to them as Mr. Compton thinks we must, perhaps for centuries, nor to attempt to destroy them, as Mr. Compton thinks the Greeks did, and as perhaps in effect the totalitarian states are attempting to do now, but to control them in terms "of those important things of life" which Socrates could not find accounted for in physics. It is true if we underline the right word that "the world's leadership must go to those who are *served* by science and technology"; but only those are capable of being served who are capable of leading. I do not wish to be misunderstood; neither science nor any scientist is to be led by the nose; mutilation is not leadership; the independence of science is conceived as absolute within the limitations of the scientist; no, leadership consists in making full use of science under a policy of which only the means and never the ends are affected by technology, which is the active side of science.

How far Mr. Compton is from discerning any such need on the practical level is clear when he comes to examine *The Human Meaning of Science*. "But perhaps of greatest importance is the fact that science is making man develop into a social being." The exact opposite would be nearer to significant truth. Without philosophical or imaginative control the general effect of science has been to permit the appearance and to encourage the growth of an a-social society, a society which is an aggregate of units and not a fellowship of individuals, a society held together, as in our great cities, largely by the concatenation of technical services, but otherwise, so far as the community of interest and act is concerned, evidencing a disintegrating culture. It is only fair to add that Mr. Compton is probably not "for" such a society, he sees it as inevitable, and perhaps he is right. At any rate he uses various senses of the word society indiscriminately and takes them as more or less equivalent to each other, which is a clue to the trouble we find him in. A first necessary distinction is certainly that between society conceived as a fellowship and having an ethos, and society as a body of men having no naturally necessary connection but having an urgent economical or technical relation, and society thought of as such an aggregate of persons as, in different circumstances, is necessary for survival. It is not that Mr. Compton does not feel the need for a fellowship society but that he takes it for granted. Thus he refers to a "law" of history which says that the trend of history is towards "a greater consideration of one's fellows as society grows more complex." Social welfare is neither identical with nor a substitute for Christian fellowship, and to pretend that they are is in the end to lose the conception of both. It is demeaning to think of fellowship, whether Christian or not, in terms of welfare; just as it is futile, as we saw under Hoover, to deal with welfare merely in terms of fellowship.

Mr. Compton, if he reads this, may think my objections quibbling, and perhaps in terms of his own ultimate frame of thought he is right. Further, I am sure that we could force a kind of tripartite agreement between his point of view, Mr. Mumford's, and my own. But insofar as words may be held either to predict or to express action, the quibble—the tilt, the idiom, the twist of thought—makes the difference between life and death. Thus, I share the point of view which makes Mr. Compton say: "The man of science may not feel qualified to choose for others that which gives dignity and worth; but he can at least supply the data on which that choice must be made." But it seems to me that the tilt of his language is all wrong and towards obfuscation if not death when he concludes: "Science must clarify the vision of the seers who would point out to us the goal of life." Tilted the other way, we would have found Mr. Compton saying that science must *implement* the *policy* of the *imagination*—common in source, only articulated by individuals which would express the dignity of life. But Mr. Compton himself makes the whole matter clear and dreadful when he makes his last contrast. "Whereas to Plotinus it appears that: 'It is through intuition rather than through reason that we may approach our highest aspirations,' the scientist finds that in the discipline of unprejudiced search for truth lies the beginning of wisdom." It seems out of place, but there is no recourse else, for a man of letters to remind a scientist that physics—from Maxwell to Kelvin, Planck, Gibbs, Bohr, and Einstein—has succeeded, in fundamental matters, in pushing order but to the brink of chaos; which is indeed the purpose of physics as it is of every orderly or reasonable form of knowledge. But reason alone can neither maintain an order nor discern its significance. Reason, as Lord Kelvin said, is not enough; only faith goes beyond. Without faith—and this applies to looking backwards and forwards and at the present day no less than to looking at science—without faith, chaos is come again.

The Enabling Act of Criticism

There is a kind of resolute candor necessary to a full approach to literature which is impossible to any particular approach. The best that the individual can do positively is to insist that his particular work aims in the general direction of that candor, and the least that he can do negatively is not only to admit but to insist that other particular approaches also aim in that direction. Failure to make either insistence leads to irrelevance and arrogance of judgment, and if persisted in at the level of practice—whether in book-reviewing or in major criticism—tends to complete the separation of the literary critic from his proper subject-matter. Instead of practicing literary criticism he will find himself practicing self-expression or casual philosophy, practices which will be deceptive in the degree that they were not candidly undertaken. Thus when the critic takes Criticism itself as his subject—when he faces his own practice, when he confronts other critics with their own practice—he must concern himself sooner or later with the relative stage of candor or deception which that practice discloses. And the sooner he does this the better, because for the life of me I cannot see how the critic judging of Criticism can do much more. Further, if he takes his job seriously, I cannot see how he can content himself with attempting less. Surely it is a tenable view that criticism must in the end come back to the task of saying what its objects are in terms of themselves; as surely, then, it is of first importance to distinguish in the work of a critic what is criticism from what is something else.

To put the matter quite practically, on the level where we actually use criticism, which is to say in our efforts towards a better understanding of literature, let us set up a series of questions designed to show the distinctions we want. We have a critic before us. What, when he is all done, does he tell us about the works he says he is examining? Is what he tells us everywhere subordinated to what we may call the interests of the works themselves: precisely, what it is within the work that interests us or defeats its own interest? Or, on the contrary, is what he tells us subordinated to some interest, no doubt worthy in itself, independent of the work in hand? If so, which interest predominates? And, if the extra-literary interest does predominate, can it yet be said that it nevertheless enlightens the literary interest, by situating it, say, among all the interests that go to make up a culture? This last, if we rephrase it, makes up the crucial question; for does it not ask, really, whether we can accept or reject a literary work by the application of literary standards alone? That is, to make one more rephrasing, do we in fact ever understand literature only by literary means?

If we can answer these questions as it were backwards, it is possible that we may come out somewhere near right in the end. At least we should have a beginning not merely provisional or wayward but with an end already and firmly in view: namely, a focus for literary experience, and a vantage for looking. We can think of the whole backward process as the enabling act of criticism.

Well, then, it is plain that we never do in fact understand literature solely by literary means any more than we understand water solely by drinking it, solely by chemical analysis, solely by looking at it, or solely by damming it up. It is the unified mind and sensibility that is engaged in the act of understanding; the act is imaginative; and to try to compartmentalize the act so as to emphasize one faculty over another is to invalidate the imagination and abort the act. Looked at in this way, the question of the final understanding of literature becomes either an artificial or an irrelevant question. If we do not use the whole mind we shall understand nothing; if we do use it, we do so as it were inarticulately, as the product of our whole culture: that is, we take it for granted.

But what is taken for granted must be attended just the same, like breathing; and in this case especially; for the unified, imaginative character of the understanding was not brought up here for nothing but indifferent acceptance. It was brought up in order to emphasize the fact that at the other end of the rod from criticism—in the act of the composition of literature itself—the process is the same. Serious writing is done under the full tolerable weight of mind and sensibility. Imagination is in that sense absolute. All that can be made to bear, bears. That is why the critic must bring his full tolerable imagination to bear before judgment is possible.

In the word tolerable we introduce a consideration which brings us to the next question in our backwards moving series; the question whether, really, we can accept or reject a literary work by the application of literary standards alone. Here the answer is double; partly yes and partly no, only good sense—the taste of practice—determining which. T. S. Eliot's remark is initially in order, that while we can only tell that a work is literature by literary standards, we cannot tell whether it is great literature except by other than literary standards. A first qualifying reflection is that there is not very much great literature; and a second is that, even when a critic is concerned with great literature, most of the problems he handles will not directly affect his estimate of its greatness. Greatness is come up to, felt, discovered; not handled. A critic who tried to handle merely the greatness of Shakespeare or Dante would see it disappear before his eyes. And a critic who attempted to establish the greatness of Joyce or Eliot or Yeats would be largely wasting his time; for greatness is established by custom, by time, by the apprehension in the minds of many men of inexhaustibility, and even so greatness is transitory and variable. Milton is not so great to-day as a century ago. Dante is greater. And I use the copulative deliberately, for greatness is an act of estimation not an assertion of fact, and hence may be expected to vary, but not, once estimated, ever to disappear irrecoverably. It would be intolerable as well as impossible for us today to look at Milton either with our own full mind and sensibility or with those of his own generation, or with those of the eighteenth century. We use of our own what will bear, of the others only what will elucidate—and then only putatively. On the other hand—and this is the aspect of critical activity to which we shall return—it would be intolerable if we did not bring the full force of our literary standards to bear in order to determine what of Milton is literature and what is not. Equally, the other way round, we should bring as much as possible of Milton's literary achievement to bear on the products of our own time; and the extent to which this can be done will constitute a literary judgment on both Milton and our own time. Those other, extra-literary standards, the standards of the convictions of our whole culture, will thus tend to disappear or be transformed into the literary standards.

A very different thing happens—at this time; though it may not be at another—in the example of Dante, whose greatness has grown so in our estimation that the force of his work seems almost a quality of the air that poets must breathe to invigorate their own verse. Dante, said Yeats, was the chief imagination of Christendom; and I think it may be hazarded that his greatness lies in the fact that he showed the highest and fullest unity the Christian order ever reached actually at work in light and air and earth. As Eliot says, the Divine Comedy is a vast ordering of actual human feelings and emotions;

which are our own feelings and emotions, and as we apprehend them expose us, as little in our own poetry is able to do, to the conviction of our own fate. This is to say, perhaps, that no matter how much of our extra-literary standards we bring to bear on Dante, it is not enough; it is rather that Dante's standards enlighten ours; so that, as far as actually accepting or rejecting Dante goes, we have only our literary standards to resort to. (I suggest that it is not our Christianity that brings us to Dante, but our desperate lack of it.) If this statement of present affairs is provisionally correct it constitutes a profound judgment of defect in our culture, established, in the fact, by literary means alone. Thus, in effect, we witness literary standards operating the Christian order as a "mere" principle of composition. This is not offered with approval or disapproval, but hazarded as a possible mode of approaching the problem of judging literature; namely, by the transformation of literary standards to the level of general conviction. It should be added that there does not seem to be any other poet—certainly not Shakespeare, who dramatized inertia rather than order—where such a possibility shows itself, Dante is alone in achievement.

You would not think so from a quick rereading of the principal literary critics since the middle of the nineteenth century—since, that is, the specific decay of the Christian order began to be felt as a shifting towards disorder, towards dismay, towards corruption, in the general order of culture. In Taine and Saint Beuve; in Arnold and Pater; in Babbitt and More; in the psychologists, the aestheticians, and the Marxists; in the critics associated with the *Action Française,* and in the secular neo-Thomists as well; indeed almost everywhere that men have taken literature seriously, you will find the tendency prevalent, at varying intensities, to estimate the value of writers in the degree that their *literary* standards did or did not operate in the place of other standards. Writers have been generally judged, along the lines of the critic's particular interest, as to whether or not they were able to effect deliberately such a transformation of standards as we have just been suggesting that Dante effected as it were inadvertently. There is not a writer of the last century of any stature who has not been condemned, or at least run down, for his failure in this direction by one or more of these our most eminent and best trained critics.

Now it may be that these critics are right in their preoccupation. It may be that the vast task of ordering human feelings and emotions has been imposed upon the arts and especially upon literature by the present lack of any authority otherwise derived. It may be that we are committed—I will not say condemned—to a wholly secular culture. Faced with the immediate alternatives in the wave, as Mrs. Lindbergh calls it, of fascist and soviet culture, we may even hope for a secular culture. But if assent is given to that idea, it does not follow that the literary critic in emphasizing the Dantesque aspect of literature can escape his obligation to explore and to master the primary aspect of literature: that aspect in which it represents the experience of the actual which is beneath and beyond merely moral experience, and which alone grounds or situates moral experience. Eliot's remark holds true that as morals are only a primary consideration for the saint, so they are only a secondary consideration for the artist.

This brings us up sharp on our next question, as to whether the extra-literary interest, if it predominates in the critic's mind, enlightens the literary interest. With regard to the general mass of critics to whom we referred above, the answer is plainly negative, and may be drawn from two approximate facts about their work. They seem, in the mass, seldom to have enjoyed literature, and they seem as individuals, and especially when concerned with the literature of their own times, to have been concerned with what a given work did not do to the virtual exclusion of what it did do. In short, and this is what makes one most suspicious of their candor, they not only made their criticism autonomous, which is a sin of pride, but they also made criticism appear to do the work of literature, which is the sin of putting God in second place. They defiled their literary knowledge to the point where it hardly seems recogniseable as knowledge of literature at all; with the curious but natural result that their morals or politics or sociology or theology seemed second-rate, vitiated by isolation from the actual world which lay before them in the literature which was their declared subject-matter. That the literature has survived in spite of its criticism and continues to arouse the same sort of attention suggests that it was not that the intent of the critics was mistaken but that their method was inefficient and their attention inadequate.

It is not the business of this paper to decide to what uses literature may be put, and it is not the predilection of this writer to see literature made into a kind of Pandora's box of panaceas, or even into the source of a merely moral order; but if there is a demand for that sort of thing, and there is, then it had better be done along lines that admit the possibility of success at the beginning. Those lines exist, are available, and may be taught; they are indicated in the frame of questions around which these paragraphs have been laid down. Assuming that literature, being imaginative, is understood if at all by the whole imagination before it is understood or used in any other way, acknowledging that many interests not literary but moral, political, spiritual, are nevertheless imaginatively present in literature, and even insisting that it is in the light of those interests that literature shows its stature (thereby adding to our own) and must be judged, it remains necessary to approach those other interests through the interests of the works themselves: through what is told, shown, expressed. It is there, in the interest of the actual, shaped and composed by what Santayana calls the enormous burden of perception—all that the intellect ignores or merely schematises—it is there, straight in front of you, in the words and the motions of the words, that the artist has focussed, or failed to focus, those interests you want. It could not be otherwise.

If you think otherwise, there is a primary defect in your contact with literature such as you would not permit yourself, say, in your contact with philosophy where it is a commonplace that the words are important and often difficult: where a universe is heaped in a phrase. If you think it is so but easy, you are rash and inexperienced. In the very degree that the work of literature does focus the interests you want it will be difficult—indeed an inexhaustible labor—to grasp the text. And until you have grasped the text you cannot paraphrase it; and to paraphrase in intellectual terms an imaginative experience is I suppose a generalized description of what you mean to do. But if you can grasp the text the rest will either come naturally, though arduously, or will seem irrelevant or superfluous. You will have either the labor of articulating your judgment of interest, or you will see that, so far as literature is concerned, it does not count.

The real difficulty lies further back, and is double in character. It consists, first, in being willing to concentrate your maximum attention upon the work which the words and the motions of the words—and by motions I mean all the technical devices of literature—perform upon each other. Secondly, it consists in submitting, at least provisionally, to whatever authority your attention brings to light in the words. In doing this you will be following in pretty close parallel the procedure which the writer followed. Whether your submission is permanent or must be withdrawn will be determined by the judgment of all the standards and all the interests you can bring to bear. These will differ with the work in hand. But the act of submission must be made before you can tell; it is an act of imagination, not of will; and it is the enabling act of criticism. If it does not provide you with another Dante, it will at least provide you with an interest in literature; and without that you would not know a Dante if he appeared.

The Undergraduate Writer as Writer

I suppose it will be all to the good if we limit the kind of writer we are talking about to the creative writer—more particularly, to the writer who tries to be creative under the peculiar but pressing distractions of undergraduate life, which very likely are only a very little more distracting than distractions elsewhere. As everyone present is no doubt obsessed with his own version of what these distractions are and as no two of you would agree as to their relative distractingness, we will say no more about them but merely pretend that they do not exist. As to what a creative writer *is,* the conditions are much the same. Everybody knows about him in his own way—a way that is short of satisfactory definition. We shall merely insist that he does exist and that in so far as he busies himself about writing he is quite admirable. In short, we put up with him.

Another good thing will be to say what the creative writer—and especially the undergraduate creative writer—is *not.* He is not likely to write easily, except when he has nothing to say. So accomplished a poet as Yeats remarked that the difference between a good and a bad poet was that the good poet wrote with great difficulty what the bad poet wrote easily. If your undergraduate writer finds himself writing easily, the chances are that he is not writing creatively but is writing off the surface of someone else's mind or out of the bottom of the vast reservoir of dead commonplace. If he looks, he will see that he has not written what he had in mind or, worse, that he has not discovered anything in his mind capable of being created on the page. The usual thing is, at this point, to give up the effort, to succumb to the nearest distraction, and to find satisfaction in getting by. Your truly creative writer cannot be the fellow who gets by; that is the privilege reserved for the merely popular writer—I do not say the good writer who grows popular, but the merely popular writer. As he writes to get by, he will do to pass the time. No. I think we may end our negatives and hazard it that the truly creative writer for the most part fails to get by precisely because he is so deeply concerned with the struggle, not to pass, but to *occupy* the time; which means to fill up his words as brimful as may be with the actuality, the quality, the whatness, the substance of what he has seen as possible to create. To borrow again from Yeats, he will have chosen of all things not impossible the most difficult.

This is to put the matter on a high plane. It is the plane of longterm judgment. It is the plane on which the writers of the past survive, if they do survive. Thus it is the plane at which, whether they are conscious of it or not, contemporary writers try to write and which they naturally for the most part fail to reach or reach only partially, for the moment, in a line, a passage, a paragraph, a parenthesis—almost, as it were, by accident. In other words, most writers necessarily fail most of the time. There is a radical imperfection in even the greatest art, which you cannot get around except by great effort and which you cannot overcome for sure at all, no matter how long and hard you try. As a consequence, we are bound to enjoy, and to value, the incomplete, the inadequate, the imperfect piece of writing, provided only it aimed in the direction of the complete, the adequate, the perfect: provided, in short, that it is the best job of work possible amid the distractions of a lifetime and the various privations of disability. I suggest that this is about as far as you can go in making a high initial standard. If you insist on anything more highfalutin, you will spoil your fun. If you refuse to enjoy or to do anything short of the best, you will never understand what the best might be. You will be damned, as you ought, for a kill-joy; and that is the end of you.

Here the undergraduate writer comes in pat. No one expects him to be perfect; everyone makes allowances for him; even his friends will invent reasons, if they find none, for enjoying what he writes. I suspect things would be better in the literary world all round if all writers were treated with the same generosity; there would be both more and better reading and more and better writing. Generosity, like friendship, is more demanding than snobbish spite or indifference.

Let us make the assumption, then—and I think it is a true assumption—that the undergraduate writer is naturally on the right track and try to see what some of the problems are, which, as he fails to solve them, knock him askew. I have in mind only those problems which are open to solution through the practice of the profession of writing. Some of them have to do with writers of any age or skill. Some have to do more with relatively young and inexperienced writers—a class of persons not necessarily the same as young and inexperienced men. But all except one of the problems which I shall mention have this in common: that they can be solved only for the occasion, in the particular act of writing. One way or another they are problems of the trade, the craft, the profession and thus have the double characteristic of all technical problems: that, while the skill needed can be learned by example, precept, and practice, the application is always in some sense fresh, novel, unique. I suppose that that is where the creative part of writing comes in: the use of the words is yours, though the words themselves—even your neologisms—cannot be.

The problem which makes the exception, the problem which is not primarily technical, has nevertheless certain secondary technical features through which alone we are able to get hold of it in practice. Let us take hold of it first because, no matter to whom else it applies, it applies almost without exception to the young writer and because, for the most part, the writer is aware of it only as an intruding, alien, vague ill-ease: the way an interrupted dinner sits within you before digestion is resumed. This is the problem of writing before you have a theme. I don't mean plot or subject matter or point of view; I mean precisely an *intention*—as some critics would call it—big enough to give direction and meaning and conclusiveness to your plot or your subject matter or your point of view. I mean, a little less precisely, an omnivorous central notion—a kind of magnetic core of imagination—which will digest and order and compose all or almost all the material that comes to hand. It is perhaps the definition of a great writer that he has such a theme. It is the possession apart from mere peculiarity—his accidental oddities and imperfections—that defines a great writer's character: it is what puts and holds his material together into a unity. It is the sort of thing we mean when we say Hemingway writes about doomed men, Thomas Mann writes about the delicate man, the outsider; the thing we have more vaguely in mind—it is so much larger!—when we say Dostoevsky dealt with the injured, the insulted, the humiliated; the thing we know, but do not know in words, when we say Shakespeare or Dante or whoever—and stop short if we have good sense. A major theme is one of those things we know and do not know. Even with themes less than major, we cannot predict them or in any way say what they are until they have emerged; and it is with lesser themes—themes just big enough to keep us going—that we have to do, because, no matter how big a theme is in itself, you will make a small theme out of it until your skill has become very great; until you know how, so to say, to let a great theme have its way, until you have the technical means of supplying it with material.

Here, perhaps, is the best place to say that about the only way you can go about looking for a theme is to write, regardless, what you know, that is, you must write only where you have authority over the details, over some major aspect of your subject. If you do that—if you find you are *able* to do that— you may come to the condition of having authority *as an author*. This is not a mere verbal play. For you cannot know what you know *as an author* until you get it on the written page; and it is only what you get on the page which counts for anybody but yourself. The maxim, if you want it, is this: Writing alone increases authority in an author. It follows that, as you increase your authority in this sense, you also increase your chances of finding your material involved in a genuine theme. The inner stress of the things you have put together will become plainer, will seem to be their meaning, their intention; and you will find suddenly that your words and the pattern that runs among them have an organic life of their own—quite different, even alien perhaps, to anything you expected.

It may be observed parenthetically that one of the commoner sources of authentic themes, in the sense that we have been developing, has been in some deep conviction about life entertained quite aside from the author's experience and derived from some external authority. One thinks immediately of the great religious art of the Middle Ages; of the classic revival in the Renaissance; of the infusion of Platonism into seventeenth-century English poetry; the cult of nature in Romantic poetry; the effect of anthropology (Frazer's *Golden Bough*) on Eliot's *Waste Land;* and so on. I do not think that writers today are very likely to find their themes in this way, or if they do that they will be able to do much with them. In the examples given you will notice a diminution of external authority and an increase in the effect of the writer's authority as such. We have become, whether we wish to or not, largely dependent for our convictions on our own resources; there is only the actual world outside us, the rest is within our heads. It is a curious and I think illuminating fact that there is support for this statement in a poet with all possible external authority available to him in the Anglo-Catholic persuasion of the Church of England. I mean, of course, T. S. Eliot; yet it is Eliot who insists that only in his prose reflections can he be concerned with the ideal; in his poetry he must be concerned with the actual. Only over the actual can his work have authority.

This is a very alarming state of things if you think about it; but it will be only your thoughts that make it alarming, for you will most likely think that you are on your own. You are not. You were never less so. You are something much worse from the naive point of view; at any rate you are in a predicament harder to get out of than has been the lot of writers and artists and thinkers in most civilized times. You are more than ever the random creature of every idea that blows; and your predicament is which way to turn, what ideas if any to use, to get back into imaginative relation to the life you actually live. Whatever you do in religion, philosophy, politics, and society generally, I suggest that *as writers* you go about it the other way round: start with the actual which confronts you and stick to it. I do not mean to be anti-intellectual or antirational. I don't want you to think with your blood or your bowels or your adrenal glands—you do that more than enough by nature. I mean that when you write, and especially when you come to write with the beginnings of authority and are on the edge maybe of discovering a genuine theme, you should stick to what you actually know and feel, even to what you *actually* think (for there are occasions in actual life which are open only to thought, which is why we think at all), using all along as your chief and sufficient discipline your native language.

This is not easy; it is the hardest thing in writing. The temptation is everywhere to use thought without relation to the actual, to use thought to conceal or distort the actual. But if you do not stick to the actual you will never come upon a theme worth having; you will have merely a mechanism—a trick beginning as well as a trick ending—a formula of dead shells of words without sound or motion; and as an author, a creative writer, you will have lost your birthright. Words are your medium, and as Professor Woods used to say at Harvard—rubbing his hands into the desk in front of him—the reality in words is greater than, and anterior to, any use to which you can put them. It is the reality in words that makes the actual experience permanent. If you think it is the other way round, you may be right, but you have no business being a writer.

Perhaps you will recall that at the beginning of these remarks about having or not having a theme I said that, although in a sense the whole problem was outside the practical, immediate problems of writing, yet it did exhibit certain connections with those problems and that it was, indeed, mainly through those technical connections that you might be expected to grasp—or fail to grasp—the problem of the theme. It is not that I have ignored those connections but that I have been leading up to them. What else, indeed, is technique for but to establish your theme? Or put the other way round, from the point of view of the practicing writer, what is a theme for but to exact the greatest possible use of your full technical resources? Without the demands of your theme—and this is the point of connection—your technique could not come to exist.

The burden of these remarks should be very comfortable to the aspiring writer—that it is only by writing what you want to write, only by writing what you are, as it were, *haunted* by the need to write, that you can make any real growth or can keep the growth you have made. This should relieve you—perhaps fatally, but never mind that—of the horrible problem of looking for something to write. We are all familiar with the one-poem poet, the one-novel novelist, who follows up his success with bad poems or bad novels, until the publishers give up all hope of a second coming. What we sometimes fail to realize is that if you look closely at the careers of successful writers you get a similar picture; the peaks are far between either in time or in books. The graph of most good writers is mostly below par, sometimes from a relative failure in technique, sometimes from a relative failure in theme, more often from both. I think of the poet Yeats who had a fallow period of five years preceded by a peak of 1890-ish poetry not now to our taste and followed by a range of high peaks of a very different order of poetry. I think of T. S. Eliot, a poet of very small production to begin with who had a peak in 1917, 1922, 1930, and 1935 and would I think, if it were not for the war, be ready for another peak now. I think of Henry James who in a writing life of forty-odd years had four peaks of high achievement and was rearing another when he fell ill and began to die. The levels between—the flat places, the arid plains—have puzzled many critics to explain. To me they seem the topography to be expected. The comparison I mean to make between such writers as Yeats, Eliot, and James and the one-poem poets is this: There are at their various levels—some of them good enough for the permanent anthologies—literally thousands of the one-poem poets, and each one of the good writers, is you might say, the rough equivalent of several dozen of the one-poem poets.

Here I want to make two deductions. One is that neither the good writer nor the one-poem poet can tell when the next good work or the one poem is under way. The second is that the drudgery that goes with the production of the failures is necessary to the production of the successes in both classes. There is no way out, drudgery is always necessary, to which I might add, as a warning of punishment to come, that there is probably more drudgery—I think certainly more—in executing a work of what we loosely call "inspiration" than there is in executing a work without inspiration, precisely because there is a growth in technique.

You, as undergraduate writers, are naturally in the condition of one-poem poets; and I mean to encourage you by saying that if you drudge enough when you think you have got your poem—or your story—by the tail, you may find yourself suddenly making such a leap in technique that you have him by the throat. I see, that is, sudden technical advances in the work of undergraduate writers which I can explain only on the ground that their themes have suddenly become more available to them. The thing works, as I said, both ways. Growth of technique gained from reading and discussion, of course, opens up access to the theme; but I repeat and insist that the other operation is far more important. It is the discovery of the theme that demands of you the use of technique which you must already have possessed implicitly or it would not have been there to use.

If what I have been saying seems largely offside or irrelevant to the problems that actually bother you, when put in the more or less general and ramshackle terms I have employed, perhaps I can make the matter clearer— and more formidable—by taking up in series some of the overt problems I have seen bothering you, with my general remarks still serving, I hope, as a background and perspective.

There is, first, the problem of problems, which afflicts some of you with the peculiar irritation of the itch of which you know neither that exact location nor the cause. The problem of problems arises, the practice of writing, when you learn by hearsay that there are all sorts of technical facilities for doing this or that; without knowing really what they are, you want to use at least some, and probably all of them. It is like introducing a man moderately handy with a tack hammer into a fully equipped carpenter shop after watching, once, a good man on a job. Of six saws with teeth of different shape and length and different set, how will you know which to use to saw a green pine board? As if that were your only embarrassment, you will probably suffer from alternating desperate desires to use, for the same job, either the fret saw or, if you are a chunky fellow like the late Thomas Wolfe, the adze and the ax by turns. Whatever choice you make you are likely to ruin either the tool or the job. The analogue in poetry is the attempt, say, to use the Petrarchan sonnet for the expression of ballad material, the effort to put domestic dialogue into rhyme royal. It is usually not as simple as that; it is usually such a complex thing as using the wrong mode of language, which you have caught from a particular poet, or the wrong vocabulary, or using association when you want contrast. I only mentioned the sonnet first, because there is an addiction to the sonnet in the wrong place which no amount of free verse has been able to wipe out. The result is the abortion which you do not see because it does not get printed, or the obfuscation of theme and material which bothers you so when it does get printed. In stories the analogue to the carpenter shop turns up more often as the artificial problem of how to lead up to having somebody say or do something, how to move somebody from place to place; and it often happens because the writer has chosen to tell the story from the point of view of the person least able by nature to display the substance to its best advantage. The usual answer to the writer beset by the problem of problems must always be to tell his story or write his poem any way he can, letting the drive of his subject matter, for the nonce, take over everything else. The very nature of technique—that it is traditional and has thereby gotten into the language itself—will help him considerably. It is surprising how well a story will tell itself if you let it alone as much as you can. However, my own suggestion would be, if undergraduate writers were not, like other writers, so lazy and impatient (as no doubt they must be), to try anything not immediately ridiculous that comes to mind. If it does not work, try again. But in any case do not try to use any device, no matter how beautifully used—so you think—by someone else, which after the first touch is seen to prevent you from telling your story or your poem at all. Not only the ultimate technique but, quantitatively, almost the whole of technique is in the words of the language you use and in the patterns or connections they make of themselves. Any form, any structure, any convention, will do which does not defeat your use of words. I suppose that is the hardest lesson that a writer has to learn.

Let us take something easier—a double problem which may at one end be described as the problem of self-expression and at the other end as the problem of deliberate ambition. Here I have only the usual things to say. If you have enough self to express objectively and on the page, go to it. So far as you are a writer, your self is only the focus or funnel for your experience; and there is no ambition more impossible to achieve than the common attempt to make your immediate autobiography do for a novel or the emotions of a summertime do for a sonnet sequence. If you think of yourself as the mere focus, rather than the substance, of experience, the same material will become immediately susceptible of objective expression. You will limit yourself to what you can put down on the page, all that and only that. What I am driving at is what I think Wordsworth was driving at in his remarks about emotion recollected in tranquillity. To recollect is in this sense to create; and, if you must write about yourself, you must first create yourself—a very arduous problem which I will not go into and which in fact I would not have the slightest idea how to tackle. I don't expect you to follow my advice on this matter, yet I think it is true that each of you will realize in the work of your friends that their best work is done when they are furthest from any immediate version of themselves.

Similar observations hold, if to a lesser degree, in the field of overambitiousness in what is apparently the objective field of poems which attempt to imitate the *Waste Land* or the *Inferno* or *Faust* or the *Bridge;* and they hold precisely because overambitiousness—the attempt to do something plainly beyond your powers of intellect and experience (I do *not* say your feeling or suffering)—is hardly more than a glorified form of self-expression. It is your self at work as you would like to see it; but the work that comes out will be beneath your least abilities. Naturally, you will try to do more than you are able, else you would never reach your ability. There is the maxim of Robert Frost, out of Robert Browning, that a man's reach should be larger than his grasp; but beside that I should like to put the remark that Henry Adams' wife once made about Henry James, that it was not that he "bites off more than he can chaw, but that he chaws more than he bites off." As to what a proper ambition is, I don't know, but as poetry is supposed to be a more persuasive form of words than mere speech I will quote two lines from T. S. Eliot:

> Ambition comes when early force is spent
> And when we find no longer all things possible

After thinking about self-expression and overambitiousness, it is a natural step forward to think of the problem of imitation and emulation. Here there is a vast amount to say which can be boiled down to saying: I am all for both. You learn more by imitation than any other way but you will achieve little until you get beyond the stage of imitation and approach the stage of emulation. You can read Eliot and Flaubert and Henry James and James Joyce and Shakespeare and Dante and anybody else you want to, and, if you are also a writer, you can no more escape imitating them than you can escape using the English language. Your imitations will make up for the work you cannot do for yourself: the work of articulating the inner skeleton of your poems or stories or plays. You will use the outsides of your models for the insides of your work, until you can make your own insides. That at the same time you will take over a great many effects without also providing any ground for them to stand on is regrettable, natural, and necessary. This is the evil we call being "meretricious": where you do anything to pick up custom, using as your standard of conduct only your success in making sales, meanwhile demeaning your own talents. To be meretricious, I need not remind you, is to be something befitting a harlot, which, in literature as elsewhere, is the oldest stuff in the world.

I mean there is a little of the harlot in every literary man, and especially in the first part of his career. You can apply this to suit yourselves. But one application I should not want you to overlook is that, no matter how good you turn out in the end, for a long while you are going to hawk your wares only if you disguise them, fill them out, enrich them, in the wares of others. Because of your own poverty and confusion with regard to the conventions of writing, you will be bound to use the conventions of the writers whom you admire. And in using these borrowed conventions, which seem so strong and rich and clear, you will not even know whether or not you have freshened them in the instance with new substance. They will seem fresh, seem substantial, seem, indeed, inevitable at the very moment when they will seem to others stale, empty, and altogether chancy affairs. This unconscious duplicity does not, however, reflect upon your character or your future—only upon your achievement. There is nothing else you can do. You cannot imitate from another writer more than an ape can, until you reach the point where you no longer need to imitate but can, at your own level, rival your master. To rival is to emulate; and, with the exception of one field, you cannot emulate until you have done a vast deal of empty aping. That field is, once more, the field of your words themselves. With enough care and with a subject matter appropriate to your powers of apery, you can tackle the details of your writing with almost the ability of the master himself. You have come so far by being able to speak and read and write at all that all you need in this field is a master.

T. S. Eliot has some very interesting remarks on this point in his paper on Dante. Dante, he says, is the great poet for the young poet to imitate rather than Shakespeare, because Dante is the great master of common speech: the universal common speech common to all Western languages. More of the vitality of his images comes over to foreign ears, to ignorant and unskilled ears, than comes over from any other poet—from Racine, say, or Baudelaire or Catullus or anyone you please. Thus, says Eliot, if you imitate Dante you will get something done in your own words; but if you imitate Shakespeare you will make a fool of yourself, until you are much nearer Shakepeare's sophistication of language than you are likely to come.

Here we come to two problems which would seem especially to bother the undergraduate writer. There is the problem of the ear for poetry, which includes the ear both for the speech around you and for the written speech of the great poets. It is a problem which ought to take care of itself as a matter of course; and in other societies than our own would naturally have done so. Judging by the verse which I see, the natural ear has fallen to so low an estate that we might well say that it has approached desuetude. No doubt the radio and the "talkies" have something to do with it. Possibly the fairly widespread training in visual as opposed to auditory reading in the primary schools has even more to do with it. Whatever the causes of tone indifference may be, the writer who is afflicted by it—and he naturally won't know it—must overcome it. There could be nothing more probably fatal for poetry or imaginative prose than the cumulative effect of such indifference. You cannot write well without music in your words. Nor can you read unless you can hear the music in the words you read. Not only is the meaning of imaginative language inseparable from its sound, but the sound is a major engine of meaning, without which your meaning will not move, in any sense of that word.

None of the aids to poetic hearing which I can suggest at all touch the fundamental deafness—the vast indifference to the creative values of the sound of language—which seems to infect the great quantity of contemporary verse. Indeed, there is just a chance that I may be wrong—not about the disappearance of sound from poetry—but about the future medium of poetry. We may be in for visual poetry to the virtual exclusion of audible poetry. There are examples broadcast in the topographically designed poems of E. E. Cummings—a poet with a native ear of high quality—poems which cannot be spoken aloud or inwardly heard and make sense, no matter how hard you try. You can work them out, but not in your auditory imagination. The prospect seems dismal because it is not my prospect; I prefer to think of it as a decorative heresy rather than the emerging orthodoxy. Meanwhile, I had rather suggest that you deliberately attempt to tune your ears to all the verse you read. If you cannot tune to the old poets, the fault will be most likely yours, and you had best try till you can. Read it over three or four times to yourself to establish the musical drift of it and then aloud to the best of your executive ability. Further, never let a page of your own verse go until it sounds right when you hear it in your head. If it sounds wrong, the meaning is not there, the words are not at work, there is nothing there.

There are tunes to prose, too; and I think of the example of Hemingway as one that may clinch my point. Hemingway's dialogue receives a great deal of praise; it is everywhere imitated; many writers have rivaled it for their own purposes. I would praise it also and should be glad to rival his dialogue in my own way. But what I wish to rival is not its patness to "realistic" speech, its equivalence to the phrasing of bar and barrack and bedroom. That patness is Hemingway's minor accomplishment. What I wish to rival, what any writer should wish to rival, is the clarity and cadence, the musical idiom of the speech, for it is that—the music of it—that makes it work. And the music did not spring from the haunts that Hemingway keeps. It reminds me, in fact, of nothing so much as the music of *The Way of the World*.

And here is a good note to end on. If you can grasp the importance of having music in your speech—your written language—you will have understood quite enough of what creative writing is to get on with. If you cannot grasp that importance, it matters little what other problems you may think you have solved. You may have a great theme and many skills; but, if you cannot make your words sound and, when need be, sing, your best readers will be indifferent to what you say. Indeed, you will not have said it. Ben Jonson perhaps put it as well as any. You will not, without music, have that within you

> That must and shall be sung, high and aloof,
> Safe from the wolf's black jaw and the dull ass's hoof.

The State of American Writing

It appears to me that your first three questions have to do with that fraction of the self-elected who write and criticize literature in its relation to the whole society; that your fourth, fifth, and sixth questions have to do with the inner doings of that fraction in relation to their work, when they can get to it; and that your last question, as put, is the swindling chasm which lies between all of us and our work. At any rate, such a division gives a practicable shape to discussion.

My initial assumption is that the elite of writers in America, and so far as I know in other countries, is at present not only self-elected but is also without adequate relation to the forces which shape or deform our culture. (Malraux is only an apparent exception: he represents something that will only be obliterated by the success of the forces with which he allies himself.) There is not even an adequate relation of rebellion. We have instead a vogue for the terms anxiety and euphoria; and we have a growing literary expertness in the techniques of expressing the experience of dismay, and the general techniques for creating the conditions of trouble. With us the role of hero is taken by the impotent, the defective, the psychotic, or by the artist himself. All these are inadequate forms of rebellion. It is neither divine madness nor diabolic; neither inspired nor destructive; it is the anguish of letting go, the agony of the hellish drop, expressed as a kind of taking hold, a struggle in flight. It is as if one's private hysteria were the matrix for public disorder. It is as if we believed the only possible unity and enterprise were those of crisis—against any enemy, for survival. We have a secular world stricken with the mood of religious war. That is an aggravated way of saying how the literary elite responds to its feeling of the actual momentum of society.

Its feeling—its works of art—is what has happened to its culture, not what has happened to society; perhaps only what has happened to the elite itself. In point of fact, society persists—in America with extraordinary buoyancy, in Europe with the ancient tenacity. I see no fellaheen. In the elite (whether literary or not) there is a dare of consciousness as to what has also persisted, if only we would recognize it, in the culture of society; and indeed one would think the future of culture (the state of American letters) hopeless did not the writers so well express its present disrepair. They see the risk of spiritual fellaheen everywhere, and, rightly, they see it in the proliferation, in America already, and shortly in Britain, of a new intellectual proletariat; and in their writings they make dramatic prophecy.

I do not know about new literary figures, but it seems to me that there is a new literary tendency and that it comes under the head of this notion of spiritual fellaheen and may be explained (in the sense of diagnosis) as a consequence of inadequate relation between culture and society. What else in their various ways and with the varying degrees of consciousness in their authors are the recent novels of Lionel Trilling, Robert Penn Warren, and Saul Bellow—what else are they about? Why does Robert Lowell call his verse *Lord Weary's Castle,* Randall Jarrell his *The Losses,* John Berryman his *The Dispossessed?* Why do the young rejoice in—seeing analogues in themselves—all those aspects of William Faulkner which cheat or deprive the intelligence? Why is the negative mysticism of T. S. Eliot's *Four Quartets* satisfactory poetry to those who have no positive Christianity at all? Why are the alternatives Ernest Hemingway, Evelyn Waugh, Kenneth Patchen, and Aldous Huxley, if not that each of them, in his own way, reduces the human figures to a muscular, or authoritatively sinful, or apocalyptic, or magical-mystical jelly of principles without values: they are all of them easier to take, than those who hold on to their values no matter what else they let go.

If American middlebrow culture has grown stronger in this decade, I would suppose it was because the bulk of people cannot see themselves reflected in the adventures of the elite, or only so as a pastime, not as a touching possibility. The middlebrow does not want to be dragged through the adventures of his culture; he wants to enjoy it, to escape from it, and to be given the cold dope. His enjoyments and escape, but not his hankering for cold dope, probably rather bolster than threaten serious writing; his needs keep alive a kind of mechanical competence in the old modes of drama and narrative for the hand of the master when mastery again becomes possible. Neither O'Neill nor Hemingway by themselves have enough strength. We need the whole ruck of competents besides. Somebody someday will see what the commitments of our society really are, and will make them actual, and so illuminate much that is now doing in relative dark; he will have found what survives and what has been added and what the resultant new aspect is of our culture. Meanwhile there is the adventure of the intellectual proletariat.

Meanwhile there is also the literary revival in its various forms. It seems to me that James had the subject of the intellectual proletariat beautifully in hand before it existed; almost by himself he invented the artist as hero in defeat and made up the conventions by which his heroism could be expressed. That he had also the vision, and the courage to use it, of the Medusa face of life, has little to do with the success of his revival. That, representing an older elite, he yet makes an excellent bridge between the present elite and the middlebrow, is the whole secret of what is genuine in the revival. I do not see that either Forster or Fitzgerald serve any similar purpose. Forster is up a little, as he should be, in the cycle of reputation. Fitzgerald, I expect, is a kind of backwards prophecy: as a characteristic figure of the twenties he ought to mean something—some incompleted threat, perhaps. My prejudice is sharp; as I can see little ever alive in his work, I see only his figure to revive.

If these remarks carry any weight at all, it ought to seem the natural sequence of things that the writing of the late forties should be less experimental in language and form than that of the twenties. The job of *what the writing is about* has become the job of experiment and form, or, let us say, form and experiment in language have become attractive at a deeper set of levels than in the twenties: those levels where the substance of the thing expressed has to be created into form. Experiment in language requires more of a culture safely assumed than we seem to possess; and, on the contrary, when a writer is responsible for much more of the substance of his culture than the profession is accustomed to, he will tend to submit as much as possible to the controlling aspect of executive form. I imagine this has something to do with the formal influence of Henry James—quite apart from his revival. Certainly, also, it has something to do with the renewed sense of prosody and the re-assertion of the magical-architectural values of metre. The shift in emphasis is not at all because experimentation came to a dead end, and it will be a great pity if in the effort to make a poetry of statement, reaction should lead writers to make statement without poetry—which seems to me to have happened already in some painting and some music. It is not unlikely we might have an intensifying warfare in the arts where on one side you got insistence on unmediated perception and on the other insistence on the absolute matrix of form. This would result if, freed from both tradition and purpose, the impulse to experiment came to a dead end. But this could only come about if—

to remember an earlier PR symposium—there were a real failure of nerve: a loss of the real delight in imaginative risk.

What is ominous about the agglutination of writers in the universities is just that it declares such a possibility, especially if you look at it from the point of view of the old free-lancing risk those of my age grew up with as natural. But I do not know that the mortality of talent need be any higher in the universities than in other possible situations; it is merely that different precautions—different measures in public literary health—need to be taken now from those needful at an earlier time. Principally, these are measures of resolution that the leisure that exists for scholarly work shall also exist for literary work, and that the temptation to do more teaching—to make more money—and the other temptation, to lead more than two kinds of social life, both be resisted. This is a matter for the individuals concerned; some will fail all round, some will become wholly teachers, some will succeed. In any case, the writers will be in the universities. The economic, political, and cultural drifts of our society are towards the institutionalization of all the professions; their special freedoms will lie *only* in their own work, which to those with the American experience seems too little. As a people we are unused to taking our risks in our work. But even if society did not push writers into the universities, the enormous absolute and relative growth in the number of writers— a by-product of the geometrical progression of college graduates in the last fifty years—would do so. No form of free-lancing in the old sense could take care of them; and what room there is will naturally be taken up by the less serious writers, who make better free-lancers. It is also of course true that with the growth of the academies there has been an increase in the number of academic writers moving into serious fields.

Here we come hard on the sixth question; the remarks above in their various ways all marshall themselves about it. The "new criticism" naturally concentrated upon the analysis and interpretation of poetry because the language of the poetry itself was, like the elite who wrote it, self-elected; because its character was highly experimental in language and form; and because, so to speak, its authors were internal free-lancers—without adequate relation to the society of which they expressed the substance more and more as an *aesthetic* experience. (I duck the relation of this to poetry's "ever-diminishing audience," because I am not sure we have not merely returned, for the kind of court poetry we write, to the audience which preceded the era of universal education, and I suspect that audience is larger, not smaller, than it used to be. We have not been *able* to turn up any poetry to go with the new situation; it is either a failure or—more likely—a difference in our cultural structure.) It would seem to me that, just as the practice of writers now forces them to experiment with the very substance of their work, so criticism ought to analyze and elucidate, ought somehow to get at and bring to judgment of maximum knowledge, what is going on in these deep experiments at bringing the substance of culture to aesthetic expression. To the degree that critics become conscious of the job, they will transpose their skills to such a purpose. Re-examination is a perpetual need, since what is examined turns always a new face.

It is only one aspect of that face—and by no means surely the Medusa face—that shows through the tension between Soviet communism and ourselves. So far as we make it seem more than one aspect, or make it the dominant face, we create a swindling chasm between ourselves and our common enterprise; and so far as we do that, we cannot handle the tension except by forcing it to that crisis of which the cost is "not less than everything." That extravagance is the swindle, and it seems to me we tend to that extravagance because we do not understand our own culture very well, and do not know to what it is we are committed. To find out is partly our job.

The King over the Water:
Notes on the Novels of F. M. Hueffer

It would seem now, after re-reading some seven or eight of his novels, that Ford Madox Hueffer belonged to that race of novelists whose facility for the mere act of writing is so great that their minds never quite catch up with the job under way, and whose writing seldom stops on the difficulties that make the job worth doing. If you have the ease of too much talent you cannot benefit from the hardships of genius. Twenty years ago and more, when these novels were first read, nothing of this sort could have been said by the present writer. Let us see along what lines it has become possible now.

Ford Madox Hueffer—or Ford Madox Ford; to me he remains Hueffer—wrote a great many novels, publishing the first at the age of nineteen, and between 1920 and 1928 I read as many as I could lay hands on, without ever a twinge of reaction which might lead to judgment until it was asked for in the present circumstance. The twinge will appear later, but I do not think it will reach judgment; I do not think Hueffer was the kind of writer who takes to being judged much, because he did not diplay the materials, or the order of materials, suitable to our means of judgment; the twinge is enough.

Meanwhile, there is the memory of reading, and how it came about. Joseph Conrad just then in 1920, had come to the height of his reputation with *The Rescue,* and in reading Conrad one found that he had twice collaborated with Hueffer, in *Romance* and in *The Inheritors.* These being read and indiscriminately admired, one went on and read *The Good Soldier* out of curiosity to see what Hueffer was like all by himself, and came out with an admiration out of all proportion. Hueffer at the time seemed to belong to a group: he belonged to Conrad, W. H. Hudson, Stephen Crane; but that was only part of it, for he belonged also to Henry James, Ezra Pound, and T. S. Eliot; he belonged to two generations and to the bridge that over-arched them. He occupied, mysteriously but evidently, all the interstices between all the members of both groups, and somehow contributed an atmosphere in which all of them were able to breathe. He had something to do with the *life*, the genuineness, of the literature written between *Lord Jim* and *The Waste Land*, between *The Dynasts* and *Ulysses*. All this was actual enough at the time; *The English Review*, dug up and read in old numbers, and *the transatlantic review*, both of which Hueffer edited, make the history stand. Yet to think of Hueffer in this way involved a view of him which has little of the truth in it that goes beyond history, the kind of truth which must somehow be our subject here. Atmospheres do not last, and can be re-created only in the living memory. Ford Madox Hueffer bore no real relation to Conrad and Hudson except the editorial relation; he had in his own writing, what corresponds there to the editorial, he had the relation of the chameleon-response to them. When his work was in the felt presence of their work, the skin of his writing changed color accordingly. What he responded with was partly the stock baggage of English literature and partly his own sensibility. I do not see how anybody who had not read Conrad and James could see what Hueffer was up to by way of form and style in their separable senses, or for that matter how anybody not knowing Conrad and James could feel the impact of Hueffer's sensibility attempting to articulate itself in terms of what it had absorbed of theirs. Without that knowledge, Hueffer's novels seem stock and even hack on the formal side and freakish or eccentric on the side of sensibility.

All this is summary description of the sensibility articulated in *The Good Soldier*, and in the four novels of which Christopher Tietjens is the central character, *Some Do Not, No More Parades, A Man Could Stand Up*, and *Last Post*. The first was published in 1915, the Tietjens novels in early twenties. Aside from *Romance*, written in collaboration with Conrad, I take it that these novels are what we mean when we speak of Hueffer as a novelist. If they stand, we have to put beside them at least one Utopian fantasy, *Ladies Whose Bright Eyes* (1911) and perhaps the late Napoleonic romance, *A Little Less than Gods* (1928); because his serious novels lie always between fantasy and romance. *Ladies Whose Bright Eyes* is gay, light, tender: the fantasy of a commercially-minded London publisher (himself a fantasy rather than a caricature of the type) transported in a traumatic dream to the England of 1326; in terms of which, when he wakes, he undergoes a kind of backwards conversion, and unearths a corner of fourteenth-century Utopia in modern England. *A Little Less than Gods* is the historical romance of an Englishman who finds himself, a kind of chivalrous traitor, in the service of Napoleon between Elba and Waterloo; it is pompous, stuffy, and sloppy both as romance and as history; but is written, so the dedicatory letter says, in the belief that it is—or means to be—a true sight of history. Each of these books has something to do with the glory of an arbitrary prestige resting on values asserted but not found in the actual world: values which when felt critically deform rather than enlighten action in that world, so that the action ends in the destruction of the values themselves. Like the idea of Napoleon, such values have all the greatness possible without virtue, and like the Napoleonic and the medieval ideas, they have a genuine and universal popularity. Many people—or parts of many people—find life tolerable only because they think it is like that; other people find literature tolerable only if it furnishes such ideas for getting back at life. In writing light novels—more or less unconscious pot-boilers—in the exemplification of such ideas, Hueffer was certainly on the track of what people want in a light and preoccupied way.

In his serious novels, *The Good Soldier* and the novels about Tietjens listed above, what makes them serious is that these same ideas are treated seriously, with all the fanaticism that goes with fresh conversion or the sore point of fixed prejudice. Edward Ashburnham, the hero of *The Good Soldier,* is an extravagant princely sensualist, a wrecker of lives in the pursuit of life; he is also a soldier and he is seen by the narrator as a model of glory—a glory which is brought to a climax when, because his manners make it impossible to accept the body of a young girl brought up in his house, he cuts his throat and drives the young girl mad. Edward is feudal and Protestant; what moden Protestant feudalism cannot do to ruin him through his sensuality is done for him by his wife's Roman Catholicism. Feudalism, sensuality, Roman Catholicism, are, all three, forces which prevent the people in this book from coping with the real world and which exacerbate their relations to it.

In the Tietjens novels Toryism replaces feudalism, as it is the modern form of it, and as Tietjens is a Tory public servant in a world of 1914, or Lloyd George, liberalism; the sensuality is given to the wife rather than to the husband; the wife, being both Roman Catholic and sensualist, is thus more exacerbated than the wife in *The Good Soldier.* Otherwise the ideas are much the same. The virtues of the deprived Tory and the deprived Catholic are seen as the living forms of damnation. The Tory becomes the object of undeserved scandal, leading to disinheritance and his father's suicide, and thus, as a result *only* of his held beliefs as to the proper relations between father, son, and brother in a Tory family, to his own ruin. For her part, the Catholic sensualist becomes a bitch *manqué,* that is to say, an unmotivated destroyer of her own goods. There is not a person of account in the four volumes who is not animated by principle so high as to be a vocation from his or her point of view; but there is not a decent, frank, or satisfying relation between any two of them till the very end; principles get in the way by determining rather than formulating or judging values in conflict. Yet these principles are shown as admirable and exemplary in Christopher Tietjens, and exemplary if not wholly admirable in his wife Sylvia. Indeed the world is shown as in conspiracy against these principles—with the war of 1914-1918 as a particularly foul part of the conspiracy. The war, in presented fact, is only a kind of international Whiggery and interested scandal-mongering—all but those aspects of it which permit Christopher Tietjens to follow the Lord and behave like a princely Yorkshire Tory gentleman. Surely, if we want an easy name for this sort of thing, it is romanticism in reverse; it is the Faustian spirit of mastery turned suicidal on contact with classical clichés; it is also to say that these serious novels are only an intensified form of whatever happens when you put together the ideas of the medieval fantasy and the Napoleonic romance.

What intensifies them is, what we began by saying, the relation they bear to the work of his two immediate masters. And this is to say that Hueffer is a minor novelist in the sense that his novels would have little existence without the direct aid and the indirect momentum of the major writers upon whom he depended. He dealt with loyalty and the conflict of loyalties like Conrad, he dealt with fine consciences and hideously brooked sensualities like James. But all the loyalty he did not find heightened by Conrad was obstinacy, and all the conscience and sensuality he did not find created by James were priggery and moral suicide. Adding this to what has already been said of the chief novels, makes a terrible simplification: it says that Hueffer supplied only the excesses of his characters' vices and virtues, and only the excesses of their situations; and it suggests that his sensibility was unmoored, or was moored only in the sense that a sensibility may be moored to lost causes known to be lost.

Known to be lost. If there is an image upon which Hueffer's sensibility can be seen to declare its own force it is in an image of devotion to lost causes known to be lost; that is what his more serious novels dramatize, that is what his characters bring to their conflicts and situations, otherwise viable, to make them irremediable—for the law is already gone that could provide a remedy. In politics and philosophy we call this the cultivation of ancestral Utopias; in literature, since we can recognize these cultivations with the pang of actuality, they make a legitimate, though necessarily always subordinate, subject matter. They are real, these causes known to be lost—as real as the King over the Water—but they depend for their reality on their relation to causes not lost, much as history depends on the present which it disturbs, not for its truth but for its validity. So it is with Hueffer's novels; the validity of his dramatizations of men and women devoted to causes known to be lost depends on our sense of these same causes in the forms in which they are still to be struggled for. To the purposes of his obsession he chose the right masters in Conrad and James. His lost English Catholic women, his lost English Tories, his lost medievalists and his strange inventions of lost Americans, depend on Conrad's sailors and James's ladies and gentlemen (since they are not men and women) of the world—in whom only the milieu, the ambience of positive sensibility, is strange or lost. The difference is that where the people in Conrad and James are beaten by the life to which they are committed and by the great society of which they believe themselves to be at the heart, in Hueffer the people are beaten because they believe themselves animated by loyalties and consciences utterly alien to the life and the society in which they find themselves. Not only their fate, but also their ideals are intolerable to them. They make of their *noblesse oblige* the substance as well as the instument of their damnation. They are ourselves beside ourselves the wrong way; and they are so because the sensibility of the novels is identical with that of the characters; there is no foil or relief, whether of aspiration or of form; only that terrible facility with the medium which goes with causes known to be lost.

That is the twinge of reaction that comes in re-reading Hueffer's novels; that as an artist as well as a man he knew his causes to be lost: which is why he had to be facile, and why he could not supply his novels with the materials for judgment. You cannot judge the King over the Water, however you may feel a twinge at the toast proposed.

The Substance That Prevails*

It is sometimes said that a man turns his thoughts into clichés in order to get rid of the words that erode the movement of thought into contortions of their sweet original agilities. It is then that we have another chance. But there is no less of a chance the other way round. Let us ignore the poor creatures of our own thoughts. Is there not a way of saying that the great experiences of thought come about when the current of our lifetimes suddenly explodes or finds expression in cliches of which the meaning had been forgotten or had not yet come to pass? In the wooing of these two chances lies much of the adventurous affair of lyric poetry; and the lover of lyric poetry must, I think, as in the adventure of other loves, choose both chances—if only because it is by the celebration of both chances, sometimes separately and sometimes at once, that our modern lyric poets come to make memorable statements. Thus, to study clichés, especially in poetry, is one way to study thought. It is good to remember at this point a remark Delacroix made in his *Journals:* that the *thought* in painting showed at its purest in sketches or initial studies. I think he mentioned Titian. I don't know if Delacroix meant it, but there is in his remark an implication that something happens to thought later on. Aristotle in the *Poetics* had an analogous observation: that you use thought or dianoia when the action isn't working. We seem to want, not thought, but something that has happened to thought. When a woman says of a man, "I wouldn't give a thought to him," it is by no means an entire dismissal: it is an initial assessment.

And there we are, tickled and bewitched with the possibilities of talking

*In *The Collected Poems of Wallace Stevens.* Knopf. $7.50. These remarks were presented in an earlier form as a Braden Lecture at Yale University, Oct. 8, 1954.

about the poetry of Wallace Stevens. It was Mr. Ransom, on a singularly hot evening in Indiana when thought was remote on some cooler planet, who wanted me to give a thought to Stevens; and he had since reiterated this want in print (and promises more). For myself, I have tried to find the "thought" in Stevens, and believe I have felt the prod of it, but as for understanding it, there seems to be an occasion for repeating the dying words of Hugo Grotius: "By understanding many things I have accomplished nothing." Grotius is very much like a name in some poem by Stevens, and his dying words are like certain of Stevens' dying cadences—that echo and echo without rhyme and never quite die.

This is in the *proprium* of Stevens. It is the intellect that dies in words, and Stevens is not—and the echoes remind us he is not—a man of intellect. When he tries for intellect, for the *ordnance* of concepts, his work becomes merely discursive and his syntax disappears into an obfuscation of sensation—indeed into a disorder of sensation. The grasping hand, too grasping, lets everything drop into a tumulus of shards. The reader will find this more apparent in the prose essays than in the poetry: he writes the other harmony of prose in an archaic and incomplete language. It is only the French who can sack the very seat of the intellect in lucid and controlled prose; I think of Mallarmé, Apollinaire, and Aragon; Stevens still uses the language of poetry in its own adjudication, the language which the intellect puts into a different order and for administrative purposes under the desperate programs of action. For Stevens, concepts are not tools of action or the worse urgency of inaction; for him concepts are merely names or reminders for thought otherwise experienced. Thought, I take it, it is the sum of human activities engaged in ordering, demolishing, and reconstructing the sensibility, both as we have inherited it and as we add to it. It has many voices and many modes besides those of the intellect, and some of those modes and voices engorge and ravish those of the intellect: they do so by the application of ideas, not as Arnold wanted ideas to be applied to life, but as an assessment of what can be made of life. Stevens is in this sense a poet of ideas: there is in his poetry *a poiesis of things seen:* he sees his ideas and the seeing is residual and resourceful in the best of his words. His poems are often concerned with what is immortal in man; but there is no theory of immortality in them in any conceptual sense, nor are there any prudential statements; his poems rather give a way of looking at ideas of immortality, and what you get is a sense of intimacy rather than a sense of understanding: "*et mentem mortalia tangunt.*" This is how the tears of things are stopped: in intimacy.

But it is not only immortality that is engaged in Stevens' verse: the scholar, the nun, the recruit or candidate, the lacerated fop, the dandy agile with hope—all these and others are experienced in the otherwise of Stevens' thought. In that otherwise—in the roaring at the other side of the silence of his mind (George Eliot's phrase)—he has been continuously engaged with the *experience* of conceptual thought as it strikes with "the clashed edges of two words that kill," and he gives it an *aesthetic* authority to which we can assent or dissent, which we can refute or praise, find thin or rich, but which neither invites scepticism nor admits proof. If you doubt or demonstrate these ideas, you cannot feel them and they disappear mere irrecoverable illusions. But if you take them in their cadence, the illusions are the very experience of the truth. In their cadence they have the verisimilitude and the coherence of the images in which they are arranged. That should be enough to ask, though it is not all that can sometimes be asked, of the adventures of ideas in poetry.

Dante was sometimes alive with the intellect in its own shape; in him logic sometimes has the autonomous force of poetry or the miraculous authority of numbers; as, to a lesser degree, and against his will, these qualities are also sometimes found in Valéry. So, too, Shakespeare dramatized his obsessive thoughts, rearing out of them an action of extreme moral authenticity; which is, again to lesser degree, the quality of Yeats in his dramatic lyrics. That is why we think of Dante and Shakespeare as comprehensive poets. We cannot think so of Stevens, but if we try we can then better see what is proper to think of him. Stevens has rather an *apprehension* than a *comprehension* of conceptual or intellectual thought. In him concepts either rise like the hairs at the back of the neck and along the spine—goose flesh of the spirit—or he moves them about like counters in a game, where the values vary according to the unexpected arrangement—the *acte gratuit*—of the moment. In the second case they become abstractions, in the first they deepen as concepts. Concepts are how we remember what we know. Abstractions type spilt blood for imperative use.

I have been saying, perhaps, that in Stevens' concepts and abstractions is the weather of his sensibility. The "otherwise" of his thoughts is weatherwise, like a weather-vane in good order. Indeed the terms of weather or of bodily presence are actually his richest concepts: they affect the sentiments without modifying the substance of his poems. His concepts afford him the moods in which to show, in abstractions, the sheer preciousness of his beliefs. This is one way of defining the whole operation of "Le Monocle de Mon Oncle," "The Comedian as the Letter C," "Sunday Morning," "Peter Quince at the Clavier," and "Esthétique du Mal." Weather and bodily presence enlighten his reminiscence, and thus illuminate all that haunts his sensibility. The body of his belief is within him and all around him and he is alone with respect to both, except as he gives the voices—aesthetic voice, which is *also* his own voice—in his poems. He does not generalize, he identifies. For him, *in nomine, numine*.

It has often been argued to the contrary, and it may be that Stevens has argued to the contrary himself. He sometimes thinks his identifications generalize his thought, but he only thinks so in his prose, especially in the essay, "The Noble Rider." That essay draws on the "The Phaedrus," but rather less so than "Death In Venice," and merely because it does so draw it lends authority to those who call Stevens a Platonist. The poems too address Plato, who is once called "the ultimate Plato, the tranquil jewel in this confusion." And so on. It may be that Stevens is alone in Plato's cave, but it is not the cave Plato thought it was. His platonic ideas seem to me ideas of weather and color and being; and are otherwise names not realities. Those who have studied philosophy at the University of Paris in the 13th Century will catch the distinction; others had better look up the terms, since our modern instincts want to reverse the distinction, and on behalf of either term. At any rate, Stevens is far more a nominalist than a realist in the technical sense—as indeed almost every poet except Plato has been. Stephen Dedalus' pledge to Aristotle and rejection of Plato in the Library chapter in *Ulysses* is not the quirk of a young artist, but an expression of his vital bent. And so with Wallace Stevens. He is a nominalist longing to find his names realities. He is a poet bitten and wincing with reason; but it is the bite and wince that make the poetry and the reason is the dominant trend of the weather. In what we name, and because we can name it, we find the divine substance. This is the nature of experience when taken aesthetically, with no urgency of action; and it ought to be what we mean by pure poetry. Pure poetry is weathered experience, weathered by naming.

The most beautiful ordering of such experience comes in the arrangements—the coherences—we give to our persistent daylight dreams, those dreams in which, because of long cultivation, our personalities and our moral consciousnesses unite. It therefore follows by nature that the purest poetry will arise when the aesthetic intelligence fastens an arrangement on disorder or chaos. The aesthetic intelligence sees at once—it is the transport of the experience—that disorder and chaos are the incipient or seed-forms of order, and perhaps the only ones they have. (This is why one suspects that God, at least when he was engaged on creation, was something of a poet.) Disorder and chaos constantly extrude from the heart of Stevens' poems; he never generalizes or censors or excludes them—unless it be one of these actions to find immense disorder the natural arrangement of truths. Instead he makes himself a connoisseur of chaos, as a normal next step in his role. Here is the first section of a poem by that name, and then something from the end.

I

A. A violent order is disorder; and
B. A great disorder is an order. These
Two things are one. (Pages of illustrations.) . . .
A great disorder is an order. Now, A
And B are not like statuary, posed
For a vista in the Louvre. They are things chalked
On the sidewalk so that the pensive man may see.

V

The pensive man . . . He sees that eagle float
For which the intricate Alps are a single nest.

The eagle disdains its nest, though it may yet return to it. We disdain what we have no compulsion to understand. The muse of Stevens is often such an eagle, and for our part we do not need to understand the eagle to see that this is so. Only the Hollywood parody of our existence requires constant understanding, and the rest of us only need it at ordinary moments; at extraordinary moments there is something better which no parody ever sees. Stevens does not, then, have an *understanding mind;* it is rather a mind seized with its own actions, and, under that standard, infinitely aware of other actions and inactions. Hence we call him a dandy and he calls himself a connoisseur. There is no dandy like a bird in flight, and there is no connoisseur like an animal watchfully at rest, where flight and rest have the dignity of awareness: of incipient disdainful acknowledging responsive agility. One side of this agility articulates beautifully in the third stanza of "La Monocle de Mon Oncle":

Is it for nothing, then, that old Chinese
Sat tittivating by their mountain pools
Or in the Yangtse studied out their beards?
I shall not play the flat historic scale.
You know how Utamaro's beauties sought
The end of love in their all-speaking braids.
You know the mountainous coiffures of Bath.

> Alas! Have all the barbers lived in vain
> That not one curl in nature has survived?
> Why, without pity on these studious ghosts,
> Do you come dripping in your hair from sleep?

That is the affirmative, the dandy in true action: like a Baudelaire crying in another night, or a Mallarmé exposing the secret of his manners, or a Valéry smiling openly. Here is the other side, which I will not call negative, which is the connoisseur, in reserve, like a quiet lion seen punctiliously, with plastic deliberation, by Rousseau or in a drawing of Leonardo.

> The greatest poverty is not to live
> In a physical world, to feel that one's desire
> Is too difficult to tell from despair . . .

These lines are taken from Section XV of "Esthétique du Mal": the immediate playful conceptions of evil to which for over a century the dandy has been drawn in his other half, where he is the connoisseur of the actions he takes as a dandy. A dandy could not live except in the physical world which the connoisseur sees dissolve all round him. The dandy survives the connoisseur by assessing the dissolution; the connoisseur sees how it is, in dissolution, that the dandy survives. I think of three old poems which illustrate this antinomy of dissolution and survival: "Anecdote of the Jar in Tennessee," "Thirteen Ways of Looking at a Blackbird," and "Sea Surface Full of Clouds"—all of which have enraged the bourgeois from time to time, and very naturally, too, since the bourgeois sees only the penalties and deprivations and never the liberations of survival in such attitudes. It needs only be said that in the 30 triplets of the last named of these poems there are 32 shifting conceptual colors, some with moral fragrance, some with moral malevolence, all with a kind of aesthetic insolence and verve of manners.

A dandy can afford with the easiest of all thoughts not only insolence and manners but also learning and inkhornism. A dandy affords Euphuism both as ornament and as the instrument of sane growth, both the Elizabethan practical misconception and the original Greek conception. Affording this, he can also afford frivolity and waste and the kind of elegance that ignores syntax or shoe-laces. His pieties are likely to be expressed in compositions of these qualities, and yet reach great dignity; and indeed that is exactly how it is in the first stanza of "Sunday Morning." I quote only the first eight lines to remind the ear already aware, and to invite the one which is not.

Complacencies of the peignoir, and late
Coffee and oranges in a sunny chair,
And the green freedom of a cockatoo
Upon a rug mingle to dissipate
The holy hush of ancient sacrifice.
She dreams a little, and she feels the dark
Encroachment of that old catastrophe,
As a calm darkens among water-lights.

This is the courage and naked dignity of the role. But the dandy—and even more the connoisseur—needs protections, and his insolence is the first assertion of the need as his manners are the second. Like a duchess, he cannot be too far from his carriage and maintain the person he really is: the product of all his effort. He needs the idea of the poet and the idea of the poem, not so much for himself as for others: the idea of a superior person making a fundamental product: himself. Along with this, in Stevens, there is the protection of the idea of a vocabulary of rare words always justly used in terms of the dictionary together with a vocabulary of ordinary words which move outside the dictionary as they come before it. The idea of the vocabulary is probably connected with the need of asserting the protection of attitudes both of disdain and acceptance, where the disdain controls the acceptance. (This is very different from contempt and consent where there is humiliation not control.) This, in turn, is allied to the need for the protection afforded by foreign words: mostly very old words choked with history in every familiar circumstance, but in the new poems of Stevens stripped of all associations, and all the drawbacks of associations, so that they behave as if they had an authentic and elite life of their own—as if they only contributed to the poems of which they are actually a part. And lastly, there is the deliberately doubtful protection of studied carelessness amidst elegance, the letting of one out of three poems run down; the pretence at sketchy perception at crisis; then the casual pulling together in one gesture where the pretence was not to bother: like a special handshake.

Such would be the sketch of Stevens (Stevens the poet: the gods forbid any other image peer over the shoulder of these notes!) as dandy and connoisseur. Yet the sketch would be lacking in the thoughtfulness a sketch must have, if we did not also remind ourselves of certain other aspects of Stevens' poetic conduct of his vast affairs. Being a dandy, he is not a symbolist, either as Yeats or Valéry was: the iconography of his mind is immediate and self-explanatory *within* his vocabulary. You need no special key, only a dictionary and a sense of life and the willingness to assume his role. He is not a symbolist, but he may be a parodist: both dandy and connoisseur make a parody of their other selves: that is how they touch the quick of their other—their previous and their final—selves. Even as a parodist, he is not given to any secret meanings, nor to any meanings not present in immediate words and attitudes under the shaping influence of his role. In the deepest possible sense his thought is in the action of his role. So he writes of "a few things for themselves," and again—as near as he comes to the statement of mystery—he says "The only emperor is the emperor of ice-cream." His ambiguities are of the nature of consciousness not of intent, of sensibility not of aspiration. There is nothing he wishes to create, there is everything he wishes to meet; nothing to transcend, much to mirror; in the clashed edges of the things his poems see. Hence he is not an allegorist, but a connoisseur of the absolute in the phenomenal; everything is said as expressly as possible in the medium of his vocabulary, in the resources of the dictionary of his mind. The mystery of his senses is enough: for him it is a full statement (in "The Comedian as the Letter C") to say that "Man's intelligence is his soil." His four-fold interpretation never reaches to the anagogue; that reach would be out of his *métier*. His four-fold is in the cycle of the four seasons—which are often reduced to three as in the triads which govern so many of his poems— notably in "Notes towards a Supreme Fiction" and "Esthétique du Mal."

His poems ring the changes on what we already know: the aids and gnomic devices he uses are also those we already know—at least if we are not wholly megalopolitan. He uses the colors Blue, Red, Green; Clouds, Sea, Wind; Trees, Lakes, and Birds; Sun, Moon, and Stars; the Scholar, the Rabbi, and the Nun; the Colonist, the Grammarian, the Poet. (The division into triads is deliberate, but not authoritative.) These are the machinery: they constitute the minimum of outside adjustment, and take up all the slack of meaning in the feelings the poems discriminate. It is these devices that focus all the meaning found in the precise and persnickety and learned words which intervene and give role to the poems. All this machinery, all these terms, belong in the area of Stevens' natural piety: how he sees things with respect, and passion, to how they are beyond his immediate experience of them. There is possibly an exception to be made for the last term in the list—Poet, poem, poetry in its various forms. Ordinarily, one thinks poets should be at home in their poetry but anonymous to all outsiders. Reading over Stevens' poetry, one gradually sees otherwise for him: here the poet is playing the role of the dandy, and the dandy is nothing if not conspicuous, even in the wilderness. Stevens says it himself in "Bantams in Pine Woods." This poem is not triads, but dyads.

> Chieftain Iffucan of Azcan in caftan
> Of tan with henna hackles, halt!

> Damned universal cock, as if the sun
> Was blackamoor to bear your blazing tail.
>
> Fat! Fat! Fat! Fat! I am the personal.
> Your world is you. I am my world.
>
> You ten-foot poet among inchlings. Fat!
> Begone! An inchling bristles in these pines,
>
> Bristles, and points their Appalachian tangs,
> And fears not portly Azcan not his hoos.

If I understand Stevens aright, it is the poet not the bantam who is left. The bantam "knows desire without an object of desire. All mind and violence and nothing felt." The poet is the other way round, precisely. The poet gives identity and feeling—gives voice to the bantam. He gives the bantam by his conspicuous presence, and so gives ourselves —in the last line of the last poem in *The Collected Poems*—"a new knowledge of reality."

For the rest, I should like to hazard it that Stevens, like so many Americans when they are poets, is a Mediterranean man with very little of the rage for order which inhabits and inhibits so many of our northern ancestors. His sense of order is the sense of what he does with his chaos; order feeds on, does not repel, anarchy; his order is, finally, his catholic self. His barbarisms are his own, too, because his violence is his own. He knows with respect both to order and violence that they spring from deep within himself and also from greatly outside himself. With his order and his violence he is at home; he does not have to resort to them. *In nomine, numine.* Let us risk a sketch of how this comes about.

It is in classical times—in the times of Plato, in the time when the Mediterranean sea predominated—that we learn how genius presided over, cherished, then entered the human Psyche by violence. In Christian times what we called the Psyche became what we call the soul and what we called genius became pretty much what most of us call talent. Talent is a violence in the soul. I suggest that genius in western history became something a little soft and unpredictable, while talent became something hard and resourceful and engaged in perpetual struggle. The suggestion may be good only for the moment or the hour. Talent is a violence of the soul, but the degree of violence differs with the capacity of the soul. Ordinary talent pours itself into the cliché; there is only enough pressure for that; and so the cliché survives, unchanged, as in proverbs and easy strategies. Of other talent, some hides; some ignites the cliché; and some creates, or finds, or reaches what we call style: the expressive, independent mastery of experience: and is thereby controlled. Only style, not society, can control the violence of great talent. Style is what talent does with the genius which has violated the soul. Hence the maxim: style is the man.

I would suppose this maxim would apply immediately to politics—to what Irving Babbitt called the problem of democracy and leadership; and indeed it first came to my mind in thinking of the joint politics of the police states of the Middle East and the relatively unpoliced states of Western Europe and North America. But if it applies there it applies all the more to what goes on in a good deal of poetry, and the thought of this application endeared itself to me particularly so soon as I began to think of the poetry of Wallace Stevens. It is the violence the soul sees in the world that most requires style to control it: to make it meaningful, or, if you like, to make it universal, more universal than history, as Aristotle, Mr. Toynbee, and Mr. Stevens all want it to be. I am not suggesting that style or poetry can save the world any more than politics can; the world is insusceptible of salvation, and I see no reason why the world should require what man's dreams do. No. I mean only that style, whether in politics or poetry, is the means of setting up a modus vivendi with the violence either in the world or in the soul; and it is with this aspect of Wallace Stevens' poetry that these remarks are meant to deal. It gives me all the more pleasure to say so because, in any ordinary sense, Mr. Stevens' poems are hardly related to politics at all. Rather, by analogy, they lend a style even to the violence of politics: even politics is seen as poetry—as a part of the supreme fiction that, as Mr. Stevens says, makes widows wince.

> Poetry is the supreme fiction, madame.
> Take the moral law and make a nave of it.
> And from the nave build haunted heaven. Thus,
> The conscience is converted into palms,
> Like windy citherns hankering for hymns . . .
> This will make widows wince. But fictive things
> Wink as they will. Wink most when widows wince.

But it was I who came from politics to Mr. Stevens' poetry; and it is therefore I, or any reader, who will think of his poems when thinking of politics: in the hope of being intimate with them, and a part of them, without being required to understand them or to put them against the times, or some other time. George Santayana once said that in most cases understanding is intimacy enough, and so it is not during all those hours when you are intent on action in the world, but when you are bent on action in the soul, and only action in the soul, then only the involvement of intimacy will do, without the impediment of understanding. It is what is called the dandy in Mr. Stevens who is the master of this deeply involved but uncommitted intimacy. There is something inelegant and not at all intimate about the statues of understanding, and there is a point, even, where understanding is only a statuesque barrier—a momentary frozen phase—sudden ice in the heart—in the elegant movement and intimate rest of the style whereby we grasp reality. Perhaps we can afford reality only when we are dandies—can only risk final affronts when we are fops—can only render adequate response when we have broken out of the community of understanding into the identity of style. Only then do we see the snowman through a mind of winter, only then see the "nothing that is not there and the nothing that is." It is Mr. Stevens who says this, not I.

> One must have a mind of winter
> To regard the frost and the boughs
> Of the pine-trees crusted with snow;
>
> And have been cold a long time
> To behold the junipers shagged with ice,
> The spruces rough in the distant glitter
>
> Of the January sun; and not to think
> Of any misery in the sound of the wind,
> In the sound of a few leaves,
>
> Which is the sound of the land
> Full of the same wind
> That is blowing in the same bare place
>
> For the listener, who listens in the snow,
> And, nothing himself, beholds
> Nothing that is not there and the nothing that is.

"The Snowman" is an early poem, and in another set of verses, called "An Ordinary Evening in New Haven" and written somewhere near 1950, and as if for this moment, he speaks thus of the two nothings:

> The poem is the cry of its occasion,
> Part of the res and not about it.
> The poet speaks the poem as it is,
>
> Not as it was: part of the reverberation
> Of a windy night as it is, when the marble statues
> Are like newspapers blown by the wind. He speaks

By sight and insight as they are. There is no
Tomorrow for him. The wind will have passed by,
The statues will have gone back to be things about.

"The Snowman" was such a cry of vision, as the "High-toned Old Christian Woman" was a cry of vision and desire. In the New Haven poem, there
is a line that says, "The point of vision and desire are the same." The juncture
may be illustrated, I think, in a very late poem called "The World as
Meditation."

Is it Ulysses that approaches from the east,
The interminable adventurer? The trees are mended.
The winter is washed away. Someone is moving

On the horizon and lifting himself up above it.
A form of fire approaches the cretonnes of Penelope,
Whose mere savage presence awakens the world in which she dwells.

She has composed, so long, a self with which to welcome him,
Companion to his self for her, which she imagined,
Two in a deep-founded sheltering, friend and dear friend.

The trees had been mended, as an essential exercise
In an inhuman meditation, larger than her own.
No winds like dogs watched over her at night.

She wanted nothing he could not bring her by coming alone.
She wanted no fetchings. His arms would be her necklace
And her belt, the final fortune of their desire.

But was it Ulysses? Or was it only the warmth of the sun
On her pillow? The thought kept beating in her like her heart.
The two kept beating together. It was only day.

It was Ulysses and it was not. Yet they had met,
Friend and dear friend and a planet's encouragement.
The barbarous strength within her would never fail.

She would talk a little to herself as she combed her hair,
Repeating his name with its patient syllables,
Never forgetting him that kept coming constantly so near.

This is an old man's poem in the sense that Verdi's *Otello* and *Falstaff* were
an old man's operas. It grasps nothing but youth. This is "the final fortune of
their desire"—the youth of style; and it is so a pendant to Verdi's operas and

to the Iliad, too, which is the greatest of old men's poems: the permanent order of style upon the violence of talent in the soul.

But this is no place to meditate the idiosyncrasy of the old man's style in prose or speech, whether it is Homer's or Hardy's, Monteverdi's or Verdi's, Renoir's or Titian's, or that of Wallace Stevens. Two fragments from poems in *Harmonium*—those which have been longest by us—will do much better than any meditation. From "Peter Quince at the Clavier" there is this:

> Beauty is momentary in the mind—
> The fitful tracing of a portal;
> But in the flesh it is immortal.

In the *flesh* it is immortal. That is one fragment. The other is from "Le Monocle de Mon Oncle," exactly half way through.

> If men at forty will be painting lakes
> The ephemeral blues must merge for them in one,
> The basic slate, the universal hue.
> There is a substance in us that prevails.

To which I add, from the next stanza, a grace note for the occasion:

> The honey of heaven may or may not come,
> But that of earth both comes and goes at once.

The Language of Silence:
A Citation

Those of us who are lovers of words—to whom a fine phrase brings a blush of response—know very well that words are merely one medium in which we express our crying-out and our salutation, our discovery and our assent, to what happens to us within and to what happens to us from without. Like all lovers, we add as much as we can to what we love: the particular from within and general from without. Our compassion is merciless because it is absolute. We have merciless compassion for the dancing bears—the ballet of our best words—because we understand they would if they could have been the moving stars—moving in their own drift and also our own. We are not lovers for nothing, but for life itself. *E pur si muove.*

That is why we blush, it is in the blush that ripeness is all, and it is under the blush, in the honey of its generation, that we know the rest is silence. It is silence that tries to speak, and it is the language of silence which we translate into our words. If we do not hear the silence in our spoken or written words—if we do not hear their voice—we find them dead or vain echo calling on something already disappeared. If we do hear the silence we know that the words are animated by and united with a life not altogether their own, and superior to it; and with the same life we respond; we blush to a blush.

Sometimes the words themselves blush with what they're made on and are burdened with the very cry of silence, the hymn in the throat. There is *King Lear* (II, iv, 56-7):

> O! how this mother swells up toward my heart;
> *Hysterica passio*! down, thou climbing sorrow!
> Thy element's below.

It may be that "mother" is a contraction of "smother." But I have seen, in a comment on this passage (Kenneth Muir's revision of Craig in the Arden edition) a citation from a contemporary of Shakespeare in which the disorder is defined as "the Mother or the Suffocation of the Mother, because, most commonly, it takes them with choking in the throat; and it is an affect of the mother or wombe." At any rate, something is being translated into words from another language. Whatever that language is it passes through thought into words bringing its rhythm with it, undismayed at the translation. It is amusing to reflect that Sir Walter Scott (in *Rob Roy*) found a mercy for his hero in this compassion when he fell aweeping, deserted of his love in the dusk: "I felt the tightening of the throat and breast, the *hysterica passio* of poor Lear." Sir Walter calls on Lear for the weight in his own voice, but the blush is there just the same.

But if Shakespeare has contracted the smother of the great storm into the inner violence of the "mother," what has Dante done in the words he gives Francesca but to turn all the mother in us into the smothering voice of the throat and breast, that yet comes clear in the words. Here again is the voice of merciless compassion, and it was Dante the Pilgrim, not Dante the author, who fainted with pity and fell as a dead body falls. Here is all the harshness of the love that moves the body in order to move the stars: it is sweet, even, and hoarse, in its fatality. We are saved from the mere ideal (as the ideal is saved from its mere self) by the throaty linkage of the voice of silence, the running rhythm through the other linkage of words and rhymes. It is as if Dante had translated his words back into the language of silence; and it is as if we listened to him to find what he had to say. There is no *tabula rasa* even in the purest expression. We listen to great men in the arts, and imitate their words, to find how our own great skill in the language of silence might break through, as theirs did, not into convention, conformity, compromise, but into the violent incarnation of style. We blush when we recognize our partners in this effort. Sometimes this is called wooing the Muse. We blush both in our inequality to our love and in our rising blood. Did we not wish to equal her, knowing we cannot, and did we not already know her voice, however imperfectly, in ourselves, the Muse would long since have become an unblushing lie. As it is, even her toes are faintly pink.

With so much for exordium (and with the substance of a peroration well in mind) let us first examine a little certain remarks of select ancestors, and then proceed to a sketch of the equivocal nature of present awareness. We shall see, I think, how the insight into inspiration has become a technique of troubles, how the sense of wisdom has become a set of schedules, and yet with nothing lost. After all this, the peroration will seem the mere hebetude of the daily disadvantageous task. But all the toes are pink.

On the ground of tradition, Scripture should come first, and here are the second and third verses from the thirty-ninth Psalm: "I was dumb with silence: I held my peace, even from good, and my sorrow was stirred. My heart was not within me; while I was musing the fire burned: then spake I with my tongue." The combination of loose idiom, basic metaphor, and an accurately stated order of procedure—almost as strict as surgery—is an astonishing witness to the depth of unconscious skill. Or, if that is too much, let us say that it is a complete example of small ritual in inducing inspiration: a ritual to persuade the reasons of the heart to translate themselves into the spoken word. Perhaps it is both; perhaps there is little difference, ultimately, between an order of procedure based on metaphor and a persuasive ritual based on the expectations of faith; between surgery and prayer. In any case, the emphatic clause is: "while I was musing the fire burned." To muse is to be out of one's mind and deeply in one's mind at the same time; musing is like ecstasy without the excess of frills, with only the slight excess of concentration in heat to receive, a ready intensity to find. Of such matters David sang.

But is it not the same, and a paradigm, in our own ordinary experience when in serious conversation we say something grossly short of our meaning? No, no, I say, that is not what I meant at all. Wait! Wait! In just a moment I'll have it; and indeed the heart is so hot it must surely burst into fire with the right musing. Sometimes it does, and we make either a mystery or a cliché. But mostly we wait and writhe, and the muse will not revisit us, until at last we make a lame issue and hope others will catch from our words the meaning that has all along been half-born between the heart and the mouth. The hope is not very strong.

The language of silence, so near in pressure, is very far away in availability. St. Augustine, in his *De Musica,* thought it was fundamental. Perhaps he thought so only because he lived under a collapsing empire where in many aspects there was a sharply diminishing *modus vivendi* between the mind and its languages. Not till the languages had almost entirely replaced the mind (what we used to call the Dark Ages) was anyone content. St. Augustine was profoundly discontented, and some of his discontent was expressed in language appropriate to these notes and to our time. It is curious that he felt what he wrote under this head was less inspired (perhaps not at all inspired) compared to his doctrinal and other religious works. To us (to myself at least) he was equally inspired; and by the same muse, or the same inspiration. Let the reader judge.

Judgment will perhaps require preliminary interest. St. Augustine was interested in metres and their relation to rhythm and the relation of the two to the truth of the arts which in his view are man's increment to God's creation. His discussion of metre is fascinating, but it does not immediately affect us so much as certain of his remarks on rhythm—the beat in words apart from but transpiring in metre. He thought there were three classes of rhythm, in memory, perception, and sound, with rhythm in perception coming first in experience. The whole matter, to him as to any of us who are interested, was very complex; the frames of discourse do not here adequately represent its subject. The mind moves by flashes and jumps, only now and then resting on the web of words. Thus St. Augustine was not sure of his words, but he could risk appearances. "Apparently," he says, "rhythm existing in silence is freer than rhythm created or extended not only in response to, *ad,* the body, but even in response to, *adversus,* the affects, *passiones,* of the body." ("Extended" is a wonderfully apt term for what happens to a bodily rhythm when it takes hold of a metre.)

The rhythm existing in silence, then, is freer than that related to the body. It is also more, and is itself subject to another thing. "Anything," he says, and I think the idiom, whether Latin or English, is as important as in the Psalms, "anything which the ministry of carnal perception can count, and anything contained in it, cannot be furnished with, or possess, any numerical rhythm in space which can be estimated, unless previously a numerical rhythm in time has preceded in silent movement. Before even that, there comes vital movement, agile with temporal intervals, and it modifies what it finds, serving the Lord of All Things." (Quotations from *De Musica. A Synopsis,* by W. F. Jackson Knight. London: The Orthological Institute, N. D.)

"Agile with temporal intervals" is a glorious phrase full of all the horrors and also the blow of beauty in actual perception. One would think Augustine had read Longinus, and a great regret rises for the loss of his treatise on Beauty. One would also think he had read Pascal in manuscript and meant to admonish him; for here, in these quotations, is adumbrated a rhythm for the language of the reasons of the heart—not the vagaries, but the reasons, of which the mere head knows nothing and is therefore, as La Rochefoucauld says, their continual dupe. There is indeed something French about Augustine when he gets to the arts; his reason shivers a little, and the logic gets a little frantic: but one learns as one shivers. There is after all a predestinate shudder at the end of things. But Augustine was also resident in Italy, and there is a flowering in him few Frenchmen have reached; a special Italian knowledge of how chaos takes form as it must. He knows that thought does not take place in words—though it is administered and partly communicated in words, and is by fiction often present in them, and though, so to speak it creates them, and creates further what they do to each other. Surely no one ever seriously thought words were autonomous. The story of the tower of Babel should have broken that fiction: every man speaks the language he can, and the angels understand them all. And if Babel is not enough, there is Coleridge, who said, with no arrogance whatever, that he *put* more meaning into his words than most people. The value we find in the writings of others is the value of the meaning they put in, as it drags out of us and expresses our own meaning: they lodged their meanings, and attract our own, into their words. They jumped from one level of skill, which we all have from the cry spanked out of us at birth to the last rattle, to another, which most of us do not have at all, and about which we deceive ourselves vastly, because we hanker so for the doubtful comfort of hearing a thing said. What oft was thought, but ne'er so well expressed. Pope was at the easy level there: the level which thinks there are words for everything; Joyce was nearer right— he acknowledged the vocabulary, but thought the words often wrong. Half the labor of writing is to exclude the wrong meanings from our words; the other half is to draw on the riches which have already been put into the words of our choice; and neither labor is effective unless the third thing is done— unless we can put into the arrangement, the ordonnance, of our words our own vital movement—"agile with temporal intervals."

St. Augustine was ancestrally right. To be agile is to be supremely responsive to every possibility—both those which can be dealt with in a given language and those which cannot. To be agile is to be inspired; the pink toes of the muse are in your lap; poets—in any mode of the mind—come dripping from the intimacy of sleep. Hence the positive obscurity of the greatest poetry in the words and hence the terrible clarity under them, pushing through. That is why, as the components of beauty, St. Thomas's *consonantia, claritas, integritas,* are not enough. Beauty hits us on both sides of the face, silencing us in the after-silence. St. Thomas left the silence to God; we cannot, even with the aid of Jacques Maritain; for it must be in another way, and much further afield, with only an alien comfort, our own silence out of which we explode. We are all—if I may be permitted a theological clench—we are all, in the modern world, enthusiasts of direct access, and the wholeness of our minds must be our own—a little tykish, a little rash, and with no rancor of a completed revelation. Our eclecticism is our only revenge upon our orthodoxy.

It would be easy, if we were not using words as our present language, to go into the field of absolute silence of landscape, even into the verging silence of

sculpture, or even into the plunging silence—the cresting then the plunge—
of the dance; and indeed we are immersed and swimming in the "vital movement, agile with temporal intervals" of these arts. But we use words, and the
farthest field we can draw on is the predatory and compassionate distillation
of Chinese verbal thought—which to a western ear is surely the least noisy of
all thought, and the least mutually comprehensible in the ordinary babel of
human voices. Their written words are voiceless pictures drawn with elegance and style: what we would call speaking likenesses when we do not call
them ideographs. (There is no better parody of what we mean by the
language of silence than the problematic image of a dozen Chinese understanding perfectly each other's written words but unable to converse
aloud.) My authority has luckily been recently twice translated into English,
and has dragged some of the original Chinese silence into both of the conflicting Englishes; and the meaning is probably as plain as that of Aristotle's
Poetics, which is all the more appropriate since my Chinese author, Lu Chi,
wrote his *Wen Fu* as a kind of *Poetics* or *Art of Letters.* It was written in A.D.
302 and the version I use is that of E. R. Hughes (New York: Pantheon
Books, 1951). It is painted in couplets, like Pope, but it is as far from Pope as
it is from Aristotle, and is much more like Augustine than either, especially if
you listen to the two with the aid of Longinus and look forward to D. H.
Lawrence, his screaming dark. He comes at Augustine's position, another
way, not from the experience of nonbeing (the kind of nothingness that can
be apprehended only from the centre of inadequate being) and from a quick
of hidden sense and skill that may yet become words. If Lu Chi's position
seems precarious by western standards, it is vital and creative (it *makes* something) with or without standards. Our western standards conform to only a
part of our experience, and to only certain aspects of that part. Hence our
silent mutiny. Hence in Dostoevsky the *boont:* the stubborn rebellion in the
soul against any standard picture of the world. Hence, too, Lear can say:
"Aye, every inch a king."

Under the right situation, says Lu Chi, every man is all that kingly
inch:

1. What joy there was in all this, the joy worthies and sages have
   coveted.
2. He was taxing Non-Being to produce Being, calling to the silence, importunate for an answer:
3. He was engrossing the great spaces within a span of silk, belching forth
   torrents [of language] from the inch-space of the heart. (*Wen Fu,* I, b.)

It should be remembered that by Lu Chi's time writing was done by a brush on silk with soot for ink. Mr. Hughes's commmentary says the word translated as "taxing" means also "divining," and that the "inch-space of the heart" has "a connotation of emptiness." This I cite only to point more firmly towards the nature and process of the inspiration wooed in the silence. In further confirmation, here is what Lu Chi says about words without inspiration.

1. It may be language has been employed in one short strain, one with no traceable sources, a foundling production,
2. which looked close to the Silence but found no friend, looked far to the Void but gained no response. (*Wen Fu*, II, g.)

Lu Chi evidently had an austere taste and had no use for ornamental verses, at least when he took to writing poetics, except to relate them to what might have been done. One would like to say he understood the potential force of the topical and the immanent abyss in the trivial—which have always been with us—or the more modern possibility that revelation itself may be unseemly, puerile, and offensive. But there is no evidence for it; one doubts if he could have done anything with Smollett's phrase (to which we shall return), "Our satiety is to suppurate." But he could do a great deal with what he had. Here is how he redeems his orphans or foundlings to their lost parents. It is the darkness before the light, then the terrible light.

1. Then comes the blocking of every kind of feeling, the will [to create] gone, the spirit held bound.
2. It is like being the stock of a sapless tree, being empty as a dried up river.
3. Lay hold of the mutinous soul by sounding its secret depths, pay homage to its vital fierceness as you search for the very self:—
4. Reason screened and obscured begins to creep forth, thought comes screaming, forced out from the womb. (*Wen Fu*, II, o.)

We are returned to the mother and the *hysterica passio* in *Lear,* but in a different construction, which I think compels us to go on to Pascal. Mr. Hughes believes Lu Chi meant poetry to be governed by reason. I would suppose any poet of magnitude to agree; but there are several ways of understanding what the term reason means. Metre is one of the reasons governing poetry; rhythm is another; and there is a third which in the cliché taken from Pascal we call the reasons of the heart of which the reasons of the head know nothing, only in the end we manage the public affairs of the heart's reasons with those of the head, especially in poetry and the verbal medium of thought. *L'esprit de finesse* is what gets hurt when the management goes wrong. Pascal gives us a great example in his pensée on silence. "Le silence éternel de ces espaces infinis m'effraie." It makes a great difference what the head does with this whether or not you hear the two words *silence éternel* as governing the insight. Mr. Eliot made a good deal of this observation a long time ago with a polemic against sentimentalists in mind. I have no polemic intent; I merely wish to keep the reasons of the heart distinct. The eternal silence is what gives vital movement agile with temporal intervals to the infinite space; as if the heart, with reason, reminded one of the empty spaces in the head by filling them, under the guise of speech, with speechless knowledge.

Erich Heller, in his little book called *The Hazard of Modern Poetry* (Cambridge: Bowes and Bowes, 1953) goes further: evidently holding speechless knowledge a special aspect of modern times. "The music of modern Europe is the one and only art in which it surpassed the achievement of former ages. This is no accident of history: it is the speechless triumph of the spirit in a world of words without deeds and deeds without words." In the general current of our citations from Augustine and Lu Chi, one could observe at once that it is when words are filled with the language of silence that they become deeds; or, Aristotle would say, that they become *praxis* or action. But Mr. Heller has more to say a little further on. In trying to define the hazard of modern poetry he cites Hölderlin's questions: Why should one write poetry in such spiritless times? Why should one be a poet at all? Mr. Heller goes on: "What was this *dürftige Zeit*, this time poor in spirit but farther than any from the Kingdom of Heaven, that made Hölderlin question the justification of being a poet; this meagre but forceful time that pushed poetry to the very edge of silence, of that 'abyss' that Baudelaire too sensed at the feet of poetry; this hostile time that yet inspired in Hölderlin, and in Baudelaire, and in Rimbaud, poetry truly unheard of before? For in their poetry speechlessness itself seemed to burst into speech without breaking silence."

It is as if Mr. Heller were giving analogies to the processes of inspiration and creation we found described in Augustine and Lu Chi; and Mr. Heller, too, believes in reason; only, if I follow him correctly, the poets named above, and Rilke also, worked against their inspiration, and in spite of reason. T. S. Eliot, in Mr. Heller's account, almost alone does better: he is a poet of civic virtue. Indeed he is, in the sense that Mr. Heller means so Roman a phrase for so obstinately protestant an Anglican as Eliot. Indeed he is, and he is so by lodging his poetry almost from the beginning in the language of silence. There is not only, "Looking into the heart of light, the silence," there is also "The silent withering of autumn flowers/Dropping their petals and remaining motionless," and there is, a little later in the same poem (*The Dry Salvages*), this distich:

> There is no end of it, the voiceless wailing,
> No end to the withering of withered flowers.

There is not much manifest civic virtue in these lines, but there is the condition of epiphany from which the several sorts of virtue, including the civic, spring. The silent withering and the voiceless wailing are working together as one explorer's cry. They "burst into speech without breaking the silence." They burst into the virtue which is the declared and sustained allegiance to the nature of things: the mother that will not down, the intractable ache of vital movement wherever it may be.

It is by means such as this that poetry avenges itself upon doctrine that has become mere argumentation (become the "mere" ideas which, to redact on Eliot's famous phrase about James, violate most minds); and the revenge is a catharsis, "a tax on Non-Being to produce Being, calling to the Silence." The wind is silent; even the winds of doctrine are silent. Even the wind the Lord tempers to the shorn lamb; that wind, and that doctrine, above all are silent. It is we who hear the wind, ruffling and re-commoding both the surface and the marrow of the mind; but we hear it truly only when we have learned how to translate it to voice-bearing or speaking forms. Again it is Eliot who says this well—avenging its impudence by transmuting it—in "the inch-space of the heart."

> Words move, music moves
> Only in time; but that which is only living
> Can only die. Words, after speech, reach
> Into the silence. Only by the form, the pattern,
> Can words or music reach
> The stillness, as a Chinese jar still
> Moves perpetually in its stillness.

I do not know that Eliot would admit that there is much thinking in these lines; there was a time when he argued that Dante did his thinking in Aquinas and such like places, and that Shakespeare did not do any thinking at all; but I would say there is a vital movement of thought here, alive with temporal intervals. Only one version of thought takes place in the medium of concepts and only another version originates in the medium of words. The weight of life in these lines is the moving weight—the momentum—the momentum and the buoyancy—of the experience of thought in its primary and final languages, for which concepts and words furnish only concentrates and analogues. The reality that drips from live words is the reality of this thought: the silence to which they reach. If this were not so there would be no thought in the other arts. We would not quake at the *thought* of the Medici tombs nor at the *thought* in the blue vault, only gradually visible, the gradual apparition of thought *each* time it is seen, in the Empress' tomb at Ravenna, which is the shiver of the thought of the last place, moving "perpetually in its stillness" because it *is* thought, the operation of the mind rendering the substance of its experience its own. This is the permanent task of the imaginative reason—of the rational imagination. But the reason must not be too clear: the cost in perception is too great: perfect clarity is a form of deafness to the human and the non-human alike. Hence Lu Chi's conclusion: "reason screened and obscured begins to creep forth, thought comes screaming, forced out from the womb."

George Eliot, in a very interesting paragraph in *Middlemarch,* says much the same thing in a less oracular but almost as prophetic language. She is referring to the representative aspect of the horror which has happened to Dorothea Brooke in her sterile marriage: and what she says represents Dorothea's five weeks of silent sobbing during her Roman honeymoon. Dorothea does not know she has company in the next stranger's house—or at least in the next to next. "The element of tragedy which lies in the very fact of frequency, has not yet wrought itself into the coarse emotion of mankind; and perhaps our frames could hardly bear very much of it. If we had a keen vision and feeling of all ordinary human life, it would be like hearing the grass grow and the squirrel's heart beat, and we should die of that roar which lies on the other side of silence." And then, as if to say what a life would be like which heard the roar the other side of silence, and yet did not die, a little down the page she goes on: "Permanent rebellion, the disorder of a life without some loving reverent resolve, was not possible for her; but she was now in an interval when the very force of her nature heightened its confusion." What was this force but that roaring? Tolstoi would have made the identification absolute; and it is a pity we do not have the language of his silence available. But Ivan Ilyitch heard the force roaring; and Dorothea Brooke is an Anna Karenina, only saved by the machinations of English novelistic conventions. The reader meditating the possibility does not require salvation; he requries a further flight of reason; for it is exactly here that George Eliot refuses a further screening and obscuring of reason. "Permanent rebellion" without resolve is one of the regular conditions of life. Reason must find it, for only reason can deal with it, and reason is not reason unless it does so: it is mere dead reason, the course of inert ideas and anaesthetized sentiments, the rubbish of lost knowledge. But she is nevertheless presenting the experience of reason, not only here but again and again: for instance, when she *shows* us, and then *proves* it, how Rosamund Vincy, that blond vampire with no blood of her own but with a charm that requisitioned blood where she set her mouth softly, "was particularly forcible by means of that mild persistence which as we know, enables a white soft living substance to make its way in spite of opposing rock." Her uncle, Mr. Bulstrode, is better still; filled with the roaring force, he makes out of a probable death a possible murder—George Eliot provides nothing if not *serious* entertainment—and mires his own act in reasonable prayer. "Early in the morning—about six—Mr. Bulstrode rose and spent some time in prayer. Does anyone suppose that private prayer is necessarily candid—necessarily goes to the roots of action! Private prayer is inaudible speech, and speech is representative: who can represent himself just as he is, even in his own reflections?"

We do not hear what Mr. Bulstrode says, but we know what it is—we would have said it ourselves; we too would have wanted both to make our action total and also to have made ourselves free of it. Our deepest prayer is to disengage ourselves from our behavior. There is no prayer for justice; we pray for mercy and for justification; and of this the reasons of the head need constantly to be reminded, if ever they are to be moved, not merely duped, by the reasons of the heart. It is not for nothing that the reasons of the head are associated with *l'esprit de géométrie;* they must be able to measure any earth—any inch-space of the heart whatever—else they are mere orts and slarts.

George Eliot—short only of the first magnitude, and often grappling with it in a furious dull fervor—could say this with specific reference, in the apprehension of the fingertips on the roughened table-top. Mr. Bulstrode in his downfall is an example. First there are the rat-shrieks of his colleagues in "the agony of the terror that fails to kill, and leaves the ears still open to the returning wave of execration. . . . But in that intense being lay the strength of reaction. Through all his bodily infirmity there ran a tenacious nerve of ambitious self-preserving will, which had continually leaped out like a flame, scattering all doctrinal fears, and which, even while he sat an object of compassion to the merciful, was beginning to stir and glow under his ashy paleness." George Eliot's own compassion was merciless, she writes with reason fired, burning in its own ashes, not yet wet. When Mrs. Bulstrode hears of her husband's downfall, the reasons of the heart are horripilated. "There is a forsaking which still sits at the same board and lies on the same couch with the forsaken soul, withering it the more by unloving proximity." That perspective inhabits without tampering with the action Mrs. Bulstrode took; heart and head work together; she dug for strength into her old aspirations, and so did her husband. "She took off all her ornaments and put on a plain black gown," and went in to see him, a lady Macbeth all milk and mercy. "His confession was silent, and her promise of faithfulness was silent." Something like ninety pages later in the book, George Eliot, moving through both perspectives, reaches her own precarious conclusion: that in looking at all these people we see all at once that great feelings wear the aspect of error, great faith reveals the aspect of illusion. So she hears the roaring the other side of silence.

Dante had a tougher mind, and took greater risks; he worked on the double war of the journey and the pity, and was implacable: he depended on the memory that cannot go wrong (*che non erra*): the roaring was not only part of the silence, it instigated reason and told him what to say. This is why one is seldom at home with the uncomforting terrors of Dante's mind. One longs always, as he did himself, for the sweet air. To Dante, feeling is absolute tidings, faith is substance. But I cite Dante only for a post of observation from which to triangulate George Eliot and Joseph Conrad. Think then of Francesca's words, and from that vantage think both of the passages quoted from *Middlemarch* and the following from *Nostromo*. It is a balcony scene, the abridged privacy, with people all round, both strangers and those eager with gluttonous interest. But the manners that left Martin Decoud alone and exposed with Antonia Avellanos, also required of them to make the most of their open chance. It is the essence of the balcony that while you are there everything is at stake. They must talk both of the world and of themselves. It is the situation where you come both on hopeless longing and hope mercilessly free of longing. Here is Conrad. "She was facing him now in the deep recess of the window, very close and motionless. Her lips moved rapidly. Decoud, leaning his back against the wall, listened with crossed arms and lowered eyelids. He drank the tones of her even voice, and watched the agitated life of her throat, as if waves of emotion had run from her heart to pass out into the air in her reasonable words." We do not hear what Antonia said—any more than we hear what Dorothea Brooke heard—in so many words; and perhaps we do not need to, for we have all heard these words and wear them as stigmata or as amulets; we have all heard the sirens and we know they sing sweetest when the heart makes reasonable words out of the language of silence. The sirens are not much given to finding words, except for individuals, and only at the moment when the individuals are themselves brimming with the language of silence into reason.

The sirens, I take it, are earlier forms of the muses; and haunt us more deeply.

Poor Decoud, in *Nostromo,* heard, and was haunted, and could not make the words his own. He died alone therefore, killed by the blow of that other silence which, when it is dominant, when the heart is inadequate to its theme, prevents human voice altogether. "The great gulf burst into a glitter all around the boat; and in this glory of merciless solitude the silence appeared again before him, stretched taut like a dark, thin string." It is the silence kills him. He "rolled overboard without having heard the cord of silence snap in the solitude of the Placid Gulf." There is no murder like your silence, once heard, when there are neither sirens, nor muses, nor the reasons of the heart to give words. What we cannot make human kills us. What we cannot keep human makes us kill ourselves. The rest is silence.

George Eliot had hope of the reforming heart. Conrad seemed to think the non-human world bears us up as a race while destroying us as individuals. Dante was implacable to see what lived. All dealt with the wastage of the precious, the erosion of belief by fact. Speaking in the same voice, but with half the register missing, yet with a singularly intimate effect upon our own ears, is E. M. Forster, and especially in *A Passage to India.* No timeless humanist he, but a rancorous doll; but the rancor is our own, the voice of the grudge we bear against what besets us and puts us about whatever tack we bend to. In Forster it is as in Yeats's poem: our creation was an accident. "My dear, my dear, it was an accident!" In Forster, I think, is the sink of energy, with no running out of awareness. Reading Forster, we know what we are aware of at our moments of the conviction of loss or of the bottom of futility: we know the hope which Luther said guaranteed the hopes in Purgatory; and this is another form of the language of silence.

In *A Passage to India,* an old woman more than senile, Mrs. Moore, speaks the language of silence; but it is others who hear it. She *says* nothing; but the young woman, Adela, who was to have become her daughter-in-law, heard, not words, but the idea in her heart and made out of it the principal action of her life. What she heard at first was echo, then an idea, then the fledging of both into words. The old woman fills the younger with the heart's knowledge which, to Forster, is neither reason nor unreason. If a great deal of guilt is built up in this way, it is because Forster wants it so. When the heart, which bites others so often, is bitten back, it winces. The heart's unreasons are the heart's offenses. Hence the guilt.

Later there is a fillip the other way. When Adela has been filled with guilt and emptied of life she has a talk with Fielding, the senior boy-scout, or catalyst of the book. When they have said all *they* could say, "there was a moment's silence, such as often follows the triumph of rationalism." In that moment silence speaks through rationalism. And when, a little later, they have their last conversation, it is the same the other way round. "She was at the end of her spiritual tether, and so was he." Their tether was very short; a snaffle. "Were there worlds beyond which they could never touch, or did all that is possible enter their consciousness? They could not tell. They only realized that their outlook was more or less similar, and found in this a satisfaction. Perhaps life is a mystery, not a muddle; they could not tell." Here the voice of silence cries through rationalism to be heard, and neither the man in the first withering of middle age nor the dying girl knows how near they come to hearing the voice they do not know they invoke. All that was left of them—as they *were*—as Forster could *see* them—was "a friendliness, as of dwarfs shaking hands . . . dwarfs talking, shaking hands and assuring each other that they stood on the same footing of insight." Dwarfs are unattended sirens.

I know no better sign that a new form of civilization, or culture, or living social anthropology—call it what you will—is afoot, than such things as Forster's reductive interpretations of the language of silence. The tower of Babel is falling again, for the voices make rancor. There is no pain, says the incredible English saint in his early senility, "but there is cruelty," and he says it—at the very end of the book—as if it were the sweetest possible thing to say—as if cruelty were the rod that struck water from the rock and brought down the light. And indeed in some incipient forms of morality abroad today, this seems to be so. We have techniques for finding moral trouble—trouble in the customs of the heart—which we can only treat with the nearest stroke of cruelty, and we think cruelty, virility, loyalty, predictability when in another time we would have thought it was the abuse of these. In applying these remarks to the novels of E. M. Forster, I know I am invidious; I mean to be—but no more so than I would be were I applying myself to Graham Greene or Evelyn Waugh or Henry Green.

What do we have? We have a clatter of lacerating facts to enforce and hold to a false and muddled and calamitous annunciation and an aborted incarnation. The facts do not acquire order (reason finding order) but descend into a deep disorder in which they have no relevant part. One's imagination grows tired, with the fatigue of any day. At the end of *A Passage to India*, the imagination is tired indeed: the god is invoked in a crash of shallow waters, in a fusion and muddle of disrelated echoes: the cobra slithering, the kissing sound of the bats, the rearing horse, the narrowing path. Rancor becomes the substance of affection. *Le lune ne garde aucune rancune*. Perhaps the moon is still there. But the sky says No, not yet, No, not there. The haunt no longer comes because there is nothing left for it to frighten. There is only the shadowy sub-deity of old Mrs. Moore, who had been filled with senility, and the dried virginity of Adela Quested, who had been emptied of echo. The haunt no longer comes.

Yet the haunts are still there; and if they do not come, then, as Mistress Winifred Jenkins is made to say in Smollett's *Humphry Clinker,* "our satiety is to suppurate." Mistress Jenkins is one of the great commentators on human experience; she believes in high literacy, and reaches higher than she knows, and higher than she could tolerate if she did know it; she is inspired by the possibilites of language itself—not the language of direct perception and momentous thought. But she uses words, and if you do not know what she means, then you do not know what she *also* means. She has the brutality of the Muse, even if she does not always furnish the transport. She deprives every word she uses of its cliché—its clutter of false and degenerate meanings. In short, she has style, in the sense A. N. Whitehead once defined it (*The Aims of Education*): "Style, in its finest sense, is the last acquirement of the educated mind; it is also the most useful. It pervades the whole being. . . . Style is the ultimate morality of mind." Whitehead goes on, that there is something above style and knowledge, which he calls Power, and then he says, "Style is the fashioning of power, the restraining of power," and, lastly, he adds: "Style is always the product of specialist study, the peculiar contribution of specialism to culture." Mistress Jenkins was such a specialist; and her function was to transmit judgments and insights that could not be direct either in the rational or in the lyric modes of language. Mistress Jenkins was a "persona" whom Smollett threw off in that ripeness he thought was old age (and which he knew, rightly, was the onset of death) through which you can hear as many voices as you have ears for. "Our satiety is to suppurate"; our society is to suppurate; our satiety is to separate; our satiety is indeed to suppurate. A *persona* is the invoked being of the muse; a siren audible through a lifetime's wax in the ears; a translation of what we did not know that we knew ourselves: what we partly are.

II

Smollett seems the right author with whom to end a series of citations relating to the language of silence. He knew nothing of such a language: it was not disengaged in his consciousness, or at any rate not in that part of it which resorted to words for its expression; and he would probably have rejected discussion of it as waste motion, though possibly he might have accepted it as a key to the hypochondria—the desperate health—of his last years. He knew the chaos upon which his reason supervened: which explains both his brutality and his goodheartedness; and he knew how that chaos twisted and impugned his reason: hence his coarseness and compassion. Whether or not he knew how the vitality of the chaos provided the elements of true order to his reason, does not matter; it happened so, and it happened by the rhythm of the full mind. In all the best of Smollett you feel the force of St. Augustine's testimony. "A numerical rhythm in time has preceded in silent movement. Before even that there comes vital movement, agile with temporal intervals, and it modifies what it finds, serving the Lord of All Things." About the Lord there may be doubt. The rest is true.

III

The rest is not only true but pertinent to practice or action where truth is only the culminating objective (is pertinent to the Aristotelian notion of *praxis:* how action transpires in the language of the mind). "Our satiety is to sup-purate" could never have been written except as a verbal translation of thought which was not verbal. Translation is what verbal language does to the language of silence. If there were no languages of silence, there could be translation from Arabic or French into English; and what is wrong about so many translations is that they pay too little attention to the silence that has got into the words. The poetry of Verlaine, for example—of a haunted sweetness craving light in French—will be empty cliché in direct English; but on the other hand it may seem packed with silence in French merely because it ought to be; we sometimes no more know how little a poet has put into his words in the way of meaning than how much. The *Dies Irae* may crack the psyche in Latin and bring a drowse in English. To say *inshallah!* in Arabic may be to say nothing, but coming out of an English throat it may renew everything that was ever meant by saying As God wills. And the children on the street speak a language between that of the parrot and that of the dove. If we regard speech as translation, it will, when it does not leave us tongue-tied, find us the right urgency and a transpiring rhythm; and thus there is something right about James Joyce's reported remark that though there were plenty of words in English they were not the words he wanted. Smollett knew this as well as Joyce. We live in a world of the *mot injuste* out of which the heart may yet create reasonable forms.

We translate most in our very own language, and so little of it gets into our words. If there were no gaps between our words—in which silence speaks, and in which we recollect ourselves (by tranquillity Wordsworth must have meant a gap)—we should never find our thoughts; nor recognize the thoughts of others; the rhythm would not transpire. In verse—the oldest discipline of words we have, older than grammar, and reaching the naked syntax—in verse the silences animate with rhythm the variations of the metre, enlivening the metronome. Rhythm is how we feel and how we translate action in the soul. The action may not be our action, though it is what moves us, but we move it through silence into words and when it is there the words remain alive. As Eliot says, "You are the music while the music lasts." And if poetry is heightened speech it is heightened with silence. Meaning is what silence does when it gets into words.

But here is Baudelaire, in his poem *La Voix,* with provisional consolation:

> Mais la Voix me console et dit: "Garde tes songes;
> Les sages n'en ont pas d'aussi beaux que les fous!"

Emily Dickinson's Notation

The Poems of Emily Dickinson. Including variant readings critically compared with all known manuscripts. Edited by Thomas H. Johnson. The Belknap Press of Harvard University Press. Three volumes. $25.00.

Emily Dickinson. An Interpretive Biography. By Thomas H. Johnson. The Belknap Press of Harvard University Press. $4.50.

Some twenty years ago it was necessary to begin an essay on Emily Dickinson with a complaint that the manuscripts and the various copies of manuscripts of this poet had never been adequately edited, and could never be properly read until they were. It seems to me now—and the reviews I have seen agree—that Mr. Johnson has done everything an editor can do, and that there remains—and on this Mr. Johnson himself insists in his preface—the second task of providing a more readable, and less expensive, edition for the ordinary purposes of poetry. This I hope Mr. Johnson will undertake because, whoever undertakes it, it will be the completion of Mr. Johnson's own work; and because it will itself be a criticism of Emily Dickinson's work at almost every possible level. The principal problem, it seems to me, will be to find within the general conventions of printing a style of presentation which will furnish a version conformable to the original notation which the poet employed. The Dickinson practice was to punctuate by dashes, as if the reader would know what the dashes meant—both grammatically and dramatically—by giving the verses voice. Within her practice, and to her own ear, she was no doubt consistent. To find out what that consistency was, and articulate it for other readers and other voices, requires more of a system than ever bothered her. Even a casual examination of any twenty pages in this new edition makes this aspect of the problem plain. Here is an example to do for the rest.

> Some—work for Immortality—
> The chiefer part, for Time—
> He—Compensates—immediately—
> The former—Checks—on Fame—

The Dickinson practice cannot be systematized; there is not enough *there*; but with enough intimacy with the poems we can see what sort of system might have emerged. The problem is not very different, so I understand, in reading the official prose of Japan in 1865; but in English poetry it seldom presents itself with such multiplicity of irritation—so much freedom in rearrangement—with such spontaneity left to the reader.

Multiplicity, freedom, spontaneity: these are terms for much deeper aspects of the Dickinson notation than that which gathers itself in mere punctuation, syntax, and grammar; or in meter, rhythm, and diction. Perhaps the deepest problem in poetics raises one of its prettiest examples in her notation. How much does a poet look to words to supply what is put down, and how much to notate what was within the self prior to the words? If words are necessarily the medium of poetry, how much do they also participate in its substance? If thought looks for words as a chief medium for turning it into action, how much, if anything, of the action is in the movement of the words themselves? Is there not in the end a nearly equal contest between the thought prior to the words and the thought already reminiscent in the words and their arrangements? If so, victory for the poem will be in the equilibrium between the two; what is in W. B. Cannon's physiology the maintenance of a precarious stable state, or homeostasis, called the wisdom of the body. This equilibrium, this wisdom, is in poetry recorded, though it is not maintained; is communicated, though it does not exist—in the words taken as notation. In this respect the words resemble the notes in music.

The words resemble the notes on the musical score. This is not said as a triviality but as a fact about poetry and music which no theory can ultimately ignore. It is said that Beethoven sometimes wrote out his initial score in words, and surely there are some poems where the words seem like the notes in a final score—as perhaps "The Phoenix and the Turtle." There is only a difference in the degree of notation. The point is that the notation is always inadequate, by itself, in predicting performance or reading. As the poet was saying much more, so the reader is left with more or less to do for himself as the notation wills him or fails him. This is why the poem which has seemed flat will spring into life when one has got intimate with that will. My friends the composers tell me that the notation in music is perhaps eighty-five per cent adequate, which seems to me high and can only be true of modern music (the music the composers themselves wrote). In poetry I am convinced the notation is at best only about fifteen per cent adequate for a full reading; the gaps jumped are *that* much greater; and indeed a single reading can never again be more than approximately repeated, and as the approximations go on, the life of the poem thickens in the reader's mind and throat. The uniqueness of each reading reaches towards the uniqueness of the poem. Thus the poet's own reading, like his own notation, is often inadequate to the poem; his voice no more than his words is not up to a final job, but yet always should be heard. We cannot do without as much of the feasible fifteen per cent as we can get from the poet or can, after sufficient intimacy, otherwise arrange for. In Emily Dickinson's case the notation in the words seldom reaches the feasible maximum even with intimacy; and it is here, I think, that the final problem of critical editorship lies, since we must not permit ourselves to lose the record of our intimacy. The editor must learn to notate the voice which in intimacy he has learned to hear; which is not at all the same thing as notating merely what he has learned to understand. Consider why Toscanini is a great conductor, and then consider how Emily Dickinson's poems, all short, have none of the self-modulating advantages of length or any of the certainties of complex overt structure. One exaggerates, but it sometimes seems as if in her work a cat came at us speaking English, our own language, but without the pressure of all the other structures we are accustomed to attend; it comes at us all voice so far as it is in control, fragmented elsewhere, wilful and arbitrary, because it has not the acknowledged means to be otherwise.

All this Mr. Johnson's edition makes plain, and makes it plain not only about the extreme case (which as in fever is only a degree or so) of Emily Dickinson, which would be merely to dismiss her, but about a great deal and to some extent all of poetry, which is why more than ever we would save her in spite of all her losses incurred on her own account. His own effort in this direction, which I hope will reach to a critical canon of the poems at their maximum potential of notation, is so far to be found in his interpretive biography; and it is with this book and its notations, and what happens to them in my mind, that the remainder of these notes will mainly concern themselves. To begin with there is more sense in his biography, and more nonsense left out, than in any of the other biographies or studies I have read. It may be that he has avoided some real problems of personal relation, but it is certain that he has obviated a good many artificial problems and mere traps of possibility. If he does not speculate about the direction or the substance of her eroticism, he allows, and even encourages, the facts which he exhibits to speculate for themselves: as we do in all our intimate interests which do not transgress themselves in gossip. Mr. Johnson is concerned in both his edition and his biography with establishing Emily Dickinson's identity and the evidences of form that declare it. In the edition the relations are made to speak entirely for themselves as they are spread seriatim and according to a chronological spirit; in the biography the relations are grouped irregularly with regard to chronology and to theme, and so are helped to speak for themselves more clearly in our tongue. Yet identity is always a mystery—precisely the mystery in others that is beyond us the more we share it; and as I become more familiar with the outlines of Mr. Johnson's figure of identity, I find myself encouraged to speculate or contemplate a little the intimations I feel. There is nothing in Mr. Johnson that would make me alter the judgment I found rising from the reading of the poems twenty years ago, but there is a great deal that would suggest deepening that judgment which is the acknowledgment of identity. There is more in Emily Dickinson of the same sort than I had seen; she has more *semblables* and perhaps less, or a different, *vraisemblance*. So one speculates.

I see in the looking-glass how much she is a nuptial poet, and I think of her in connection with two other poets who might also be called nuptial poets, Robert Herrick and Rainer Maria Rilke. I speak of course of the poetry. All three celebrate the kind of intimacy we celebrate and sometimes find as nuptial. Herrick marries the created world; Emily Dickinson marries herself. Rilke creates within himself something to marry which will—which does—marry and thereby rival the real world. Each marriage is an effort towards identity—by acceptance, by withdrawal, by rivalry in all three, but with the emphases different in each. Let us throw these up one by one with deliberate exaggeration.

In Herrick, one spends all one's life in returning from the withdrawal (the splitting off from the general) accomplished by a particular birth. The formality of verse, and the wonderful superficial experimentation around the norm of verse, and the formality of attitude, and the sensuality of both, are means of bridging gaps, are helps in anticipation of gaps, and are projections of hypotheses of particular experience—where the direct experience remains only in detail. It is as if, in Herrick's mind, the direct experience was accepted only for the sake of something else which was to be found in the plenitude of God's creation of nature. Thus it is that the clergyman wore the sexual garment sweet. He played at wearing great costumes in which we acknowledge the union of God and Nature, he played at casting himself in what roles he could of all those which God provided. I think particularly of "A Nuptiall

Song on Sir Clipseby Crew and His Lady." Herrick's order is the world's order of his time, his poetry what he did with that order with his senses and with his forms. It is elegance taking flesh.

In Emily Dickinson, one spends all one's life finding a role apart from life, an outer role within which one creates one's own role in spite of (and thereby counselled by) the world. Born in unity, one cuts oneself off, and cuts one's losses in the role of one's own immortality. What was sensuality in Herrick becomes in Emily Dickinson the flow of deprived sensation on the quick. In her, direct experience (often invented, sometimes originally contingent) was always for the sake of something else which would replace the habit and the destructive gusto (but not the need) of experience in the world, and become an experience of its own on its own warrant and across a safe or forbidding gap. This is the best that can be done with the puerile marriage of the self with the self—like the sanctity of the puerile saints in William James: a sensorium for the most part without the senses, it is sometimes the vision of sense itself. Emily Dickinson withdrew from the world in all the ways she could manage, and was connected with the world by the *pangs* of the experience she could not abide and yet could not let go. She could not perfect her withdrawal, and she found herself in successive stages of the inability to return. She had the experience of withdrawal without return; she found herself a shut-in, which was the best she could do with finding herself in the beginning a shut-out. Hence the basic formality and loose form of her common meters—her hymn forms which do not become hymns; it is the oldest form of English verse, but is very seldom long used by great poets, though often used a little. Hence, too, the wilfulness of her syntax led to irregularities rather than to new orders, which would have compelled at least a formal return. One thinks in her of enthusiastic transcendence and of lyric solipsism. Her disorder is her own. Also, which is more significant, her order is almost only her own. She withdrew from both the disorder of the outer world in experience and the outer world of order in reason. It was as if she was afraid to pay attention to what is contingent and embarrassing and scandalous—to what is pressing—either in sensation or predilection in the experience either of people or of the orders people make of their impulses in order to get along with their behavior. I do not say she did this except exemplarily in her conduct, but that under the theory of life that is in them this is what she did in her poems. Thus she made the poems of a withdrawal without a return: a withdrawal into spontaneity not experience. All her life she was looking for a subject, and the looking *was* her subject—in life as in poetry.

> Elysium is as far as to
> The very nearest Room,
> If in that Room a Friend await
> Felicity or Doom—
> What fortitude the Soul contains,
> That it can so endure
> The accent of a coming Foot—
> The opening of a Door—   (#1760)

She was not the watcher; she looked only for a focus without having a target—since the target was to *have*. This is sometimes called looking for frustrations, but in this poet it amounted to a means of making poems. There was no mountain of refuge and also no mountain of fall. She said of herself, when "someone rang the bell . . . I ran, as is my custom." Colonel Higginson wrote to his wife when he first met Emily Dickinson: "I never was with anyone who drained my nerve power so much. Without touching her, she drew from me. I am glad not to live near her." Thus she both drained and was drained by others. Mr. Johnson remarks that "the idea of an affection which in the presence of friends gives way to panic made her feel guilty." It is as if she got, at the quick, the sense of vampirage which is usually only a possible accompaniment of relation, but which is yet one of the excesses to which the soul is prone: as we see in Henry James, where it is the fate of people who know each other well to destroy each other. This is why to both James and Emily Dickinson renunciation is the "piercing" virtue. It is why, in Emily Dickinson's soul, there was something that kept her from going to church. Of a preacher she writes, "He fumbles at your soul," then

> Deals—One—imperial—Thunderbolt—
> That scalps your naked Soul—   (#315)

Here her words get ahead of—or come ahead of—and create her intuition, just as in another version of the same intuition (#501) the words lag a little:

> Narcotics cannot still the Tooth
> That nibbles at the soul—

If in Herrick one spends one's life in returning, and in Dickinson in perfecting it, in Rilke one spends all one's life in a constant succession (almost simultaneous in experience) of withdrawal and return: withdrawal from the actual world and return to the same world, with no loss of response to it, but with something added to that world in the sense he made of it. Rilke built his own death, and made all the world of it; and so he built his own life also. This he had to do because life—God's creation of it alone—had lost its plenitude, its habit of continuing creation. In Rilke, it is the chain of being that is our own, the plenitude is for us to find in order to make the chain great. This is the pull in Rilke that makes him great as a poet: he makes that sense, and draws us after. His order is his own, and we use it in our own order. Dickinson we use when we have none. In Dickinson there is the *terribilità* of our inner escape; in Rilke there is the greater *terribilità* of that impossible act, full assent in natural piety.

Both Rilke and Emily Dickinson were obsessed to create mortal images of immortality. So were Milton and Dante. I do not mean to hit Emily Dickinson over the head with Dante, but merely to remind the reader immediately lost in Dickinson of that other species of image where immortality is so much more enlivening than in Dickinson that a different part of our being quivers in response to it. Yet it is a part of what Dickinson depended on. Here is the end of the sonnet that begins *Tanto gentile e tanto onesta.*

> E par che de la sua labbia si mova
> un spirito soave e pien d'amore,
> che va dicendo a l'anima: Sospira.

Here is the best that Emily Dickinson can do in her analogous line—and it is very good. I wish more to point out what is different rather than what is missing.

> All Circumstances are the Frame
> In which His Face is set—
> All Latitudes exist for His
> Sufficient Continent—
>
> The Light His Action, and the Dark
> The Leisure of His Will—
> In Him Existence serve or Set
> A Force illegible.

In the "Dark Leisure of His Will" squirms the protestant, than whom nobody could have been more so—because more *manqué*—than Emily Dickinson. She had protestantism without the business instincts of her contemporaries and without the roast beef of Bunyan and without the secular evangelism of Wesley; she had the resignation and the loneliness and the excruciation—she had the characteristic *misery* of protestantism and a version of her own for its hysterical glee. The soul so inhabited tends to have psychogenic perception only. We like to say that misery, or suffering, matures us to the point where it is impossible to write—and yet one writes, and what one writes has nothing whatever to do with maturity or with immaturity either. Emotions are not susceptible of maturity.

> Rearrange a "Wife's" affection!
> When they dislocate my Brain!
> Amputate my freckled Bosom!
> Make me bearded like a man!
>
> Blush, my spirit, in thy Fastness—
> Blush, my unacknowledged clay—
> Seven years of troth have taught thee
> More than Wifehood ever may!
>
> Love that never leaped its socket—
> Trust entrenched in narrow pain—
> Constancy thro' fire—awarded—
> Anguish—bare of anodyne!
>
> Burden—borne so far triumphant—
> None suspect me of the crown,
> For I wear the "Thorns" till *Sunset*—
> Then—my Diadem put on.
>
> Big my Secret but it's *bandaged*—
> It will never get away
> Till the Day its Weary Keeper
> Leads it through the Grave to thee.   (#1737)

This is not maturity. What we have is a shift of phase (as from ice to steam) in the *verse*, which has its own form of maturity: the form by which one learns to deal with one's persistent adolescence. In Emily Dickinson we seldom see a completely mature verse, though we often see the elements of such a verse. Perhaps we see her own adolescence *and* her own maturity peep through. Both are fragmentary. We cannot say of this woman in white that she ever mastered life—even in loosest metaphor; but we can say that she so dealt with it as to keep it from mastering her—by her protestant self-excruciation in life's name.

It is at this point that in the pursuit of identity, as Mr. Johnson describes it, she did not "clearly find herself" in the excruciation of the lines beginning

> The Missing All—prevented Me
> From missing minor things.

One would rather say that in these lines, so far as they are topical, she found that she had missed herself. In a way—in a verse way, echoing other lines— she made a protection, a carapace of white cotton, even of brocade, so that raw life could not sack the emptiness within. She has all the pang—the expectation, the reversal—of experience without the experience. But for how much the pang may be made to count, to stand, even to *be*!

In making it so count, she is scrupulous; all the little pains of life, the sharp stones in her boots, both those that exist and those that might yet come, or cannot come, spring up and are taken into excruciating account; and there is a strain in universal behavior which needs precisely this account; and poems of this sort are what permit us to bear it. When we read them, as when we write them, we stand incriminated.

The scruple and the incrimination are like those in Gide, a comparison of which it is worth thinking a little, for it shows how Gide is a little too evil in the self-convicted sense, just as Emily Dickinson is a little too good in her sense of badness. Each is tortured by the scruple of the unexpected, what could come to the free act—as if for both, free will were found in action, without motive. Gide was tortured by the inner world of necessary insight, Emily Dickinson was tortured by the outer and frightful world of contingency. Each *gave up that* citadel; which is why Gide had to live so long and in such a hurry to come on himself, where Emily Dickinson had to hurry to die young enough. To keep going, Emily Dickinson had a resourceful barbarism of the soul which would ally itself with no tradition, where Gide had a resourceful barbarism of conduct. It is in the exaggerations of our principles that we expose ourselves to the quick and barb of truth. Each was enthusiastic, protestant (Jansenist or Puritan—in this respect there is little difference), and each was short on decency to one's equals, in the nervous drive to bring experience into a form just short of excruciation. Thus I do not think either of them much of a hand at discriminating experience; for each was under the mastery of incrimination. *La vie est vraie et criminelle!* cried LaForgue. It is ourselves who are incriminated, seems to be the thematic statement of Gide and Emily Dickinson. Hence their cruelty, the one to others, the other to herself. Hence each is playful in a primitivism, not a maturity, of emotion. Hence each has the kind of personality which is almost wholly informed by temperament and makes of it a substitute for sensibility. Yet each is powerful in reach upon the neighboring forms in our own temperament.

I do not know that the playfulness of Emily Dickinson's temperament can
be illustrated in her verse alone; I am tolerably sure her verse was not very
conscious of it. Yet I think it is there, like the playful ambiguity of a kitten
being a tiger: an ad-libbing of resources of which one is not too much aware,
but which inhabit one at the edge of being. Here one is very skilful because
one has all instinct to bring to bear. Let us look askance at one of the better
known poems, but with an ad-libbing of our own in three readings.

I

Much madness is divinest sense
Much sense the starkest madness
In this, as all, prevails.
Demur, you're straightway dangerous.

II

To a discerning eye
Tis the majority
Assent, and you are sane;
And handled with a chain.

These two versions print alternate lines without change except in the mod-
ernization of punctuation offered by Oscar Williams in his anthology. Here is
the original in Johnson.

Much Madness is divinest Sense—
To a discerning Eye—
Much Sense—the starkest Madness—
Tis the Majority
In this, as All, prevail—
Assent—and you are sane—
Demur—you're straightway dangerous—
And Handled with a Chain—   (#435)

Having experimented sufficiently, I can testify that this sort of thing can be
done with a large number of poems with not more damage than in the present
instance; and I chose this one only because it is short and would not clutter
the page. If the reader turns to "I cannot live with you" (#640), he will see
what fun he can have; and see also how manners and style can make a breach
in moral sentiments—but if that statement seems too formal, I will merely
say that these provisional re-arrangements (otherwise quite without tamper-

ing), represent something interesting about the structure both of Emily Dickinson's mind and of her verse: a cruel freedom which will not itself be tampered with; also that it represents something profound about the deeper forms of her notation, both in verse and in the movements of her psyche. It is the sort of thing that happens to poetry when it is released from the patterning barriers of syntax and the force of residual reason.

To say this is not to attack, or to diminish the value or the force of the poetry; but merely to indicate that in the dates of her life if not in her deliberate theoretic practice she was sympathetic to kinds of poetry she probably never heard of and would have repudiated morally, if not aesthetically, if she had heard of them. This is the chain of poetry which runs from Baudelaire through surrealism and, if you like, into existentialism. I look to the new French, at the next outbreak of war, to see this in Emily Dickinson, so that they may create out of her a new theory of correspondence, a new, complex, and non-architectural syntax (for by then we shall dislike like the imposition of death the modern architecture and the faded modern abstractionism) much as some of their immediate ancestors saw or felt incentive in Poe with less cause. In the meantime, I refer the reader, both of this review and of Mr. Johnson's excellent edition of Emily Dickinson, to Marcel Raymond's *From Baudelaire to Surrealism* (NY: 1950) as a means of establishing her as a member in good standing of the intellectual movement of modern poetry. Poetry in this time, says he, "tended to become an ethic or some sort of irregular instrument of metaphysical knowledge"; and it is upon this sentiment that I think the business of the reading edition and the criticism of Emily Dickinson might well proceed. It would bring her nearer our own quick, and nearer, too, to the curse of our own spontaneity.

Introduction to *American Short Novels*

Fictions are what we make of ourselves, and they cannot help reflecting something of our character and forecasting something of our fate. One of the honest commonplaces of conversation is that knowledge of a strange country is better gained from its imaginative literature than from its guidebooks, history, and statistics. There is a sense in which it may be said that Greece wrote Homer, Rome Virgil, Italy Dante, Spain Cervantes, England Shakespeare, and Germany Goethe. (I myself found that the Mardrus-Mather *Arabian Nights,* read complete just before going to Cairo, made me at home there in an old-fashioned way, and the *Tale of Genji* was a condsiderable help in Tokyo, but I cannot say that the *Mahabharata* helped much in Delhi.) In the sense in which it is pertinent today this can be detached from the mass of impertinence: every writer is necessarily in some relation to his actual society and its culture when it has one, and the relation remains actual even when the writer lies, exaggerates or denies, or revolts against that society.

It was the French *esprit* (mind taken from the effect of *spirit*) that inhabited Rousseau and assumed his romanticism, and it was made deliberately preposterous in Stendhal's wonderful almost autonomous lies. Great writers perhaps prophesy and enact the history and characters of great countries by giving their feelings form and their thought the special twist of idiom. The writers come, as each of the great masters named above came, at the time their countries reach a new stage of identity. Lesser writers perhaps reflect that identity, its lapses and recoveries, the hypocrisies and sincerities of custom and behavior by which it gets along. A new novel, or a novel newly read, is news from everywhere good every day, as if the best journalism were written ahead of time only waiting for behavior to catch up with its forms or to react against them. No matter what the lie, it is told in relation to the truth; no matter what the eccentricity, the center is at hand, and the end is missed or gained with respect to the means. Literature is the free will of the soul—as some say it is his words that make man conscious of his soul—circling about the will of things and the will of history. Literature has the great merit that it can be apt and false at once to the drift of truth, if only it knows how to say so. Thus it is we look for knowledge of a strange country to its tales and meditations about itself, and our own country is the strangest ever. But it is hard to generalize that intimate knowledge.

To an American who has not read his own serious literature for some time and who comes back to it (and I should suppose also to the unblemished reader who looks at it for the first time) its most striking general characteristic (aside from the recognition of detail and the authenticity of the idiom) is its steady habit of using the symbolic imagination, rather than the narrative or dramatic. The forest of symbols in it regards us with a frightening familiarity of glance and we see at once we must find out what those symbols mean or would mean if we could put them together. We see the problematic quicker than we see the immediate, and indeed the immediate seems often to have been left out or to have become hidden in remote motions of the imagination. Action is just over the edge of vision, and its symbols draw us on. To D. H. Lawrence, and to other foreign writers, symbolism seemed inherent in the American literary character, or if not inherent seemed the result of an effort to make up for a defect in our culture. Either we write by nature more than we know or we will ourselves to write about what we cannot grasp except through symbolism. That is to say, if you like, religiously; but I would not like to say just that. Two other things, either one or both, seem more plausible to say. One derives from the notion that St. Thomas took about allegory: that it is the habit of so writing that words shall signify certain objects which in their turn signify something else. The other is that America has reached— indeed had reached it long ago—a stage of imagination singularly lacking in training in the unconscious skills which afford immediate body to the works of our cultures; less is present by nature in our words, therefore we must put more into them. The immense sophistication of the best American writing— Poe, Hawthorne, James, Melville, and Whitman (who wrote for the most sophisticated possible of audiences, the elite of sophisticated barbarians) was the effect of the need to put more into our words—in short, to invest them as symbols—than came with them at voting age. This is the live heart of Henry James's complaint on behalf of Hawthorne about the American lack of court and church and the various other external costumes of society.

Only the other day, according to the New York *Times,* Mr. Eisenhower's appearance at his dinner for Mr. Khrushchev was accompanied by a ruffle of drums; the president was in white tie but his chief guest, like the shade of Franklin, wore what is now called a dark business suit. The problem remains the same. Was it allegory in St. Thomas' sense? Was it sophistication grasping necessity? Only that great novel of American Culture, *The Education of Henry Adams,* could make any answer, and Adams' answer is now some fifty years stale in the writing and a full century in the reference. I mean especially the chapter called "The Perfection of Human Society"—a phrase detached from Charles Sumner, who made it of England in adulation, and applied by Adams as a weapon to the English "society" of the 1860's. Adams' own regular novels of the 80's, *Democracy* and *Esther,* pushed in both directions, *Democracy* for sophisticated symbolism and *Esther* which he said was written in blood, for that kind of allegory in which the originally signified objects go on creating forever.

The student of American literature who is intrigued by this problem, and who has himself a flexible mind, will turn from description to description of it in the fictions at hand, seeing himself first in one mirror then in another, but he is unlikely to reach any one position—let alone any solution—unless he arrests his powers of observation. As Henry Adams once said on one of his many returns from Europe to America, the American mind has never held that any one form of the good was *necessarily* superior to any other form; and this is also true of the forms of American imagination. It is only in his hysterias—his flashing manias, his occasional *idées fixes*—that the certainties of the American mind are absolute, and the hysterias change with the certainties. A freshman recently remarked in an examination on his abilities in English composition that he had no time to read because he spent all this time being civilized; which I suppose was his way of saying that every American has to make his culture for himself—which might be called the American Experiment. This is not true in itself; but there is certainly an effect of its being taken as if true in most of the leading American writers—especially when they make it out of some primitive culture, which is out of their own alien innocence; and perhaps most especially when they make it out of "European" culture, which is out of a borrowed guilt. We shall be saved neither by the Eskimo nor by any form whatever of the *ancien régime,* but the gestures of trying either are symbols of our hidden action. Whitman and Eliot, Melville and James, point our way. No wonder our writers have turned to allegory in one or another combination of its forms by which they could express what they had not achieved or could create what they did not yet know—like the morals in Faulkner's novels. (This differs from the works of those still inhabited by a culture: they create what they did not know, or only partly knew, that they knew—like the chorus of the women of Canterbury in

Eliot's *Murder in the Cathedral*.) Many considerations arise from these notions. One feels the host at the back, and one seems about to see very far ahead into the possible drama of the American mind, till there is vertigo in the heart and blackness at the rim of vision. Stopping short of all that, which is the wound of incentive in the private sensibility, it is yet in the presence of these notions (and with a sense of their margins of possibility) that we can proceed to comment on some seven short American novels. But what we say will be affected by the forms of writing used.

Henry James is the only author on the list who was naturally a novelist in the old sense, earned between the time of Cervantes and that of Balzac— though Stephen Crane might have become so had he lived and found a positive talent. When you read the early James you can legitimately think of Scott and Dickens and Trollope, of Balzac, Flaubert, and Turgenev; his work is a continuous development and modification of the work of his predecessors as these were affected by his deepening sensibility and his increasing virtuosity in form and in language; but the sense of the story is never lost and the feeling for drama in the theatrical sense is everywhere cultivated. Thus *Washington Square* is both in the first and the last place a story in which the scene is more important than the episode. It was something written and something told pretty much without any external or over-riding ambition. James was already, in 1881, when he published the story, what thirty-odd years later he was to call himself in a letter to Henry Adams—he was already that "obstinate finality, the artist." He made life into stories and stories into life by skilled acts of nature. The role was perhaps not yet self-conscious, but it was there to play, not only when there was nothing else to play, but always— like what happens when you wake up—by a kind of second nature which had very nearly extinguished the first.

James, that is, was a professional author *tout court*, altogether, and at once. This is perhaps why so much of what he wrote hovers on the edge of disappearing into the mechanical forms which in his early years he borrowed and which later on he invented. Under his method a very little life could be very greatly felt. Whenever a man lives by method he seems to the outsider to live very little at all, even though, and possibly because, his every second is fatally occupied. James was impervious to every force to which he could not give a form and what makes him a writer of great stature was the gradual deepening of the themes which beset him to find them form. The deepening was into the action of the human heart, and especially a heart deprived or frustrated which had in its own beat to make up for all that it had lost or had been kept from doing.

Without that deepening, James would have become, when his early freshness was lost, a popular, amusing, and forgotten writer. In his own later
language he would have succumbed to "the platitude of mere statement."
The deepening was what turned the struggle for money, for position, for
prestige, for marriage, for all the goods of this world, into the contest of adverse wills. For James, the goods of this world expressed the desperate tangle
of good and evil: of the innocence every creature has in inexhaustible reservoir and the encroaching tide of the evil that will be done to it, not so much
by major motive as by the general shabbiness of our moral equipment. Our
goods, his tales seem to say, are not adequate to express our needs, or to reach
our ends; and yet the good, to repeat Aristotle, is what all things aim at. What
then? What must be done? Nobody has ever been able to solve the problem
of the good, except by offering bon-bons which sully the taste or apéritifs
which replace appetite. In James the heroes and heroines offer no solutions,
just as they reach no victories. Either they die, having recognized life as a
Medusa, or they make renunciations as the nearest to a positive action they
can take on behalf of life. Death leaves room for the next person, and renunciation seems to allow the momentum of life to take over. Death and renunciation are for these men and women the only available forms they can give
to life when the goods of the world fall away. We think of Strether in *The
Ambassadors,* of Isabelle in the *Portrait of a Lady,* or of Milly dead and Densher
renouncing in *The Wings of the Dove.*

And so it is that we think of Catherine Sloper, at the end of *Washington
Square,* in a limbo from which she will never be withdrawn where the quality
of life is clear and its substance missing: the heiress of the human Psyche who
has thrown away everything and insists she has lost nothing. It is a role very
near and sharp to the romantic heart we have created for ourselves. We long
for it against all our good sense, for we believe we could make ourselves
meaningful if only we could sit still, if only we could keep the glory of our
patience. Catherine is still and patient in her sitting room on a spring afternoon; it is sunny outside, but only a little way into the room the sun stops,
and the light airs ruffle no more than the curtains. They belly against the sash.
The sun is known by his shadows. Miss Sloper has a long time to live, and it
will be longer, and more alive, because of what, on one mistake, she has
given up.

Two facts are plain about the history of Catherine Sloper; its frame or
scaffolding of convention is as melodramatic as *East Lynne* or *Crime and
Punishment,* and its inner structure may be as properly related to Aristotle's
Poetics as that of any work of modern Christian imagination. That is why the

story was relatively popular when it appeared and perhaps also why it could be transformed into both a play and a movie without much formal loss. The strength was in the form of the action and in the familiarity and "natural" authority of the human types who make up its roll of persons; the reader or the spectator knew by long practice what to bring with him of immediate actuality to make the meaning and the motion of the meaning his own. The details did not matter so long as they were freshly observed, for the frame and the structure would lend force and identity to any details. We will know how to speak these lines when they are given us; the generalizations upon which they depend are already part of our private lives if not part of our culture. Melodrama is how we would like to live, if we did not know better; and Aristotle, looking at Sophocles, generalized the patterns by which we can look at life as melodrama even when we do know better. Not every scene can bring the house down, but every scene may lead to the idea of doing so. There is no sweeter vision than the world lying in ruins—while we, however ruined, remain steadfast in our purpose. That is why we distrust the good man; we know very well he sees us in ruins.

But to return to our facts. In *Washington Square,* we have the upright well-meaning father who wishes to protect his daughter from all possible worlds, especially from the wiles of her fortune-hunting lover and the follies of her aunt as well as from herself, and when she refuses to be protected threatens to disinherit her, and subsequently cuts her off with less than a fortune because she refuses to promise him not to marry her villainous lover. Thus she brings about her exclusion from the goods and evils of the world and alienates herself from her father, her aunt, and her lover—all by the exercise of her simpleton and obsessed will. This is melodrama that loses rather than that which wins. There is no true lover waiting against the folds of the portières, no posthumous disclosure of fatherly forgiveness; her melodrama has brought her house quite, quite down. There is instead an increasing distance of intimacy between Catherine Sloper and ourselves, and if we closed the distance the intimacy would be gone. Only one thing can this new-made maiden aunt treasure. Throughout her short life this plain and somewhat stupid girl has been tampered with—by her willful father, whose intelligence could not compass his daughter, by her silly aunt, and by her chosen lover. Now, after her reversal of roles and of fortune, and after her recognition that her lover did not love her even for his own sake let alone for hers, after all this one thinks she feels sure that however people may use her for the rest of her life, no one will ever again tamper with her. She turns from the window as the light fails, untouchable and faintly luminous; and to her changed heart even

the movements of human affection had become an intolerable kind of tam-
perage. In James the social melodrama was translated into an allegory of the
piercing virtue—Emily Dickinson's phrase—of renunciation. But the allegory is united with the story and needs no interpretation beyond the story, in
much the same way that human behavior requires only confrontation and
recognition.

James, then, wrote what we may call natural allegory, which is not to say
primitive or willful, for it had lost the main part of its machinery and had
become a skill in the blood of imagination whereby things put in motion
could become their own meaning without losing, but increasing rather, their
own identity. This is not at all the case with Melville's *Billy Budd,* which seems
to have been the last thing Melville wrote, perhaps about 1891, though it was
not published until 1924. Melville wrote Allegory in all the machinery of
capital letter in the hope of finding—or creating—an absolute structure
within which he could make a concert of the contrary powers of heaven and
earth. Like Shakespeare, he had to make a concord out of discord, and especially out of the shifting discords of good and evil. His story could never be
content to be a story, or its own meaning, but was compelled to assert a
meaning which had not yet come to pass. The figures of Billy Budd, of
Claggart, and of Captain Vere are something that has happened to the human
by human agency, against human interests. It is an example of Melville seeking, as he said Shakespeare did, what he must shun—but what, if you like, he
must put up with all the more because he has sought it in the lonely places of
the unmitigated and unaccommodated self. Though there is a story—a series
of connected events—the story provides chiefly a frame for a series of
meditations, and the story in the end would not hang together without the
meditations which extract, which create, meaning from the series of events in
the words of the senses. Consider, then, what takes place.

An impressed sailor in the British navy during the Napoleonic wars is
falsely accused of mutiny by the master at arms. When confronted with his
accuser by the captain, he is tougue-tied and strikes his accuser dead. The
captain tries him by court-martial and he is hanged the following morning.
There are only the antennae of human relations between the three figures
concerned, and in any case the human relations are transformed by the accusation and the blow into official relations. It is as if the human and the official relations were warring forces, each of which was unstable from internal
strife: the war we seek and shun.

Thus the facts reach immediately into a kind of form for all facts, their hidden and hideous form; and it is this form upon which Melville's meditations

cast light, but we cannot say what it is except that we feel it as a unity. It is worth remembering that the great medieval masters of allegory *believed* in a unity of the world and of apprehension as already there, as a point of departure, and their allegories were intended only as interpretation, whereas most modern allegorists, such as Melville, believe increasingly in the fragmentary and the divisive out of which they wish to create a unity. This may account for the effect of strain and the air of hocus-pocus which seems to inhabit insistent and deliberate allegory as compared to the skilled ease of the older practice. Yet the two forms face what is at heart much the same situation; it is merely that God has turned his face to a fresh profile. We are, as we constantly hear, in defect of faith both of what we know and of what we do not know. There is at least a part of us, and perhaps our most energetic part, like those in Dante's limbo who had not the chance to worship God as he ought to be worshiped, since they lived in the other time and lacked baptism. "For such defects," says Virgil in *The Divine Comedy,* "and for no other fault, are we lost; and only insofar afflicted, that without hope we live in desire. *Senza speme vivemo in disio.*" Thomas Mann used this form to describe, in *Doctor Faustus,* the hell of the furious modern imagination, and Melville wrote from an earlier stage of the same condition, the stage of incredulous mutiny. It is possible that no man could mutiny against a unity in which he believed; but which of us is in belief all the time? There are moments when nothing is precious; others when belief falters. But any of us have the inner power to mutiny against either an imposed unity or a created unity, even when ourselves have created or imposed it.

In *Billy Budd* there was mutiny of several sorts. There was the mutiny of the evil against the good, as these entered human forms (as Judas mutinied against Jesus, and as Peter came near doing so, both in the line of Adam) as new creations. There was also the general perpetual possibility of mutiny against the imposed unity of the navy. The navy is always on the threshold of mutiny, no doubt because of the sharpness and clarity of its laws. Law cannot be just to the individual though the laws are themselves just and therefore command the sacrifice of the individual. Just so we must sacrifice the good in order to put up with the evil. In his allegory of the mutinous human spirit Melville created his necessities: that the good is worth its death, where the evil merely deserves it, and I expect that something like this was what Captain Vere thought when he lay on his deathbed in Gibraltar muttering of Billy Budd; at any rate it was to such a thought that his actions had conformed. From the backward dream of the admirable there had emerged the scapegoat who must be sacrificed for the image of others' redemption, and to impose the sacrifice was the task of the rational and sensitive mind. One thinks of Brutus, in Shakespeare's play, just before the murder of Caesar:

> The Genius and the mortal instruments
> Are then in council, and the state of man
> Like to a little kingdom suffers then
> The nature of an insurrection.

But where Brutus acted upon the stage of history and in the dimensions of a hero, Captain Vere acted upon a kind of timeless stage, quite outside history, where men were mainly forces meaning things other than themselves, for their selves were incredible unless taken as gestures pointing, and beckoning, beyond. Billy Budd was an unstigmatized and unjustified saint, with a presence that put down quarrels, and made your ordinary villain love him. He was a child-man, whose "child's utter innocence is but its blank ignorance." His "simple-mindedness is unaffected by experience." He has "none of that intuitive knowledge of the bad which in natures not good or incompletely so foreruns experience." When he lies in irons and asleep the chaplain kisses the cheek of the innocent beauty. He could "in the nude . . . have passed for a statue of young Adam before the Fall." He was, so to speak, all of the good that is possible without experience.

That is a great deal too much for human nature to bear, and it is a relief for us to hear: "Baby Budd, *Jemmy Legs* is down on you." Claggart the ship's policeman is down on him, and his antipathy is called forth by Billy Budd's harmlessness. Claggart had "something defective or abnormal in the constitution and the blood," and he is altogether familiar to that part of the imagination which roves after images of pure evil in the smother of waking nightmare. He is "the direct reverse of a saint." Melville's phrases belong in the gothic dark at the end of every hall in the brain. "To pass from a normal nature to him one must cross 'the deadly space between' and this is best done by indirection. . . . a master of reason in the world, a riot of exemption in the heart. . . . With no power to annul the elemental evil in him, the reading enough he could hide it; apprehending the good, but powerless to be it; a nature like Claggart's surcharged with energy as such natures almost invariably are, what recourse is left to it but to recoil upon itself and like the scorpion for which the Creator alone is responsible, act out to the end the part allotted to it. . . . Claggart's conscience being but the lawyer to his will." He is the incarnation of evil, and when the tongue-tied Billy Budd kills him, Captain Vere cries out: "Struck dead by an angel of God: Yet the angel must hang!"

As these symbolic figures clash and reverberate in Melville's meditations, one is struck with the possibility that whenever both good and evil are raised to their ideal force a permanent civil war is discovered in the nature that raises them, yet so to raise them is a regular temptation of our wills. When Billy Budd is hanged his last words are: "God bless Captain Vere!" These words are echoed by the crew, but a few moments later there is a rising mutter which makes a "sullen revocation" of that echo; and there is no longer any truth in the matter.

Some say that in this tale Melville recorded a final reconciliation with life and assented to society and nature, human and otherwise. I do not think so; I think rather he set loose one more set of images in a continuing allegory of how it is that we seek what we must shun. The truth, as Melville said, has ragged edges, whether or not uncompromisingly told, and it is the mutinous heart or the mutinous sea equally that shows those edges. The mutiny remains, and is the action of nature. In allegories of Melville's kind we make that action our own.

It is perhaps because we make these rash allegories, which then, like all allegories of damnation and salvation, imprison us in the action they engender, that another part of the spirit rebels in another way, and in the name of reality makes a burlesque both of our morals in action and of the allegories that appear to dominate them. Burlesque is how we tolerate reality when we cannot see visions, but we often do not give these names to what we are doing and would deny the names if they were offered to us. To repudiate categories is almost an act of nature, as to make them is another. Nevertheless or because of this it seems convenient to call such works as Stephen Crane's *Maggie* and Mark Twain's *The Man That Corrupted Hadleyburg* burlesque allegories of reality. Each was written in the hope that it would mean and be what it ought to mean and be, and each proceeded from prior generalizations to the instance in hand—as if a generalization could ever create an instance, or even mirror one, except cloudily. In art of the ambitious kind it is the generalizing power of the mind that seizes upon the instance and revitalizes itself; which is what Crane did in *The Open Boat* and Mark Twain in *Huckleberry Finn*. But art does not need to be so ambitious as all that, and the arbitrary content of the mind does very well for ordinary and familiar purposes. What we already know is quite enough for burlesque allegories, and needs only skill in handling the appropriate conventions of the form used.

"A very little boy stood upon a heap of gravel for the honor of Rum Alley. He was throwing stones at howling urchins from Devil's Row, who were circling madly about the heap and pelting him. His infantile countenance was livid with the fury of battle. His small body was writhing in the delivery of oaths."

This is the beginning paragraph of *Maggie: A Girl of the Streets*. Though no particular promise has been made, yet something has been promised—in the setting of the scene, in this first action under the subtitle, "A girl of the streets." We do not want to know precisely where and what we are, because we know quite enough to go on with; and we know it most from the diction, which is the diction of burlesque—the high language of low purpose. It is the diction which promises, and at the end of the tale it is the diction which rounds off the promise. In the beginning it is the brother who writhes "in the delivery of oaths"; in the end it is the mother who writhes in a burlesque of mourning.

"The mourner essayed to speak, but her voice gave way. She shook her great shoulders frantically, in an agony of grief. The tears seemed to scald her face. Finally her voice came and arose in a scream of pain. 'Oh, yes, I'll fergive her! I'll fergive her!'"

In between, Maggie, sister of the brute and daughter of the sot, had become a girl of the streets with no other equipment for the role than her circumstances, and had died as people die in the newspapers, after the brief—or long—illness of her life, in unconscious burlesque of her own possibilities. This is the allegory of evil forgiving evil by pushing it out of sight in brutality, seduction, drunkenness and prostitution, with the good pushed out of sight altogether without qualification, like blighted innocence pushed into the snowstorm which falls for that purpose. Everything happens at the perimeter of sensibility and is only known, where burlesque joins it, through a grossness of sentiment, to reality. What gives this fiction its force, and has led it to be called a realistic work, is that this is how many people make articulate their public, and indeed even their most private, reactions to life. The burlesque and the allegory are together what makes life seem tolerable when its momentum is not felt—when no events are felt astir—to these people who are "in" but not "of" the society where they find themselves.

The Man That Corrupted Hadleyburg exposes a different relation and a different psychology, that of an outsider who nevertheless partcipated in his society as one of the gods who make cruel sport of the fragile and preposterous structures of human virtue and its Siamese twin, human cant. But it is that curious outsider at work here who has the interests of natural virtue at heart. Like the elder Henry James, the father of the novelist, he understood the horror in the market place of flagrant morality, but unlike the novelist he never tried the broken steps on the moral staircase. One cannot think of

Mark Twain wildly in air. He knew nothing of the perpetual disrepair in human institutions, and never groped for a missing handrail; his pessimism walked on solid if uneven ground. Hence his burlesque was nothing in the way of expression for the unwary and deluded, it was rather a castigation and a reduction of the canting form of the pretentious allegory whereby they managed their public relations. It is not a noble but it is a satisfying act to take revenge upon the cant one has suffered for a lifetime even when one has one-self to masquerade in fraud and cant in order to do so. There is no escaping evil for the man who sets himself up to do good, and our fictions, which tam-per with actions by giving them new constructions, make this almost as plain as our actions themselves do. It is the weakness of the human mind that it can get little help from its truths and must do the work of the world by its pre-cious lies. Thus one trembles after every moment of sincerity. As in our-selves, it is the stranger within that corrupted Hadleyburg, and in telling his tale Mark Twain followed an old tradition. *Corruptio optima pessima,* which is a little nearer truth in Latin, because of compactness, than in English. In cor-ruption the best is the worst.

"It was many years ago," Mark Twain begins reassuringly, and goes on with his fairy tale, so sonorous with his hatred of reality: "Hadleyburg was the most honest and upright town in all the region round about. It had kept that reputation unsmirched during three generations, and was prouder of it than of any other of its possessions. . . . Also, throughout the formative years temptations were kept out of the way of the young people, so that their hon-esty could have every chance to harden and solidify, and become a part of their very bone." Here again, as with *Maggie,* the title sets the course and promises a port, and the diction, so to speak, gives the weather of the voyage; so that it seems the fitting end of the sequence when, after all nineteen of Hadleyburg's leading citizens had "fallen a prey to the fiendish sack," the town changed its name by an act of the legislature and the motto on its seal is an omissive act of its own. Each of the nineteen had laid fraudulent claim to a unique act of virtue, eighteen of them flagrantly in open town meeting in a grand burlesque allegory of how unfortified virtue comes to a bad end. The nineteenth, who had been saved at the meeting by the cruel charity of Mr. Burgess, the clergyman who sat in the chair, made his claim in the agonized obloquy of a deathbed confession which was not believed and which renewed a wrong done many years earlier to the clergyman, whereby he had lost his cure of souls in Hadleyburg. The change of motto was the omission of the negative from a phrase in the Lord's Prayer so that it read: "Lead us into temptation." One wonders whether Mark Twain's might not have changed the next phrase of the prayer to read: "And deliver us unto evil," for it seems to be the meaning involved in the irony of the concluding sentence. "It is an honest town once more, and the man will rise early that catches it napping again."

It is perhaps a pity that the fiendish sack of false money should have provided the active motive for corruption when there are so many other darker temptations at hand. But Mark Twain was on sound *a priori* ground, that money is the root of all evil, which I suppose means that money is the most available agent and lever for converting the potency of evil into action—as we see in family quarrels about wills that are defective and can be broken. The point is that in Mark Twain's allegory the figure of the fiendish sack is immediately and universally believed, as is the probability that someone had made the remark, "You are far from being a bad man: Go, and reform." And if there were any that did not believe, there were none that did not delightedly and excitedly accept the burlesque excesses of the exposure that follows. What the reader believes is something else again. Perhaps he believes at a distance. Certainly what has happened in the tale does not work in him as Melville's *Billy Budd* does, nor does it hold the possibility of a personal role as Catherine Sloper does in *Washington Square;* yet what he sees is nearer to him than the accidents of circumstance in *Maggie.* What he sees is perhaps a parody of himself—he knows he is more and fears he is less than the parody shows. There ought to be an old saying, for it is everywhere illustrated, that no man is ever more than a parody of his best self.

On that sentiment we make a transition to Gertrude Stein and her story *Melanctha,* for she mined the deep possibilities of the self seen and created in parody as skillfully as any author of our time, especially in her early works, *The Making of Americans* and *Three Lives,* from which *Melanctha* is taken. What is meant by parody here is everything that goes with her best-known phrase, which so many have further parodied in quoting it: "A rose is a rose is a rose is a rose. . . ." Repetition and recurrence and periodicity in varying cycles produce changing patterns which are often astonishing, sometimes impenetrable, and occasionally full of *éclaircissement* or completing enlightenment. As these patterns move they seem bound for infinity or one place short of it, and yet suggest simultaneously that at any moment they may be arrested by death, by collapse of interest, or by a willful boredom of sensibility—as if all the different clocks should stop ticking. There is no simpler figure for how her patterns are made and how they move than the kaleidoscope, where a small number of irregular pieces of colored glass are multiplied into changing patterns by a still smaller number of reflectors as the cylinder within which they are contained is little by little revolved: they shake, teeter, crash, or faintly modulate, securing novelty and affirming pattern—making prophecy and deriving from history—as each precarious balance is succeeded by another. Thus we imitate the numerical mechanism of nature by mechanizing it a little further and by denaturalizing it (since we do not have the momentum or skill of nature) as little as may be. The chips of glass are substantive in nature and formal in their procession, color and translucence have a good deal to do with the effect of rearrangement, yet with each rearrangement a new force is precipitated, or sometimes aborted. So it is with Gertrude Stein; only her chips are not glass but fragments of human personality, emotion, action, and sensibility. Sometimes she changes the selection of the chips a little, and sometimes her creative presence intrudes to modify the tone. She cannot help trying to make up by her presence for what her method has compelled her to leave out. The method is not new; the Pindaric ode is the classical example; much Provençal poetry and the sestinas of Dante are another; what is new is the deliberate narrowness of scope in the selection of the chips and the repudiation, as far as possible, of the other and more rational modes of the mind in favor of the mode of intuition.

In Gertrude Stein intuition becomes a mode of abstraction, the thing itself is its own generalization, and the pattern of intuition takes on the obligations of rational imagination. It is as if for mastery one had to reject all help from what the mind has already learned from other minds. She is a beautiful but primitive example of Croce's aesthetic which says that poetry gives theoretic form to our intuitions of feeling; beautiful because she does so much, primitive because she ignores the further nature of the power with which she does it. It is allegory freed from all structure of belief, and imprisoned by what the solitary mind is capable of with the two helps of words and patterns. One of the things she is freed from is the plot which Aristotle called the soul—the form of forms—of the action, the shape of the myth by which we see human action rise, stretch itself upon experience, and reach its end. We can do without all that, she seems to say, and we must do without it; for it corrupts and twists and binds us, and we do not live like that. We must change our account of the world according to what we find in our natures as our unimpeded intuitions reveal them in words. Thus she is compelled to charge her words with their meanings by turning and returning them until their repetitions and modulations become a pattern. Luckily for her enterprise there is a common stock of both words and intuitions into which hers enter and to which we, the readers, can if we will bring ours: and so together we make a plot just the same.

Only, as our culture seems to desire, it is an unfinished plot. There is a shapiness to it but there is no final shape which can be repeated, perhaps changed a little, in the adventure of new experience. The mastery of life by intuition alone constitutes a surrender to it as experience; when we insist too much on our own meanings, things dwindle in their own meaningfulness. It is a sad delight to read *Melanctha,* for we are reminded as we watch her procession of gestures of every misgiving we have ever felt in our own self-confidence. The story of Melanctha Herbert caresses us as we see how she got blue and consumed away. First she tries to create love by asserting her intuitions upon reality. Reality rebelled against her, then imitated her intuitions when to her despair her lover wanted from her what she had wanted so long from him. Intuition here seems to create a world of persons who crush us because they cannot exist. As Dante says, in love things color as love wills, and only the angel of solicitude, which is reason made heavenly, can save us. Here there is no such solicitude, but there is the quick and truth of tenderness which may be the substance between people and which may also be injured between people, crucified in sentiment on the cross of loyalties.

One thinks of George Meredith, for whom tenderness in affection was the great gain and loss, and then one thinks of the difference there is in Gertrude Stein. Between Melanctha Herbert and Jeff Campbell there is not so much gain and loss as there is the positive torment of tenderness that goes with a relation without common enterprise outside and binding the relation. Melanctha wants relation for its own sake—as if the stakes could be won without a firm commitment. Indeed, Melanctha's life is a study of the intuitions of an unmoored romantic love—an illusion never more than on the verge of actuality, but which yet makes all other forms of life secondary and all other obligations nugatory. The soul dissipates in the blueness of that love in which one loves for one's own sake, that romantic love in which love creates its object and is jealous of its own creation. The losses, as Gertrude Stein says, are impossible to take up.

"In tender hearted creatures, those that mostly never feel strong passion, suffering often comes to make them harder. When these do not know in themselves what it is to suffer, suffering is then very awful to them and they badly want to help everyone who has to suffer, and they have a deep reverence for anybody who knows really how to always suffer. But when it comes to them to really suffer, they soon begin to lose their fear and tenderness and wonder. Why it isn't so very much to suffer, when even I can bear to do it. It isn't very pleasant to be having all the time, to stand it, but they are not so much wiser after all, all the others just because they know too how to bear it." The ego is driven to new vanity by its losses, and this is what happens to Melanctha and Jeff in the allegory they make of love in action.

In each, love seizes on the autonomous in a world where there is no autonomy, and in each (one thinks a little of D. H. Lawrence) love then enters into the phase of anger—so near to reason, yet its opposite—for the last assertion of the self before it reaches isolation. This love is like conversion to a private religion which turns out to have no external object; and as faith cheats after its first deprivation, so does love. A conversion, when it disappears, leaves a real emptiness, and that emptiness is replaced, in Gertrude Stein's language, by a hot love, which neither Melanctha nor Jeff can accept in the other, since neither is in phase with the other's creation, whether in what happens to the sweetness of love or in what happens to real religion when these do not happen at the same time. Almost, this story seems to show, as its pattern widens, that real sweetness crossed by real sweetness comes to desolation, and that real religion comes to devastation. What Melanctha Herbert learned from love when she made it into religion was "new ways to be in trouble." So she consumed away and died—not because she was "in" society and not "of" it, but because at every critical point she found society was not in her, only trouble. This, I would suppose, is the kind of meaning that rises in "A rose is a rose is a rose," when it is said in the poignant parody which is sometimes all we have with which to greet a rose. Intuition is good only the first time; repeated, it leaves us defenseless and we wear away, seeing further and further into the beauty of what we have more and more lost in life.

Gertrude Stein had something to do with the perpetual process of self-creation, and she was mistress of the arts of giving revery effective form: her mode was the pattern of intuition, both her own and those her words yielded in repetition. William Carlos Williams has something to do with the perpetual alliance of our senses with the objects around us. His imagination makes a constant effort to see what forms objects will take when selected from the flux and put into words, and words for him are real objects too. He does not create from revery, for his business is to create everlastingly the immediate world in immediate words. I suppose he would assent in part to the medieval maxim that there is nothing in the mind that was not first in the senses, but I am not sure he would not go further and insist that what got into the live mind was the senses themselves, with words being taken as an extension of the senses. Like Gertrude Stein he is antirational in temper and desires no gifts but his own, especially nothing of the gift of old forms, old psychologies, old institutions. It is not that he is new, but that he is older than all that. He is rather like the image in his poem to the morning star:

> It's a strange courage
> you give me, ancient star:
>
> Shine alone in the sunrise
> towards which you lend no part!

Only you must think of the star as cranky, knowledgeable, and exact, as well as a light in itself, adding to what it shines on.

Put another way, Williams is an egregiously ebullient writer, as far as possible from sophistication. His allegory consists in seeing what will happen if he relates observations in the least rational order practicable. His observations become words which are names that as they move struggle with the fixed ideas and the fixed anti-ideas which irritate him in society. But he is of course never quite free of either, any more than the freshest sensation ever escapes its ancestry or fails to leave posterity. In his poetry he has no use for the sonnet, in his fiction no use for the plot, and the questions of unity of approach or the confusion of kinds would never seem to him valid. He speaks with the authority of sensation, not sentiment, yet his sensations achieve the form as they create the substance of emotions. Gertrude Stein wove according to pattern which as you get used to it is in part predictable. In Williams, as one of his poems says, the detail is all, and as the details are turned into words they end in a pattern: the pattern is how the words love him. He is as automatic as the lively intelligence can be; in his attendance on revery he is compelled to submit to his words, which insist on an order no matter what, and to the irregular intrusions of his rational predilections, which are almost as deep as his unconscious. Besides these, he submits with insistence and glee to the long order of the seasons and to the rougher order of the immediate weather.

In *The Great American Novel* and *In the American Grain,* written during the first part of the twenties, and which by some were called impressionistic essays, Williams began a long effort to write fictions wherein the rudiments of the American Psyche would make an allegory of themselves. He asks us to listen to a tumult of fragments, selected only because it is impossible to put everything that appears in lively revery into handy words, and given in minimum order only because everything looked at gains an order by the act of looking. Order is a human invention to account for what the senses perceive in sequence. Williams seems to hold that the best orders are the most fortuitous, least human, and those we can be most nearly careless of. For example in *The Great American Novel,* there is a running white water of likes and dislikes. He dislikes England like a Chicago Irishman. He dislikes standard literature. And he dislikes the actual shift of one kind of order to another. On the other hand, he likes Esquimaus and the women of the Cumberland Mountains and yellow lady-slippers and all kinds of weather, and he is fascinated by certain shady aspects of history—especially Imperial Roman history—and archeology. But mostly he does not care whether he likes or dislikes a thing; his curiosity is equally intense, and his disinterestedness is a kind of animal recognition that something is happening or that something is there—who knows what?—namely itself. He is addicted to randomness and to identity which in combination fix and exhaust his attention.

At about the time he wrote *The Great American Novel*, and a little later, he used to call himself an Objectivist, a movement or point of view in which an intense subjectivity identfies itself with the random objects of the world. It is the practice of magpies made theoretic and fruitful; one takes title to and becomes rich in the random objects one collects. At least I suppose this to be what Williams means in the following sentences. "I know not a land except ours that has not to some small extent made its title clear. Translate this into ancient Greek and offer it to Harvard engraved on copper to be hung in the water-closets which freshmen use." It would be better if the sentiment were engraved in the language that cats and dogs can read—which Marianne Moore once said was plain American, and Williams' sentiment is very American indeed—assertive of vitality, muddled in mode, a little hysterical in tone, and quite unfair to the burden of its sentiment. Translated into something like the mode of Greek thought it might turn out roughly this way: If you insist too much on what you own, very few objects will seem appropriate to you, while in the piety of observation everything may yet come to be yours. I should like to think that at bottom this is the sort of thing that Williams meant. But he has been too restless, and in the heat of speech too eager for everything, to limit himself to saying so. Certainly it is what his poems and the best of his prose, whenever not argumentative, do say for him in great clarity. It is this clarity within his words that commands our attention even when we are bewildered by the confusion and the contrariety of their procession. Perhaps the burden is in this short paragraph.

"The sun has come back. The air is washed clean. Leaves lie plastered on the streets, against the tree trunks, upon the very house sides. The bird bath is filled to overflowing: a lame man is hurrying to the train." This is how observation, as the reader observes it again, makes itself into allegory: things which being themselves signify a further meaning. The observations are both exact and experimental.

There is more than this to say of *The Great American Novel*. Something

about the First World War made many people think that America had come
of age, or at least that she ought to have done so, and this thought raised a
great deal of talk about the necessity for someone to write the great American
novel to prove it. Writers as a class were held remiss for not producing it but
it was felt that it would surely come in the next book one opened. It is impossible to recapture the tones of exhortation, prophecy, and annunciation
with which article after article was written, and it is hard to remember how
deeply public conversation and private ambition were infected—until one
recaptures and remembers how in 1940 writers as a class and individually
were held by their irresponsibility to have brought on the Second World
War. However that may be, Williams' little book was an answer to the plea
and a scheme for an example of what The Great American Novel must be.
Hence Williams' polemic and jingoistic tone. "We must first isolate ourselves. Free ourselves even more than we have. Let us learn the essentials of
the American situation." And so on.

There is also in his book a paradigm, more individual in its elements than
random—and altogether a product of Williams' own direct reading and
observation—precisely of "the essentials of the American situation." Fact,
fancy, and the documents of autobiography are mixed and rehearsed with the
looseness and fragmentariness and enormous attractiveness of unsorted objects in a box. Anybody can add what he wants; everybody must put in what
he can; everybody must take title to this fiction. For this is a fiction the reader
must write as he reads. But it is a fiction, not an essay, at one of the extremities that fiction can reach: the extremity of expressionism which says
that things mean whatever we would have them mean and that the structures
we make will carry any weight we put upon them, even the weight of the real
world. It is the sort of fiction that tugs at us to put our own reality in to see
what will happen to it. After all, this is how most of us actually look at the
world, and not alone in our daydreams, and there is every reason why there
should be a form of fiction to correspond to a deep habit. We are all
automatons until we use that part of the mind that puts things in order under
public authority; Williams wants us to see the order things make for themselves in as near as possible their own waywardness and their own identity. It
is as if, as it was with Gertrude Stein, things could be, when we are led to see
them as their own selves, also their own generalizations beyond anything we
can grasp, grasping us.

What Williams has no use for—which yet persists in use and possibility—
is exemplified as well as anywhere in Elinor Wylie's *Venetian Glass Nephew*.
Published in 1925, just two years after *The Great American Novel,* Elinor

Wylie's book moves in every possible way opposite to the direction taken by Williams. Where Williams revolted by means of direct observation against the forms of art and the institutions of society, Elinor Wylie represents the double revolt of form and decorum against life and the further revolt which invents an artificial formality and fantasy whereby if we do not escape our compulsions we can at least criticize them and look at them in a different way. It is the sort of art Oscar Wilde had in mind when he said that nature imitates art; which is true to the degree that we believe in the art, and the calamity of collapse is no greater than that of most efforts of art to imitate nature. The creative mind is unequal to either task taken separately. Pygmalion is a pessimist at heart, but he does not discover it until Galatea turns out to have met only his known desires; yet those desires were very great, and the despair is earned in the gaps between the heart beats, and it is rightful to express it so long as one keeps to the mockery of good manners and polishes the details. We can polish the details only of what we ourselves invent out of forms and in fantasy, out of what has been received and in the mode of polite allegory.

Elinor Wylie made a pastoral allegory on a velvet lawn—perhaps our oldest formal tradition in the mode—but with no rough pasture of actual society behind her. She was the living flourish of those who were rootless in the New York and the Paris of the America of the twenties, and she made a great ado of liking it that way: why should she have roots since she had legs and great agility moving them and a great skill in getting nowhere a long way off. In this case she got to the never-never land of Italy at the end of the eighteenth century, just before Stendhal and Byron got there with their flourishes of ingenuity and freedom, disdain and desperation, and what she found was a mixture of the gothic extravaganza of the late eighteenth century and the art-for-art's sake of the *Yellow Book* at the end of the nineteenth century. One thinks of Mrs. Radcliffe and Beckford, of Aubrey Beardsley and Oscar Wilde.

Out of such cross-fertilization she made alchemy for fun and gave shape to the most archetypical of all daydreams, that in which we secure our immediate ends without human penalties, and in which the supernatural is at first on our side—until we realize that we have ourselves become inhuman and must make others become so if we are to survive. But it is a daydream with manners, elegance, verbal delicacy, and a feeling for hierarchy. Everything in the book is very "literary" in the sense that Virginia Woolf was; it could not have been written except in the presence and with the aid of the elite institutions of literature and the kind of culture that makes snobbery

possible and enjoyable. It is, in short, a fairy tale written from above, a form
not drawn from the depths but imposed upon them.

What do we have? An eighteenth-century Cardinal who has just found
that it is intolerable to be without a nephew and secures one, perfect in every
external detail, with the aid of alchemical magic and the glassmakers of
Murano. He has then, a Pygmalion *manqué,* to preside over the life and loves
of his creation. The nephew marries a paragon of youthful talent, beauty and
spirit, and is of every service to her except those that go with exercise or any
form of physical stamina. His hands splinter a little if too warmly grasped and
he cannot for his life pursue his bride through the garden alleys; and she, for
her part, would rather die than lose him. So the Cardinal arranges another
creation, this time backwards. This infant Sappho, this Rosalba, must be
turned into Sèvres porcelain that she may be proper wife to the Venetian
Glass Nephew, an alchemy she is eager to experience: "It will not hurt me if I
am not afraid."

To this the alchemist responds "in a terrible voice" with a classical allu-
sion: "Non dolet"—words which a wife addressed to her coward husband as
she hands him the knife with which she has stabbed herself: Non dolet—it
doesn't hurt! (Martial's *Epigrams,* I, xiii is the best locus; it was once
schoolboy Latin.) The scene continues with the poor Cardinal expressing the
anxious hope that the transformation will require beneficent, or white, magic
only.

"I can assure you of nothing so absurd, your Eminence," was the beginning of the reply. "The Deity may justly approve of the affair of Virginio; He
cannot seriously object to the vivification of a few handfuls of Murano sand
and a pipkin of holy water. But it is another and very different matter to deprive one of His creatures of the delights and powers bestowed upon her by
Himself; we shall require the devil's aid in murdering Rosalba."

So begins the fable for frigidity with which the tale ends—though with
luck and skill she will be in the simple biscuit state, without glaze. What
fathers have done to their daughters out of envy, and husbands to their wives
out of egotism or incapacity, this girl brings on herself out of romantic love.
Thus the allegory of fantasy fastens itself upon reality with elegant iniquity;
and if the result shocks us still it cannot very much surprise us, for the offense
is within ourselves. If we are to succeed in romantic love we must be glass and
porcelain and do without fear and pity—though we may arouse them. The
allegory of fantasy will in meditation give rise to anything you like and much
you dislike. But here is how the tale ends: "At any moment they may awake;

Virginio will put on his pearl-coloured great-coat and wrap an ermine tippet about Rosalba's throat, and the season being winter and very clear and cold, they will hurry to a fashionable pastry cook's to eat whipped cream and wafers."

These remarks on seven American writers have repeated the word allegory so many times that its meaning must have become nearly obliterated, and it is to be hoped that a reading of the seven stories will make the word seem apt again, in different but related senses, for all of them. Our authors do not depend for the form in which their good things appear upon narrative, or drama, or the exhibition of character, anywhere near so much as they depend on allegory, and I think they do so because allegory is germane to their sensibility and appropriate to the culture they represent. Allegory is how they set the things of the mind in motion so as to make their words meaningful beyond themselves. As St. Thomas said, in allegory the words signify objects which themselves signify further. Some of the discriminations here made between the allegories in the different authors may seem unnecessary or trivial—if so the stories will repair the damage; but I hope none of them will seem forced, for they are meant only as provisional indications of the nature of American literature and the American psyche. Furthermore, for a last repetition, allegory is not taken here as a mode of interpretation, but as one of the great traditional creative modes of the mind, which it sometimes dominates.

Religious Poetry in the United States

After meditating off and on for three years about American religious verse, I find that it seems to reach in different directions and by different routes than those taken by what is called English or French or Italian religious verse; and it appears to have used, or cultivated, different forces in the Psyche than those within the specific familiar limits of traditional Christian feeling and dogma. It is as if religion itself had reached, or is in the process of reaching, another and different stage in its history than our regular historical sense would have predicted. Some of our Protestant theologians—as Reinhold Niebuhr—say this in their own way when they refer to present times as post-Christian; and they shall have all the rest of the words on this aspect of the subject, which is American religious verse and especially the small amount of it which is also poetry; but I want to keep in mind that unexpected forces of the Psyche are at work in it.

Which is also poetry. Anyone has enough talent to write verse within a body of recognized conventions, but very few have enough talent to make their verse poetry. We are all poets in little, else we could not read it when large; it is a matter, as Croce insisted, of quantity not quality of talent. Most verses written out of love are drivel, and most versifications of the psalms take the poetry out of them and substitute mnemonic rehearsals of doctrine and archetypal images. Hence the morals, like the love, are flagrant, and all the substance of the writer's faith and passion which he would have made public is missing forever. He is not there in front of us, and he has not put his presence into his verse. It is the presence of the human Psyche in words that makes the scandal of poetry as its presence in action makes the scandal of religion.

The distinction is worth insisting on, and I can think of no better language for it than a short passage from George Santayana's preface to *Interpretations of*

Poetry and Religion where he outlines the single idea to which his whole book leads. "This idea is that religion and poetry are identical in essence, and differ merely in the way in which they are attached to practical affairs. Poetry is called religion when it intervenes in life, and religion, when it merely supervenes upon life, is seen to be nothing but poetry."[1] It is a matter of choice, chance, and tact or grace, which is which; and religious poetry, I take it, is when the two are taken together. As religion takes new forms and changes the nature and scope of its interventions, so the poetry associated with religion supervenes differently upon our reading lives in manifest presence. There is an area in us where religious poetry at one and the same time both comes among our actions and overcomes them, an ordering together with a ravishing.

The second of the Homeric Hymns to Aphrodite is like that, and the *Pervigilium Veneris,* and perhaps the invocation to Venus in *De Rerum Natura.* They intervene and supervene at once as they persuade us of our occupation. Though the first is a narrative of events, the second an incantation, and the third a part of a philosophical discourse, in each the intervention is religious, the supervention poetic: they touch on behaviour fused with aspiration. Reading, we act and breathe and lose the action in our breath. It is the same thing, I think, when we come to the *Cantico delle Creature* of St. Francis where the gap between God and nature is annihilated through the salutation of both in single breath and all our occupation is gone and come at once. Reading St. Francis' Canticle our substance is ravished with all weathers—*onne tempo*— and all the weathers have their own meaning in the being of God. The first three poems we know are not Christian; of the Canticle we know that it is a Christian who wrote it, and one who changed Christianity through the forces that led him to write it. Here are two lines of Iacopone da Todi (of whom it is said that he wrote the *Stabat Mater*) taken from the beginning of his poem on the incarnation of the divine word:

> *Fiorito è Cristo nella carne pura:*
> *or se ralegri l'umana natura*

> Christ has flowered in pure flesh:
> Now let human nature rejoice

and three from the beginning of his poem "That it is the highest wisdom to be thought mad for love of Christ":

> *Senno me pare è cortesia • empazir per lo bel Messia. . . .*
> *Ello me sa sì gran sapere • a chi per Dio vol empazire,*
> *en Parige non se vidde • ancor si gran filosofia.*[2]

Sense and nobleness it seems to me to go mad for the fair Messiah. . . .
It seems to me great wisdom in a man if he wish to go mad for God; no
philosophy so great as this has yet been seen in Paris.

Iacopone was a Franciscan, too, of the second generation, and a splendid
Christian struggle had begun in his poetry, of which St. Francis was free in his
simplicity of salutation—the struggle, the wrestling of spirit, to join himself
to God. It is a man we know who speaks, as it was in the others a voice we
discovered. We hear a voice like this in Donne (in "Batter my heart"), in
Crashaw ("The Hymn to St. Teresa"), in George Herbert ("The Pulley"),
even in Milton ("Samson Agonistes"). In them all there is a spiritual sensuality behaving like a prodigal mathematics. Religious poetry was for them,
as it is somewhat today, a natural technique for the speculative framing and
the dramatic solution of the problem of the troubles that beset us when we
would play the role of God in our own way. Those who care for the word
may say that this was the Baroque spirit at work, and this might be apt from
St. John of the Cross to Milton; but it does not help with Iacopone, and helps
very little with later poets in the nineteenth and twentieth centuries, like
Crane and Eliot and Auden, nor with all those who have read too much St.
Augustine and Gerard Manley Hopkins. I would say rather that it is the great
wrestling tradition which has inhabited the great majority of religious poets
since the Council of Trent, and it makes no difference whether they were
Catholic or Protestant or non-juring or simple abstainers. The Reformation
and the Counter-Reformation alike put upon us the compulsion to a wrestling (and to an irregular metaphysic to account for the wrestling): a wrestling
with God, with the self, with the conscience, and above all in our latter day
with our behavior. Pascal stands as a natural monument of one form of this
wrestling, Baudelaire as another, and Henry James and James Joyce as a kind
of composite for our day. But the mind roams and needs a point of return
which is in Genesis (xxxii, 22-32):

> And Jacob was left alone; and there wrestled a man with
> him until the breaking of the day.
>
> And when he saw that he prevailed not against him, he
> touched the hollow of his thigh; and the hollow of Jacob's
> thigh was out of joint, as he wrestled with him.
>
> And he said, Let me go, for the day breaketh. And he said,
> I will not let thee go, except thou bless me.
>
> And he said unto him, What is thy name? And he said,
> Jacob.

And he said, Thy name shall be called no more Jacob,
but Israel: for as a prince hast thou power with God and with
man, and hast prevailed.

And Jacob asked him, and said, Tell me, I pray thee, thy
name. And he said, Wherefore is it that thou dost ask after
my name? And he blessed him there.

And Jacob called the name of the place Peniel: for I have
seen God face to face, and my life is preserved.

And as he passed over Peniel the sun rose upon him, and
he halted upon his thigh.

Therefore the children of Israel eat not of the sinew which
shrank, which is upon the hollow of the thigh, unto this day:
because he touched the hollow of Jacob's thigh in the sinew
that shrank.

It is astonishing that we do not have poems called "The Place Peniel" and
"The Sinew that Shrank"; for there is in this adventure of Jacob half the
subject-matter of modern poetry—which is why we can fill in so well the
bareness of this original account with the muscle and nerve of our own wrestling with God, man, or angel, as it may turn out—at any rate a damaging *and*
saving confrontation of the self and the "other" self. What seem to be the
beginnings of American religious poetry—Anne Bradstreet and Edward
Taylor—illustrate the theme in its simple form as the versification of typical
experiences and enthusiasms, of doctrine and behavior, where versification is
a kind of rehearsal for an act or a role yet to be undertaken. Mrs. Bradstreet,
for example, has a dialogue between Flesh and Spirit which precisely fits this
description. Her much lovelier, and more sensuous, poem beginning "As
weary pilgrim, now at rest" has a feeling in it of a longing, a wooing, of confrontation; but we do not feel either instance or instant. There is no architecture, and the last line ("Then Come, deare bridgrome, Come away!") seems
merely pious where it had struggled to be an act of piety. This, at the furthest
imaginable reach, I should like to compare to Henry Adams' "A Prayer to the
Virgin and the Dynamo," a poem which he carried for many years as a kind
of amulet in his wallet, and in which there is present both all the architecture
of the cathedral at Chartres and all the space in the Hall of Dynamos at the
Paris World's Fair. This is, I think, one of those poems in which the poetry
ceases to matter—in which, as in Mrs. Bradstreet, the verse does some
damage to the moving thought under the words; but there is a great struggle
for the confrontation of a vision gone: the vastation in which one still lives.
Here is the last stanza:

> Help me to bear! not my own baby load,
>   But yours; who bore the failure of the light,
> The strength, the knowledge and the thought of God,—
>   The futile folly of the Infinite.[3]

One thinks of a Pascal of our days: *Le silence éternel de ces éspaces infinis* . . . and there is a regret only for the *words* of the last line. Under them there is a full act of piety to the numinous power, and Jacob's adventure is very near.

It is near perhaps because, not very good poetry itself, it is in the mode of poetry rather than the mode of religion. Herman Melville left a manuscript poem (which is said to have been much rewritten) that may be taken as evidence as to how these modes may cross—how two prayers may be said at the same time—in the special self-consciousness of American imagination. The poem is called "Art" but it deals also with Jacob. Since it is short it is quoted entire.

> In placid hours well-pleased we dream
> Of many a brave unbodied scheme.
> But form to lend, pulsed life create,
> What unlike things must meet and mate:
> A flame to melt—a wind to freeze;
> Sad patience—joyous energies;
> Humility—yet pride and scorn;
> Instinct and study; love and hate;
> Audacity—reverence. These must mate,
> And fuse with Jacob's mystic heart,
> To wrestle with the angel—Art.[4]

The poetry—the art, the Angel Art—at which these lines are aimed, is, it seems to me, one excellent way to describe what has happened to religious poetry in America, and it is possible to religion herself, too. To keep to the poetry, it has simultaneously insisted on the value of what it can itself create and on the pressure (who knows its value) of the numinous power within us, and the relationship between the two is mutinous; as for God—the intervening power—there is discontent, distrust, and dismay for what he has created, but with a lingering addiction of first and last resort. It is Melville again who put this in the final quatrain of an otherwise undistinguished poem about a picture called "The Coming Storm" by Sandford Gifford. For Melville it was the storm in the lull of which we live.

> No utter surprise can come to him
> Who reaches Shakespeare's core;
> That which we seek and shun is there—
> Man's final lore.[5]

Of these lines F. O. Matthiessen observed that they "constitute one of the most profound recognitions of the value of tragedy ever to have been made." I think tragedy an accidental word here, which might have been any other whole word, and especially the word religion; and Shakespeare is another accident. Melville fought the archetypes he sought, and he sought the God he fought. The lines represent many confrontations and many visions, and are therefore always ready to exact from us the details with which to fill them out in what we have done with our own behavior, or in the qualms it has left in us. If it were not so long there is a poem of Melville's called "After the Pleasure Party" which I would quote in illustration at full length; but I content myself with a few lines plus its subtitle, "Lines traced under an Image of Amor Threatening":

> 'Tis Vesta struck with Sappho's smart.
> No fable her delirious leap:
> With more of cause in desperate heart,
> Myself could take it—but to sleep! . . .
>
> Could I remake me! or set free
> This sexless bound in sex, then plunge
> Deeper than Sappho, in a lunge
> Piercing Pan's paramount mystery![6]

These are matters which had been exorcised by Christianity, but they are none the less the very earth of religious concern, and they have been creeping back into the articulations as well as the blood-stream of Christians. Though the argument (since it is the argument of our actual motion) would be worth pursuing for its interest and vitality, for present purposes we can get about as far ahead by thinking of Edward Taylor and Robert Lowell in single context. Both are characteristic New England wrestlers with the spirit. Each has the ghastly sophistication of the Christian Puritan Protestant—a hangnail may be taken as excruciation—and each is aware of the bottomless resources of Enthusiasm and Antinomianism generally. (I remember that T. S. Eliot once in a hot moment reprehended certain addicts of the Inner Voice by saying that it was the eternal voice of Vanity, Fear, and Lust; and he was right.) Lowell wrestles—or behavior wrestles—against the conscience of his faith as revealed to him at the moment. Taylor wrestles against his private conscience. Taylor is full of the *strong lines* of the late metaphysicals, and Lowell writes in strong lines of his own making; each—and I mean the words literally—is obstinate in the spontaneity of his corruption, arrogant in his inadequacy: each is fiercely humble. The chasm between them is like the chasm each saw in himself: upon no razor's edge can this be crossed, and yet one's feet are upon razors. One of Taylor's poems is called "The Souls Groan to Christ for Succour" and it is of such groans that the majority of Lowell's poems are made. Another pair of Taylor's poems make grating accusations of the inner and the outer man where each, so to speak, is stripped into a reversal of role. In each the "other" self confronts the self; and, again, so it is with Lowell, the devil in him wrestles with the man, the angel with the god, in such poems as "To Delmore Schwartz" and "To Speak of Woe that is in Marriage." The difference is that Taylor pushes his sensibility into conceit (almost into formal allegory) and the conceit is the meaning of the sensibility, while Lowell drenches his conceit (the position he has been forced into) with his sensibility and the sensibility, like a road-barrier, is the meaning we are stopped by. Taylor cultivates the numinous or religious force for a purpose already anticipated, Lowell makes the force the purpose itself. For Taylor unity already existed and had to be acknowledged as a mystery that enlightens; for Lowell what unity there is you make yourself and it darkens you forever.

One can imagine Lowell repeating the remark in Gide: God woos us by his calamities, and that is how He shows His love for us; but we cannot imagine Lowell repeating what Taylor heard as "Christ's Reply" to "The Souls Groan to Christ for Succour," for it would have done this latter-day or post-Christian Christian no good. Taylor can write at the end of "Upon a Wasp Chilled with Cold":

> Till I enravisht climb into
> The Godhead on this ladder doe:
> Where all my pipes inspir'de upraise
> An Heavenly musick, furr'd with praise.[7]

Lowell writes at the end of his "Memories of West Street and Lepke":

> Flabby, bald, lobotomized,
> He drifted in a sheepish calm,
> where no agonizing reappraisal
> jarred his concentration on the electric chair—
> hanging like an oasis in his air
> of lost connections . . .[8]

The difference is absolute, and we have come again full circle to Iacopone:

> Fiorito è Cristo nella carne pura:
> or se ralegri l'umana natura.

That is, we can speak of Whitman, for he could have written the Italian lines with only the substitution, to him simple and natural, of himself for Christ: All of me has flowered in my flesh, so let us rejoice in human nature. Indeed it is not in his naive barbarism (in which the artists and intellectuals of the last century found such companionship) but in his direct and deeply civilized piety, which is precisely where he resembles Iacopone, that his poetry endures. Since it is more familiar to more people than most of his poems, we can let "When Lilacs Last in the Dooryard Bloom'd" stand for the rest, the more especially because in this poem it is very clear how he met his archetypes—his governing and vitalizing images—the symbols that made him fruitful in words—both in the open road and in the thicket of the Psyche: in what man does and in what he finds doing in himself, in which is included what man has in the past done with his poetry. Whitman, says Northrop Frye in his *Anatomy of Criticism*, was "perfectly right in feeling that the *content* of poetry is normally an immediate and contemporary environment. He was right, being the kind of poet he was, in making the content of his own 'When Lilacs Last in the Dooryard Bloomed' an elegy on Lincoln and not a conventional Adonis lament. Yet his elegy is, in its *form,* as conventional as *Lycidas,* complete with purple flowers thrown on coffins, a great star drooping in the west, imagery of 'ever-returning spring' and all the rest of it. Poetry organizes the content of the world as it passes before the poet, but the forms in which that content is organized come out of the structure of poetry itself."[9]

This is very fine; but I should like to add for present purposes that this is how *religious* poetry operates—when poetry comes nearest to positive intervention in the actions of the soul. As Mr. Frye says, it is not only the Adonis material; there is also the sprig of lilac with its mastering odor, the hidden bird and the secluded swamp, and the "tallying chant" in which all come together: "Lilac and star and bird twined with the chant of my soul." There are two progresses in the poem, of Lincoln's body and of the images, which join in the sacred knowledge of death. Lincoln, Lilac, and Thrush are merged in a full act of piety.

It is a difference of half a century as much as a difference of sensibility in the particular poets that strikes us when we look into the thicket of Robert Frost: in which there are obstinate possibilities and obstinate forces, not

human themselves, that yet—as they are cultivated into the sensibility—
change the human dimension and alter, a little, the reticulation of the elements of the human Psyche. To acknowledge this is a religious action: a
momentary conversion. The consuming or purifying fire is always at hand in
such acknowledgments, and the more so if, as in Frost, the individual is held
on to, nevertheless and because. But one does not wish to exaggerate. Here is
an example in the poem "Come In."

> As I came to the edge of the woods,
> Thrush music—hark!
> Now if it was dusk outside,
> Inside it was dark.
>
> Too dark in the woods for a bird
> By sleight of wing
> To better its perch for the night,
> Though it still could sing.
>
> The last of the light of the sun
> That had died in the west
> Still lived for one song more
> In a thrush's breast.
>
> Far in the pillared dark
> Thrush music went—
> Almost like a call to come in
> To the dark and lament.
>
> But no, I was out for stars:
> I would not come in.
> I meant not even if asked;
> And I hadn't been.[10]

Frost exposed himself to the thrush in the wood—the *selva oscura*—the
thicket where perceptions not one's own become a part of one, and found
himself confronted with himself. There is no doctrine here and no dogma,
but there is the perception out of which many doctrines have sprung and the
kind of grasping imagination which has made dogma vital. Those who have
need of doctrine and dogma first, before they risk perception, may bring
what they will and it will work. Let us say only that there are two
remotenesses here: of what is dark and at hand and of what is light (the little
that is known of it) and afar; and there is a double invitation to loneliness. Intimations spring from one to the other through the man between, changing

and remaining in the graininess of his voice. This is Frost's way, I hazard it, of recording the light in the dark and the dark in the light and the coiling movement between them of the self confronting the self.

It is perhaps unfair to make a foil for Frost's poem of Edwin Markham's "The Man with the Hoe"—once so famous for its perception of man's lot and man's need; but I can think of nothing that shows so well the difference between poetry and good will as to think of the two poems together. Let us put it baldly. Millet's painting was in natural piety to the land and the man with the hoe was very close to being a part of the land which was his life, which it takes deep knowledge to perceive. To my mind Frost's poem and Millet's painting are two versions of the same perception of the human condition, which it is damnation to ignore and a strange redemption to accept. Markham made of the painting a poem of social protest and flagrantly righteous indignation. Out of a false naiveté he saw a false archetype and constructed a faulty iconography. It is the condition in which every perception disappears and hope is thereby hollow. In Frost's poem, not Markham's, the dumb Terror replies to God.

For the other type of foil to Frost, the type that sustains and protects, there is the poetry of Emily Dickinson, which puts the hand upon the quick within her and sings hymns to the actuality of every illusion, and every crowding hope, that struck her. In her, religion supervenes and poetry intervenes upon her secular life without discrimination. Faith, she thought, was the experiment of our Lord.

> The auctioneer of parting,
> His "Going, going, gone,"
> Shouts even from the crucifix
> And brings the hammer down.
>
> He only sells the wilderness.
> The prices of despair
> Range from a single human heart
> To two—not any more.[11]

The variety is sufficient, but I should not like to stop lest it be thought I would set up categories into which religious poetry should, or must, fall. I think of Hart Crane's "Voyages," of Wallace Stevens' "Sunday Morning," of Archibald MacLeish's play about Job, and of the new Catholic poets such as Daniel Berrigan, Thomas Merton, and Ned O'Gorman. All of these poets, and no doubt many more, write poetry which can be understood only if it is taken as religious; and yet the variety varies more than the winds. To repeat, since there is no seal upon us in this post-Christian time, our religious like our other emotions come out of Pandora's box; or, to repeat more precisely, as religion takes new forms and changes the nature and scope of its interventions, so the poetry associated with religion supervenes differently upon our reading lives. If there is anything in common not only with itself but with the past, aside from its impulse, I do not know what it is, but it is possible to make a few unaligned suggestions. We are likely to be concerned with the excruciation (as Jacob was not); with Jacob's wrestling with Angel, Man, or God; with the dark night of the soul that never ends since it was a darkness we ourselves made; with the nightmares of the numen or the night-life of the spirit rather than its waking wide safety; and altogether with the great sweep of rival creation since, like Ivan in *The Brothers Karamazov,* we can accept God but not His Creation. We are lost, as Eliot seems to suggest (in his essay on Dante), in our new immersion in our lower dreams, with the higher dreams gone by the board or unavailing; and indeed only Eliot seems to see the place where the two dreams cross, and it may be only his language that sees that, for he himself calls it "The unread vision in the higher dream" and "the brief transit where the dreams cross." These are the hardships we come by in our daily life, and our poetry reflects them since they are actual.

What is actual, when we would be religious, invades us like a nightmare of our own behavior suddenly seen, and it is our own monsters that keep us from God, and no mere scholarship of the dark will save us, only acknowledgment. We must remove the obstacles, as Pascal saw, that keep us from falling into the abyss; and the obstacles are of our own invention. I think of Allen Tate and his poem "The Wolves," of W. H. Auden and his poem "Petition," and of Eliot's "Little Gidding." Each of these poems, by way of those intrusive monsters anthropology, psychology, and behavior, finds it time for human nature to rejoice, each tries to construct something, as Eliot says, upon which to rejoice, but each is left impaled upon the nature of man. Each therefore is the prayer of what is terrible in human nature (which is nature herself) addressed to the "honor of man," to "a change of heart," and to the "refining fire."

What then are they doing? As one reorganizes one's life one sees that one has been religious all along in the poetry one has made of it. Religious poetry has to do with the modes of power and powerlessness, of glory and misery. These it asserts. With these it wrestles and argues; to them submits; on them rises; in them dies. These are the terms of the poem's relation with the numinous force; the force within the self, other than the self, greater than the self, which, as one cultivates it, moves one beyond the self. Poetry is one of the ways of cultivation; and the harvest is vision. One would see God and die—so Petrarch put it. In any case there is a confrontation, and in the confrontation a flowing of force ending in an access or filling of being, else in a vastation or desolation; and the two are much the same: in calm of mind all passion spent, or *In la sua voluntade è nostra pace*. Who can say which is which?

> And courage never to submit or yield
> And what is else not to be overcome . . .
>
> O dark, dark, dark, amid the the blaze of noon . . .
>
> *Sunt lacrimae rerum et mentem mortalia tangunt . . .*
>
> Myself, my Sepulcher, a moving Grave . . .
>
> *or se ralegri l'umana natura.*

NOTES

1. *Interpretations of Poetry and Religion*, New York, 1922, p. v.
2. *The Penguin Book of Italian Verse*, George Kay, ed., Bungay, Suffolk, 1958, pp. 13, 17.
3. "Prayer to the Virgin of Chartres," in *Letters to a Niece*, Boston and New York, 1920, p. 134.
4. *Collected Poems of Herman Melville*, Howard P. Vincent, ed., Chicago, 1947, p. 231.
5. Ibid., p. 94.
6. *Poets of the English Language*, W. H. Auden and Norman H. Pearson, ed., New York, 1950, V, 310, 312.
7. T. H. Johnson, "Edward Taylor Gleanings," NEQ, XVI, June 1943, p. 283.
8. *Life Studies*, New York, 1959, p. 86.
9. *Anatomy of Criticism*, Princeton, 1957, p. 102.
10. *A Witness Tree*, New York, 1942, p. 16.
11. *Poets of the English Language*, W. H. Auden and Normen H. Pearson, eds., New York, 1950, V, 396.

Afterword to *The Fall of the House of Usher and Other Tales*

One of the extraordinary things about Poe is that in our own country he has been most popular with the young. Many a boy or girl, on reading him, has wanted to become a writer. Juvenilia up to 1920 or so were likely to have a strong flavor of Poe; since then, Hemingway, Salinger, or Eliot shows most clearly. All of us who are old enough have used Poe, but none of us has ever got to be a better writer—a manager of words—by that use. On the other hand, great writers in France—Baudelaire, Rimbaud, Mallarmé, Valéry—made out of Poe a great figure and, indeed, a master craftsman, whom it is very difficult for us to recognize in his own language. This difficulty bothers T. S. Eliot in his essay "From Poe to Valéry," and it is another version of this difficulty that seems to have led Allen Tate to write his two deeply grasping essays, "The Angelic Imagination," and "Our Cousin, Mr. Poe"—an essay which he ends with this sentence: "He is so close to me that I am sometimes tempted to enter the mists of pre-American genealogy to find out whether he may not actually be my cousin."

Those who feel this temptation should go to Mr. Tate; they will see how genuine his temptation is and out of how near a reality it springs: the reality of the "undead" within us and the worse reality of the condition of the individual who sits in the place of God. My own speculations wish to look into a different dark corner. Children and young would-be writers read Poe with excitement, French poets find Poe a master—Valéry even finding "Eureka" genuine metaphysics. But we also find (in Eliot's words) that "If we examine his work in detail, we seem to find in it nothing but slipshod writing, puerile thinking unsupported by wide reading or profound scholarship, haphazard experiments in various types of writing, chiefly under pressure of financial need, without perfection in any detail."

Eliot suggests that we must look at Poe's work as a whole, but that would not explain the excitement of the child or the admiration of the French. Children read one thing at a time perhaps even more than the rest of us, and the French poets named above are not thought to have loved slipshod writing or puerile thinking. Where then is the force in Poe that will explain the extremes of his active reputation? Let us say to begin with that Poe gives us a chance at a make-believe world and that he seems also to be about the business of remaking the world within his own scope if not quite in his own image, thus satisfying what children and French Symbolists are supposed to be up to. The important thing to say at once is that this force seems to operate as nearly as possible without regard to the language. At his best, like Blake on vision, his force works through, not with, the language. At his more ordinary levels, his force gains nothing and sometimes loses a good deal because of the language in which he deploys it. The words do not matter much but what does matter would not be there without them. It is rather like reading a love letter during a crisis in the affair; it would be meaningless to anyone but yourself, for it is only you who can know, however dubiously, the meaning that passes through the words without touching them. You must know ahead of time and also find afterwards the charge of force. Such letters can be very shattering, and so can be some of the tales and poems of Poe. Both raise make-believe to inclusive action and both require a world that cannot exist unless we create it.

Here we have vast resources. Mr. Tate, in his essay about "Our Cousin, Mr. Poe," remembers what he read as a child, and how he had so much to meet it with. I read Poe in Cambridge, Massachusetts, rather than in whatever part of the South Mr. Tate was a fourteen-year-old boy, and found different things to put into such tales as greatly struck me—say "The Cask of Amontillado" and "The Fall of the House of Usher." I thought then the cask might be found in the walled-up tunnel under Christ Church parish house, which Washington was supposed to have had ready for escape from the British, or if not there then in the secret passages thought still to lurk in Warren House. Right now, I think it might be found under the lower church at Assisi. But I also remember the hysterical laughter which I gave to Poe's joke about Masons, for I had two uncles of that order, one diffident, the other diligent, and it seemed to me the diffident one, a doctor with black lustrous eyes and fierce mustaches, might play the mason with one of his patients as the Lord of Montresor did with Fortunato—for how did I know what either my uncle or I myself might do next?

"The Fall of the House of Usher" concerned more the force of the external world which might give way—on Cambridge Street between Quincy and

Sumner Road—and we all fall into the gap. For the House of Usher was for us a square blank gray house, with shutters mainly drawn, and with a deeply recessed portico and an invisible colorless door. No one lived in it—though it was large enough for a great family and great entertainments—except a man to whom the owners had lent it and whom we identified with Roderick. The Lady Madeline was dubiously within; this we knew, for all the dubious signs were about, especially on gray or wintry days and at dusk. The resident emerged or disappeared within, as it seemed to us, without aid of the door, yet the door seemed just to have clanged. He was a dandy, as Roderick was, and our mothers warned us away from him. Later on I learned that he had one probable thing in common with Roderick, which was heraldry; but at the time he was an Usher throughout our expectant selves, and there was no night storm in which the house did not dilapidate in our hearts. As the narrator says of the "disordered fancy" of Roderick Usher, so it was with us. "The idea had assumed a more daring character, and trespassed, under certain conditions, upon the kingdom of disorganization." There the tarn was greedy to receive us along with the Ushers and their house.

"The Pit and the Pendulum" was more private. Neither the outer world nor any of my relatives had anything to do with it, and if the Inquisitor and his agents were in any way responsible it was in the role of the Holy Ghost of immediate evil. This sort of thing cannot be anywhere but in one's created self, and in the farce of horror that oneself knows. I think of the rats in the dungeon who had the formal job of chewing loose the victim's bandage which held him under the descending strokes of the pendulum. "Forth from the well they hurried in fresh troops. They clung to the wood—they overran it, and leaped in hundreds upon my person. The measured movement of the pendulum disturbed them not at all. Avoiding its strokes, they busied themselves with the anointed bandage. They pressed—they swarmed upon me in ever accumulating heaps. They writhed upon my throat; their cold lips sought my own; I was half stifled by their thronging pressure; disgust, for which the world has no name, swelled my bosom, and chilled, with a heavy clamminess, my heart." He was, of course, gnawed free, to find himself "in the grasp of the Inquisition." That bit about the cold lips of the rats is possible only in the self-welling farce of nightmare; and it is to this farce that Poe applied his method. He made a clear form out of nightmare, farce of spirit, and melodrama.

"The Pit and the Pendulum" will do as an archetype for the form, and if the reader wants another, where more of what we generally think of as the person is engaged, I suggest "William Wilson." There the identical twin of the self pursues the self, is slain, and slays the self. "I could have fancied that I

myself was speaking," says the narrator. We are all familiar with our consciences pursuing us, and some of us know that there is a chance that our better selves might catch up with us—or even with just our behavior. William
Wilson catches up with himself, and it is himself speaking, and a new form of
the unforgivable sin has been discovered—new precisely because it is one's
own. I remember how easily, at thirteen or fourteen, I could identify myself
with both the William Wilsons—Eton, Oxford, riches, cheating at cards,
Italian seductions, and all. I was as near them as Poe. I also remember, at the
same age, running after dark as hard as I could and hearing in the pelt of my
feet the avenging monster of my pursuing self; and here no doubt Poe and I
were on the same footing.

It is easy and apt to say that all this is romanticism, obscurantism, symbolism, and, if you like, a retreat from humanity into an ideal realm where as
much as possible of the human is left out. Yvor Winters, Leslie Fiedler, and
D. H. Lawrence have in their different polemics said this very well. The Lady
Madeline, or Ligeia, or Berenice will not do as a heroine or as a solvent for
passion, only as a fetish or a kind of taboo of the self—something to stand
for, or something to prevent the self, as the self commonly exists between the
wind and weather of daily life. There is a puerility about all our visions of
paradise, even the hellish ones; but there is an attractive force in such visions
which seems to be only the greater because of their puerility, and in certain
moods of groundless anxiety or even of ordinary sloth there are no visions we
would rather see than these. They have the advantage of giving the sense of
extremity and the sense of mystery (what people loosely call the "mystical")
without any initial cost beyond a surrender to spontaneity. Illusions always
seem free. Poe provides us the near thing to such illusions and such visions in
forms which we can readily make our own without any serious commitment
precisely because Poe never made them much *his* own, and never had in him,
one thinks, the capacity to make a commitment at all; he had no grasp of
the particular.

It is the particularity the reader brings that fills out the form, whether as
children out of their hereditary active natures—so near the mistakes of their
ancestors—or as permanent adolescents. There is hardly anyone who has not
enough of the adolescent in him to apprehend as heroic the sentiments as the
opening of "The Assignation," and they will be very little devalued if we call
them the sentiments of the Byronic man. "Ill-fated and mysterious man!—
bewildered in the brilliancy of thine own imagination, and fallen in the
flames of thine own youth!" And so on. Which of us has not the authority in
him to lend particularity to "The Assignation" for the length of the tale?
Who is not this hero? or if a woman, who is not the Marchesa Aphrodite? The

scene is Venice, which was Poe's Venice because he did not know it, and which is our Venice because we do not know it: we can do anything we like with it so long as we keep within the gothic and romantic frame. All that counts when Poe's gondolier loses his single oar is the idea of oarlessness. Nothing matters in Poe but the frame of suasion. The authority is ours—almost the authorship—which is not true of many writers we greatly admire, but it is handy to have authors like Poe because we can always feel equal to them. We do as much work as they do.

I have been talking of the reaction to Poe which has to do with his popularity, and now ask again how it was that Baudelaire made him a great writer. Was it not that Baudelaire wrote down his reaction and gave it, in his French, the authority, the genuineness, to which it never pretended in English, both in his actual translations and in his critical expansions? As readers we make personal translations. Baudelaire made a permanent and public translation, the difference being between his sensibility and ours, and between Poe's command of English and Baudelaire's command of French. Poe provided the opportunity, and Baudelaire provided the authority. It is almost as if Poe were part of Baudelaire's juvenilia. But it is also, and more important, as if Baudelaire could see in a foreign language imperfectly understood not only what was imperfectly present but could supply in his translation what had never been there at all. He made solid Poe's loose provision of opportunity. The Italian *traduttore, traditore* for once does not apply. The translation, rather, transfigures. This is a matter worth much discussion since it touches on how it is that all authors, to the degree that they command their language with style, translate from one mode of thought to another, in every act of writing, and perhaps more so when they work in their native rather than a foreign language. It is worth reflecting, too, that Baudelaire and his successors down to Valéry got from Poe a leading idea: that neither the intellect nor the language of a writer need be committed to the understanding or the use of the society which he intends to re-create or at least to change. The French Symbolists made Poe into a sacred book, and the original contents being thin and frustrate, the gospel disappears more rapidly than usual into the theology—but still affects their tone and bent. There is something of Poe in the structure of culture that contains the fusion of the senses and the purity of poetry, symbolism, and existentialism, the Ivory Tower and The Ivory Cellar. Whether this concerns the substantive nature of French culture I leave it to the French, and their enemies, to say.*

---

*The reader may find an excessive account of the damage Poe did to the French, and ourselves, in Mario Praz' *The Romantic Agony,* or, for an earlier work, Max Nordau's *Degeneration.* But these are the works of enemies who saw no fun.

If one wishes to withdraw from these high considerations, one can say that it was Poe who invited us in for an entertainment where our weaknesses became tottering strengths and our quaverings gasping cries—and that it was Baudelaire who closed the door of commitment, of seriousness, upon him and us. It is like the spirit of perverseness in "The Black Cat," the ventriloquy in "Thou Art the Man," the great ape in "The Murders in the Rue Morgue," or the blackness of the vegetation in "The Narrative of A. Gordon Pym"—they are all out of this world and do not touch it, or us, unless we invite them to do so. They are, so to speak, only reflections of a method in the results of which we believe only so long as we know they are impossible—like the ski tracks on both sides of the tree in Charles Addams' *New Yorker* cartoon of twenty years ago, or like Poe himself in "The Man that Was Used Up." It is partly the method of spiritual farce and partly the method of ratiocination and partly a lapse of humanity. Poe knew this, and something extra. F. O. Matthiessen makes a quotation I have not located. "Poe," he says, "once commented on his tales of ratiocination that 'people think them more ingenious than they are—on account of their method and *air* of method.'" Every reader will choose for himself what value to set on method and on the air of method as aspects of what was called above the frame of suasion. On the whole it is better to worry about method and the air of method—control and pretense of control—than it is to worry about the sort of thing that Walter Pater could say of Coleridge, from whom Poe got so much and whom, in a lesser way, he resembles (the difference being that Coleridge put more meaning into his words than most people and Poe put less.) "More than Childe Harold, more than Werther, more than René himself, Coleridge, by what he did, what he was, and what he failed to do, represents that inexhaustible discontent, languor, and homesickness, that endless regret, the chords of which ring all through our modern literature." I do not mean that Pater would have written just this of Poe, but it does quite sufficiently for what people like Pater thought about Poe through the end of the first World War. I prefer either the French transfiguration or method and air of method.

Nevertheless all these points of view apply well enough to Poe, and no doubt many more (as for example the view that the power in Poe is in his manipulation of the great archetypes of the human psyche in action) would apply with greater immediacy. But I do not think we want much immediacy for Poe; we want barriers and remedies: we do not want to enact what we see and we do want to be able to explain away, to disinfect, what we do see. We cannot be between sleep and waking all day. Perhaps Henry James was right

when he complained of the unrelieved prodigies in most treatments of the supernatural. "Intrinsic values they have none—as we feel for instance in such
a matter as the would-be portentous climax of Edgar Poe's 'Arthur Gordon
Pym' where the indispensable history is absent, where the phenomena
evoked, the moving accidents, coming straight, as I say, are immediate and
flat, and the attempt is all the horrific in itself. The result is that, to my sense,
the climax fails—fails because it stops short for want of connexions. There *are*
no connexions; not only, I mean, in the sense of further statement but of our
own further relation to the elements, which hang in the void." James is
perhaps right, yet Poe is nearer ordinary reality in "Pym" than in any of his
stories except, perhaps, "Diddling." (In that story the possible edges into the
impossible; in most others it is the impossible that trespasses.) "Pym" is based
on and indeed includes a great deal of documentary material, and there are
potential and virtual connections up to the very end, when a farce of
nightmare descends and we are left to grasp what shadows we will.

What shadows we will. But it is a maelstrom into which we shall never be
wholly swept, for the most extreme addict is swept only into illusion. While
we read, as while Poe composed, but not while he wrote, we have the habit
of thinking the obscure richer than the clear, the recondite better than the
known, the glamour better than the grammar, other reason better than our
own, superstition better than religion, the inhuman better than the known
human: just as we all have a permanent fear of being buried alive, and so
would wish to destroy all of ourselves that could be injured walled up. These
are barbarous games to which we are all prone, and the proneness shows in
much of the literature which we make popular but which does not reassure
us: the literature which deals with our discontent with every practiced or
practicable debauchery; the fruitless search for the unseemly; the anxiety for
the spiritual substitute for physical failure; above all the foreknowledge,
more a fear than a knowledge, of the constant intruder, whom Poe called the
spirit of perverseness. One should almost give the appropriate passage from
"The Black Cat" in Baudelaire's French, since he set great store by it and
quoted it separately; but we are not bound to the French tradition. "And then
came, as if to my final and irrevocable overthrow, the spirit of PERVERSENESS.
Of this spirit philosophy takes no account. Yet I am not more sure that my
soul lives, than I am that perverseness is one of the primitive faculties, or sentiments, which give direction to the character of Man. Who has not, a hundred times, found himself committing a vile or a stupid action, for no other
reason than because he knows he should *not*. Have we not a perpetual inclina-
tion, in the teeth of our best judgment, to violate that which is *Law*, merely

because we understand it to be such? This spirit of perverseness, I say, came to be my final overthrow. It was this unfathomable longing of the soul *to vex itself*—to offer violence to its own nature—to do wrong for the wrong's sake only—that urged me to continue and finally to consummate the injury I had inflicted upon the unoffending brute." As it happened, the speaker only hanged the cat from which he had already gouged one eye; the sort of thing which one became acquainted with in other children at the age of eight and in undergraduates at eighteen or twenty. But what underlay or overtopped it at other and ultimate ages, whatever ages we like to call adult, was the subject of Poe's discourse all his shortened life. We have a part in that.

The Chain of Our Own Needles: Criticism and Our Culture

It hopefully seems to me that an intimate commentary on the following passages from Montaigne, all but the last from his essay on Cato the Younger, would provide every approach and much of the substance we need in thinking about what criticism must be up to in our own culture, both its problems and its chances.

> I am singular in my desire that we should all be judged apart from others, and that I may not be expected to conform to the general pattern.

> Give me the most excellent and blameless action, and I will straightway provide it with fifty vicious intentions, all having a semblance of likelihood. God knows, if one tried to multiply them, how many interpretations may be placed on our real intentions [our secret will]! In all their calumnies their ingenuity is not so much malicious as clumsy and ignorant.

> It is matter for astonishment that we have many more poets than critics and interpreters of poetry. It is easier to write than to recognize it. At a certain low stage it may be judged by precepts and by art. But the good, the supreme, the divine, is above rules and reason. Whoever is able to discern the beauty of it with firm and steady sight sees it no more than he sees the splendour of a lightning flash. It does not beguile our judgment, it transports and overwhelms it. The frenzy that spurs him who is able to penetrate into it also strikes a third person on hearing him discuss and recite it; as a magnet not only attracts a needle, but refuses into it the power of attracting others. This is more clearly seen in the theatre, where the sacred inspiration of the Muses, having first stirred the poet to anger, grief, hatred, and transported them at their will outside of himself, through the poet again strikes the actor, and

through the actor consecutively a whole people. It is the chain of our needles hanging one from the other.

From my earliest childhood poetry has had this power to transpierce and transport me. But this very vivid calling that is natural to me has been differently described by differing styles, not so much higher and lower (for they were ever the highest of each kind), as differing in colour: first, a sprightly and witty fluency; afterwards, a pointed and exalted subtlety; lastly, a mature and constant power.

One thinks at once how Montaigne has swept away all the old nonsense about styles which did so much to cut an author's force and to impair the pleasures of reading. Every great style has been mixed. Every purity is a simple well-compounded. But intimate commentaries belong to the reader, and I will say here only that none of the passages quoted formed part of the original essay; Montaigne added them late in life—his own commentary on his own thoughts. What I now add is not commentary on Montaigne, but I should like it to be read in the presence of his remarks, for that is how I now put them down.

The great risk of criticism is that it may operate when literature has been forgotten, and seem an independent mode of the mind; and this is especially so in a culture where will and choice give way to wilfulness and chance irritation. Every skill breeds its own passion, and what lasts after the skill is gone—as jealousy lasts after love—may be all the more passionately obsessive the more the point is gone. This may be why we distrust criticism and deny it all serious application to the experience of reading. We do not think jealousy valid—though we know it may be fatal.

Yet we must have criticism (even if it is *only* appreciation) or we might not know otherwise that we had a literature. It may be that providence could have given us some other means than criticism for getting hold of literature and keeping it alive and renewing it: some means free of fashion and carping and infatuation, above all some means free of error and partiality. Providence has not done so. We could be reasonably sure, if we could somehow survive so long, of seeing our own errors in the light of the errors of kingdom come. In the meantime, we can trace the recurrence of what looks like error and what acts like truth along some of the regular paths of literary history.

We accept criticism because we have it, and we will accept the risk of criticism (that it may supplant or ignore the literature it was supposed to criticize) because we think we can minimize that risk by constant resort to the trick of keeping literature in sight, among the right and wrong in whose endless jar justice resides. Let us keep in mind, say, *Antony and Cleopatra, Lycidas,* and *The Dead:* a play, a special kind of lyric, and a long story or nouvelle. The play and the poem have a long history of controversy, and the story would have it if it were older and if it were not overshadowed by its author's other works. There is hardly a rule of the older schools of criticism, and hardly a prejudice of any of the more recent schools, which each of these works might not be held to have broken. On the other hand, there is hardly an insight of these same schools which these works do not exemplify. I do not say rules are errors and insights truths; only that it seems likely that when rules are made to act like insights error results—and it may be that when insights are made the chief *source* of rules we sometimes catch sight of truth. We seldom remember our insights when we do not have rules.

What I am getting at is this. If we can really apply the lessons of literary history to the works in front of us, then I think we shall see that it is the permanent inescapable business of criticism to explain and to justify—or to condemn—the total irresponsibility of the work of art. This is not my phrase but Thomas Mann's, towards the end of *Dr. Faustus;* and of course what he had in mind was not at all what you might think. He had not at all in mind the irresponsibility of children or young animals; nor irresponsibility in any form of life. Art is not life, but an abstraction of its nakedness; art is a response to life, but not necessary to any one form or institution of that life, and with more or less in the way between the response and the life. The purer the response, and the more complete the response, the more totally irresponsible it is to any of the means whereby we control life or keep it going. There is a mystery here—because art is also the most *prescriptive* of all our activities at the formal level: we can learn ahead of time how it will be done, but we can only learn afterwards what has been done. It is this aspect and this mystery of literature and art that many have condemned—from Plato to Tolstoi; it is also what some have been troubled by—from Johnson to Paul Elmer More; and it is what others have justified and explained—from Aristotle to Eliot. It is this, too, I believe, that makes the most useful criticism in our time in the job of relating literature to society and to ourselves. It makes a bridge between those who read and what is written.

But we have a history to think of in which certain types of criticism have been persistent or at least recurrent, and none of them have been very satisfactory for very long at a time. Why, then, should there be a criticism at all? If art and society were either wholly settled in their relations, or were perfect in themselves—that is, if we ever wholly understood each other the first time—then there would be no need for criticism. Then art and society would be very different from anything we know. One of the great and steady subjects of literature is our failure to understand ourselves; another is a new, or an old recurring shift, in our unsettled states; and a third is our aspiration towards one or another impossible form of perfection. Art and especially the art of literature may be described as the effort to put into concert some of our conflicts about these relations. It expresses our experience of these conflicts. The art is imperfect in itself; and the audience has an imperfect or at least a debatable—relation to the imperfect art; and the art and its audience change their attitudes towards each other—and change themselves too—at different rates. The moments of being in step are accidental and transitory and incalculable.

Men have wanted to clear up this incongruity for at least 2500 years—for themselves as individuals, as elites, and as whole societies. There has seldom been a living literature for long at a time without its criticism, though there have sometimes been criticisms which sought for literatures to come, or contorted the literature at hand from the past. Different types of relation between literature and its audience produced different types, and sets of types, of criticism to clarify the relation or to bridge the gap. Sometimes a single type had to carry the burden once carried by several types; sometimes a number of types have cut each other's throats, and very nearly that of literature. An example of the single type is the almost exclusive dominance of Rhetoric from Quintilian roughly to Dante; some of that time Rhetoric did a pretty full job extraordinarily well. A set of types committing suicide and nearly murder, might be found in American genteel criticism of the late 19th and early 20th centuries, which either ignored or attacked living literature, as in Melville, the early Eliot, the middle Yeats. And so on.

For convenience I think we can separate out the persistent types of criticism into three kinds: those which have to do with us and literature; those which have to do with literature in relation to itself; and those which have to do with the relation between literature and us or society. Presumably there ought to be a fourth kind which would triangulate the relations between the first three. When that happens we get great criticism, but we can hardly call it a type.

The first kind—those types which relate us to literature—roughly halves itself into a concern for genesis and a concern for history. What they have in common is interest in what is variously called Inspiration, Authority, and the Nature of Authorship. They make some answer to the questions: Who wrote it? Where did he get it? The notions that collect around these questions give some sense of the types, and the deepest and perhaps the oldest notion is that of Wooing the Muse—as in our own day Robert Graves has written a book about The White Goddess, the Muse who gives and destroys, which attracts the backward demons in us. A milder form, found in Plato, Shakespeare, Milton, and Henry James, is the notion of the presiding guardian or Genius; as we would say (or some of us) a dominant neurosis or obsession with one's role. Then we have the ancient notion of the frenzied poet, the madman, the drunk—for which the 19th century invented the "pure" poet, and the 20th century invented expressionism, and both found solace in the idea of the artist as hero. Or again there is the notion, no doubt older than history, that poetry is direct intuition—where Freud would give us the relation between the preconscious and the conscious, Jung that between the collective unconscious and the conscious, and Croce would give us poetry as the theoretic form of feelings. All of these notions involve some idea of possession, of a seeking or wooing of possession, or a cult or cultivation of possession. There is a relatively early rational form of these notions in Dante's invocation of the Muse for aid in his Comedy, which is always worth quoting again:

> O Muse, o alto ingegno, or m'aiutate!
> O mente, che scrivesti ciò ch'io vidi,
> Qui si parrà la tua nobilitate. (*Inferno II*)

This is a rational notion of Memory that may be acquired, wooed, invoked, revealed, but above all acquired, and this, with a little jump, brings us to our own general attitude in literary criticism. We have turned the wooing of the muses into the study of genetics. We have turned the notion of memory—the current of tradition—into the study of history.

This explains (for the old addictions are still at work, as our poets and our scientists show)—this explains our wide practice of genetic and historical criticism. We try to find in the poet's own life and in the conditions of his own time what previous ages tried to find outside the poet and outside the time. We justify the poet's strength by the trouble in his soul or with his family, and we explain his weaknesses as the result of his environment— usually by his isolation from or in that environment—as Dante said he was a Florentine by birth but not by character. That is, we deal with poetry by finding correspondences for it in the life of the poet and the life of his time, and we judge him by his relative success in expressing both. This is how we get at (to make up for) a doctrine of inspiration, the source of authority and the nature of authorship. We like to find the genesis of the poem and the biography of the man who wrote it, which allows a high degree of relativism and makes difficult the ascertainment of judgment in the appreciation of a particular work.

The other or historical half of this first kind of criticism is composed of a larger and more varied set of types. Since we are a race that has come to live much in time—and with 2500 years of literature simultaneously on our hands—it is not surprising that we should have invented historical criticism even if we did not thereby take care of inspiration. Historical criticism takes care of two problems which are always of pressing importance as soon as recognized. It shows us what the poet did not have to put into his work— explicitly, in detail, so that another generation can recognize it—because it was taken for granted in the state of culture, the climate of ideas, the temperature of the soul, or the topical interests, under the influence of which he wrote. Secondly, historical criticism shows us what the poet got into his work by conventions, assumptions, symbols, uses of language, of which we have lost the native skill. It is these two ideas of historical criticism which have developed the whole race of literary scholars, all of whom in their specific tasks provide types of criticism under our general head. We have a scholarship in interpretation, in the establishment of texts, in history for itself (as a corrective), and genesis both biographical and environmental and that having to do with the technical situation. Historical criticism is our way of dealing with those aspects of the radical imperfection of the poetry of the past. So also, historical criticism—if we take it as our cultivated and acknowledged memory—our way of wooing the muse as readers—should suggest how to deal with the radical imperfection of the poetry of the present— of all poetry: to let it sink in, to bring to it all we can: to ask Who wrote it, Where did he get it?

Perhaps the sum of what is meant by historical criticism and scholarship is this: it gives a body of conscious knowledge to occupy our minds while we acquire—or re-acquire—the deep unconscious skills of combination and selection of perception of which literature is made. No skill is *known* in the arts until it has run down into the fingertips of second nature. Meanwhile we have to busy ourselves at the portals, as if we were inside.

What we have been talking about is a general rehearsal of facts about the body of literature taken as granted—all having to do with our relation to literature from the outside. The direction of thought is *from* us *to* literature— with a mass of theory or attitude about the source of literature, of inspiration, authority, and authorship, attracting us, so to speak, from the other side. But none of these types of criticism inquire whether a work in question is or is not literature at all, which belongs to our second batch of types, those which have to do with literature in relation to itself. Here we want to deal with facts concerned with the medium and the form of literature. We get into questions of standards of taste, of interest, and skill. Above all, we get into the question of genuineness, which depends on the answer to the other questions and something more. We ask here, How did he write? and What, as a thing written, did he write?

It must be emphasized—always—that unlike the questions of history and genesis—we are concerned with matters largely prescribed though gradually changing; with matters that must be learned and may be modified. The medium of literature is language; most of it, with respect to its immediately preceding state, is unchanged: yet that little change is what keeps it alive. The form of literature is the corpus of technical matters as they get into language; technique may change more sharply than language in a given time, but changes within a narrower compass on the whole. The technique of Chaucer is nearer that of Hardy than the language; so with Virgil and Dante, Shakespeare and O'Neill. We deal then with prescriptive studies when we deal with the inner relations of literature.

As we had genesis and history as names of our first batch, we have even more venerable names for our second. Rhetoric deals with matters of the medium of language; Poetics deals with matters of the form of literature, though of course these cannot be segregated in practice, only in theory and analysis. But rhetoric comes first, as it is anterior to and larger than the poetic use of it.

In Rhetoric we have these types of criticism or what sometimes is criticism: We have grammar or the means of the declaration of the subject; syntax or the ordnance of relations; figures and tropes or the means of expansion; semantics, or the recovery of the seed, and history brought to bear; meaning or the creation and discovery of specific experience; communication versus expression, or the characteristic problem of discrimination; the purification of the language of the tribe, or the *merely* primary obligation; the reality in language, or the inexhaustible reservoir of what we did not know that we knew; and the logos, or the word within a word unable to utter a word: the mystery in the medium. In short we are dealing with the control of the medium: the endless thing which requires true and everlasting cooperation.

In Poetics we have these types of criticism under the following words and phrases: We have genre, which asks what kind is this? with what is it cognate? with what incongruous? We have comparative criticism, which asks How does this illustrate what? We have technical analysis, which handles the questions of such things as rhyme, rhythm, metre; plot, surprise, recognition, discovery, etc.; point of view, mode, etc. We have non-technical analysis, which deals with the questions of habit and possibility and scope, with iconography, symbolism, story, character, and psychology. We have also the confusion of genres, or ambiguity of intent, and confusion of technical forms, or ambiguity of execution. And we have, if we like (for we do not need it till we come to philosophy) a theory of the imagination. In short, we are dealing with execution in the medium: the specific thing, done alone, and for once, but an example, perhaps seen with others, or against others, whether good or bad. Here we are enormously aware of standards, of prescriptions, of their arbitrariness and of their necessity: of the interminable training and practice that goes with them. And we come blank on the need for gift, for genuineness, if anything is to be done with them. We are back wooing the Muses; with the greater sense of incentive and the more haunted.

We also come upon the institutions of literature—which is how we come on our third batch of criticism: those which have to do with the relation between literature and us or society, between literature and the powers that be; between literature and the censor; between literature and the individual who is faced with—and is not merely escaping—society.

Here the question is neither one of the history of what has happened nor prescription of what ought to be done. It is the question of determining between prescription for, and assent to, what has been done, what has come out of the affair between men and the muses. And this is locked up with a kind of lock-jaw locking in the question of value. We ask of what use is it? What will it do? It is because these questions cannot be avoided, because other people ill equipped will rush in to ask them, that some at least among the body of critics must train themselves to ask these questions and force themselves to answer them. It is no defense that in a really decent society they would not come up, for the conventions and institutions of a decent society would be constantly refreshed with reality, and such a society we have never had.

These last types of criticism divide, like the other batches, roughly in halves: into those which are pragmatic in relation to existing society and those which have to do with the principle of any possible society, though the two halves may become confused and shift their roles, depending on the kind of gap there is to be bridged between the audience and the society. My orders, then, are provisional, schemes for discussion.

Of the pragmatic types, where we have to do with unabashed direct use, there is first literature as news. Here is the book-review and the topical interest. Then there is literature as the carrier of ideas, which is literature taken as propaganda high or low or indifferent. Near that, but older, is literature as active psychology (as Ortega says of the novel that it may provide us with new psychologies) where we deal with knowledge of character and "practical" human relations. Beyond this is social or political literature where we see how the general causes of society are enacted, frustrated, or recruited. Then there is literature taken as the exhibition of epistemology, as a contribution to the general means of access to experience. Last in this group there is the type of criticism which we may call creative where one writer reacts in his own work to the work of his ancestors and his peers. These are the neutral uses of literature, the supplemental uses which few believe wholly legitimate but everybody uses and argues.

In parallel to these there are the uses by principle, having to do with ultimate or aspiring use. There is the defensive use, the assertion of the voice of passion, the voice of the poet, of the inspiration of the muse. This has its correlative in moral criticism, or the relation of literature to conduct. Aesthetic criticism comes next, which deals with the problem of created perception, of perception at a remove. Then there is philosophic criticism which assesses what happens to our systems of ideas when these are incorporated in experience. In the same way religious criticism examines what happens to vision and mystery and piety when these are found in experience. Lastly there is judicial criticism, the establishment of identity in truth, purpose, or inspiration. These are the "committed" uses of literature which are believed deeply but are in our society difficult to prove.

To learn to do sums about criticism is hard. None of the digits or numbers used seem to belong to the same kind—as analysis, comparison, elucidation, and judgment. These are all moneys, or all forms of criticism, and even with the best standard of conversion you can add them up only with a sense of loss and wild injustice with regard to their particular values. What is analysis if taken as judgment? It is the insistence on rhyme or alliteration. What is comparison taken as judgment? It is the insistence on the unities, on heroes in high places, or on purity of genre. What is elucidation taken as judgment? It defeats every judgment which is not genetic and puts a greater premium on sincerity than on truth. And so on: Let us try one more from the other end. What happens to judgment if it is taken as analysis? Morals (usually in the guise of charged immorality) get forced into art instead of being found there. Whoever heard of a judicial critic given to moral analysis as a preliminary obligation who could judge favorably the characteristic literature of his own time? Not Plato, not Irving Babbitt. What is wanted is tact: the delicate submission of the arrogance of thought to the movements of life.

Various combinations and permutations, with their subtypes and small heresies, could be continued to some unknown position of "n"; and the more we put down the more surely we would approach the conviction that criticism, so soon as it touches theory, is a mass of contradictory, in-congruous, and untenable positions. Yet literature has got along no matter what the theory of criticism. Art has a vitality and a momentum, a kind of habit of survival, like society itself; though according to every law and every rational expectation both ought to have perished long since. Art and life are rebelliously themselves. What is much more surprising is that the works of intellect including criticism, though mortal in the given instance, also have a way of surviving in the *next* instance; and they do so by reminding us that the job is always to do over again. We can always see that the criticism of the past, though useless and wrongheaded to us, was for itself right and just; it is rightness and justness gone by that give us incentive for our own renewals. What we need is always the same: some sort of intellectual account of the transactions between us and the arts.

If art does not in itself substitute for or serve or transform or transcend all the matters that daily and greatly concern us, yet it does something to the felt experience of them. It discovers or creates and then gives conventional and memorable form to the felt experience of them. Sometimes the form leads to the feeling, sometimes the feeling leads to the form. Most likely the motion is double and the relation mutual. In any case, the process is dubious, confused, problematic, equivocal, and radically imperfect with regard both to the feel-ing and the form, the experience and the intent, so far as they reach the arbi-trary conventional medium of the art. That is where criticism comes in: to get into those feelings in art, to get the art back to life, and to determine the uses to be made of the art as understood in both ways; and all along to fill in the gaps where that is possible and to make jumps where it is not. It is a fact, whether of poverty or of riches, that the great activity of criticism will be on past art in terms of the present world, and on present art in terms of past art, which are not at all the same thing. The future drags us along.

This is our chain of needles.

A Poetics for Infatuation

There will never be, I hope, by some chance of scholarship, any more authoritative order for Shakespeare's sonnets than that so dubiously supplied by the 1609 quarto. It is rather like Pascal's *Pensées,* or, even better, like the *order* of the Psalms, as to matters of date or interest. No one can improve upon the accidentally established order we possess; but everyone can invite himself to feel the constant interflow of new relations, of new reticulations—as if the inner order were always on the move—in the sonnets, the *Pensées,* the Psalms. Thus the vitality of fresh disorder enters the composition and finds room there with every reading, with every use and every abuse we make of them. Each time we look at a set of things together but do not count them, the sum of the impression will be different, though the received and accountable numerical order remains the same. If we complain of other people's perceptions it is because we feel there is greater vitality in our own; and so on. We had better persist with the received order as a warrant that all of us have at least that point in common.

That point is worth a good deal more with Shakespeare's sonnets than with Pascal or the Psalmist. It is thought that the text follows that of original manuscripts or fair copies, and no intuition bids me think otherwise. Furthermore, till private interests rise, the sequence we have seems sensible with respect to their sentiments, and almost a "desirable" sequence with respect to the notion of development. Anyone who feels weak about this should try reading the sonnets backward all the way; they will turn themselves round again from their own force. At any rate numbers 1 to 17 make a preparatory exercise for the theme which emerges in number 18 and continues through number 126. With number 127 there is a break, not to a new theme but to a new level or phase of the old theme which lasts through number 152. The remaining pair of sonnets sounds a light echo on an ancient model, but with fashionable rhetoric, of the devouring general theme.

That theme is infatuation; its initiation, cultivation, and history, together with its peaks of triumph and devastation. The whole collection makes a poetics for infatuation, or, to use a slight elaboration of Croce's phrase, it gives to infatuation a theoretic form. The condition of infatuation is a phase of life; not limited to sexual attraction, though usually allied with it, it also modifies or exacerbates many matters besides—especially, it would seem in these sonnets, matters having to do with the imaginative or poetic powers. The story of Pygmalion is one of several ultimate forms of infatuation, and Pygmalion is a name for sonnet after sonnet because the problem of personal infatuation is turned into a problem in poetics. If I cannot have my love I will create it, but with never a lessening, always an intensification of the loss, the treachery, the chaos in reality. To say this is to say something about what is overriding whenever we think either of infatuation or poetics. The maxim was never made overt but it was latent—in the undercurrent of the words— throughout much of the Renaissance: if God is reality, I must contend with him even more than I accept him, whether as lover or as poet. So it is in the sonnets. Like all of Shakespeare, they contain deep grasping notions for poetics; and this is precisely, as we master these notions, how we make most use of his poetry. We beset reality.

Let us see. The first seventeen sonnets are addressed to a beautiful young man who seems unwilling to settle down and have children. They could be used by any institute of family relations, and they must have been a great nuisance to any young man who received them. The most they tell him is that he cannot stop with himself (which is just blooming), that he cannot conquer time and mortality and reach immortality (which do not now concern him), and indeed that he can hardly continue to exist unless he promptly begets him a son. If these sonnets were paintings by Titian they would swarm with naked children—little Eroses, or putti—but Venus would be missing. There is no bride in the marriage. The argument of these first sonnets proceeds with an end in view; the prudent member speaks; but there is no premise, and no sub-ject. There was no real "young man" in these poems—though he could be invited in. As they stand, Shakespeare was addressing not a young man but one of his unaccomplished selves; the self that wants progeny addressing one of the selves that does not. The voices of the children in the apple trees can be heard whenever this set of the sonnets stops in the mind: a deep strain in us all. Perhaps it is this strain in the feelings that makes Shakespeare the poet ad-dress the other fellow as the unwilling father—the chap who never answers. Montaigne's thoughts on the affections of fathers for their children (II, viii) reach the same sort of points Shakespeare dandles a little, but cannot yet accept, in sonnets 15 to 17. "And I know not whether I would not rather have brought forth one child perfectly formed by commerce with the Muses than by commerce with my wife." Sonnet 17 goes only so far as to offer both immortalities, the child and the rhyme.

In 18 ("Shall I compare thee to a summer's day?") there is a rise in poetic power and the poetic claim is made absolute. At the same time the "young man" gains in presence and particularity, and the emotion begins to ring. The "other" self has been changed. Where the lover had been using verses around a convention, now the poet is using love both to master a convention and to jack up his self-confidence. This is of course only the blessed illusion of poiesis: that what poiesis seizes is more certain as it is more lasting than any operation of the senses. The couplet illuminates:

> So long as men can breathe or eyes can see,
> So long lives this, and this gives life to thee.

There is a burst of splendor in the tautology of *this*. Every essence is eternal, but Shakespeare wants his eternity in time (which as Blake says is the mercy of eternity). He keeps both "thy eternal summer" and his own "eternal lines," and these are the tautology of *this*. But the sonnet contains also premonitions of the later Shakespeare, especially in the seventh and eighth lines where *we cannot trim sail to nature's course,* and it is this sentiment which haunts the whole poem, its special presence which we get by heart. Shakespeare hung about not only where words were (as Auden says the poet must) but also where sentiments were to be picked up. A good poem (or bad) is always a little aside from its particular subject; a good (or bad) hope from its object; or fear from its horror. Shakespeare could take the nightmare *in* nature as an aspect of unaccommodated man—whether on the heath in *Lear* or in the waste places of private love. At any rate, in this "this" sonnet there is a change in the theoretic form one makes in order to abide nature, a change from convention to poiesis. Poetry seizes the eternal essence and the substance (here the poem) ceases to matter. We *give up* the fertile self; one illusion succeeds another, one self another self. The last illusion would be to create or find the second self of second sight. For this a poem is our nearest substitute and furthest reach.

Sonnet 19 ("Devouring Time, blunt thou the lion's paws") comes, for this argument, as a natural digression, where Shakespeare announces and explicates the doctrine of rival creation (creation not adding to but changing God's creation). If in this sonnet we understand time to be God in Nature, the matter becomes plain. We save what is ours, we save what we have made

of it: beauty's *pattern* to succeeding *men*. Only the pattern saves and salves.
Even the phoenix burns in the blood; only in "my verse" shall the phoenix of
my love "ever live young." Perhaps this is to take the sonnet too seriously,
for it may be only an expression of vanity—yet vanity may be as near as we
come to expressing our doctrine, and vainglory, in this world of time, as near
to glory. Poetry is a kind of vain glory in which we are ever young.

Sonnet 19 is not only a digression, it is a nexus to number 20 ("A woman's
face with nature's own hand painted"), where the notion of verse—or
love—ever young sets up a fright. That in us which is immortal is never free
of time's attainder. Nothing in us is free, for there is no necessity with which
we can cope. We cope with what passes away, necessity leaves us behind.
Whenever immortal longings are felt, one begins to learn dread of the immortal. Who has not seen this in the pupils of his beloved's eyes?—that if the
immortal is the ultimate form of paradise, it is the immediate form of hell.
One's firmest decision is only the early form of what transpires as a wrong guess. In the
sonnets Shakespeare deals with the reckless firmness of such untranspired
decisions, and I would suppose this sentiment to be in vital analogy to the
puzzle-phrase of sonnet 20—"the master mistress of my passion"—a phrase
at the very heart of the dialectics of infatuation (which is a lower stage of
poetics, as our master Plato shows in his *Phaedrus*). Master mistress of my passion! It is the woman in me cries out, the smothering cry of *Hysterica Passio,*
which Lear would have put down as a climbing sorrow. The notion is worth
arresting us. Poetics, hysteria, and love are near together—and the nearer
when their mode is infatuation. In sonnet 20 Shakespeare "found" (we may
find) the *fabric* of what we call his sonnets—his second-best bed—the fabric,
the Chinese silk or Egyptian cotton or West of England cloth or Scotch voile
or some animal fur to your choice—some membrane to your touch. Shakespeare is *il miglior fabbro* in another sense than either Dante or Eliot had in
mind; he found the fabric of raised feeling. But when I say "found" I do not
mean that Shakespeare (or we) thought it up. It was the other side of the
lamppost or when you opened the bulkhead of the cellar in your father's
house. I cannot speak of the particulars: but I fasten for one moment on the
rhyme (lines 10 and 12) of "thee fell a-doting" and "my purpose nothing."
What is that aspirate doing there in that completing rhyme? Is it the breath of
doting in nothing? It was behind the lamppost and in the cellar; and what did
Hamlet say to his father's ghost? If that is not enough to get from a rhyme let
us go back to the distich of lines seven and eight. Here bawdiness is com-
pounded with metaphysics in the new simple: the master-mistress:

> A man in hue all hues in his controlling,
> Which steals men's eyes and women's souls amazeth.

There is a rhyme of meaning here if not of sound between "controlling" and "amazeth," and the one confirms the other; it is one of the many places where Dante and Shakespeare rhyme—I do not say they are identical—in what they signify. In Canto XIX of the *Purgatorio* Dante converts a thought into a dream of the Siren, and in that dream things change as he wills, all hues are in his controlling, for the object of attention changes complexion or color: its colors—as love wills—*come amor vuol, così le colorava.* The second line in Shakespeare's distich is the confirmation. The hues attract, draw, *steal* men's eyes, but penetrate, discombobulate, *amaze* the souls or psyches of women. There are infinite opportunities but no direction. A minotaur lives at the heart of this dream which if it lasted would become bad, but the dream wakes in the last line: "Mine be thy love, and the love's use their treasure."

If you do not like the minotaur with Theseus and Ariadne, then let us repeat that word which superbly rhymes with itself: Narcissus. If so we must leave Narcissus at once and come again to Pygmalion. Narcissus and Pygmalion are at the two extremes of every infatuation. Of Pygmalion alone we had a hint in sonnets 9 and again in 15 to 17; but in sonnet 21 we begin to move toward the poetic Pygmalion making not Galatea but Narcissus. In short we come on Pygmalion and the Rival Poet, the poet who cannot tell the truth but only its convention. Pygmalion works in private on the making of his Narcissus. We follow the Rival Poet; he can only be the will o' the wisp of another self—in reality the anticipation of this self, and so on. We are among the executive hypocrisies by which we get along. Treachery becomes a fount of insight and a mode of action. Indeed, there is a honey-pot of treachery in every loving mind, and to say so is no more than a mild expansion of these lines:

> And then believe me, my love is as fair
> As any mother's child.

When there is infatuation of soul or body in it, love is always my child. Sonnet 22 has two examples, one of the child, the other of the treachery. There is:

> For all that beauty that doth cover thee
> Is but the seemly raiment of my heart

where the child exaggerates, perhaps corrects, certainly gets ahead of the
father; and, for the treachery,

> O therefore, love, be of thyself so wary
> As I, not for myself, but for thee will . . .

lines which tell that wonderful, necessary lie without which we could not
tolerate the trespass we know that our affections make upon others: I love
you on your account, not mine, for yourself not myself: a lie which can be
true so far as Pygmalion and Narcissus make it so. When I say love, I speak of
Eros and Philia but not of Agape who is with the sun and moon and other
stars, and under their influences torn to other shreds. I think, too, of Rilke's
Prodigal Son who ran away because he could not abide the love around the
house. Shakespeare, however, in the couplet, lets the pride of lions loose—
the very first *terribilità* in the sonnets:

> Presume not on thy heart when mine is slain:
> Thou gav'st me thine not to give back again.

In short, you are nothing but what I created. Put out that child.

However accidentally it is achieved, the sonnets proceed, at least from
sonnet 23 through sonnet 40, in an order wholly appropriate to the natural
consequences of the position reached in sonnet 22. If we insist on what we
have made ourselves, nothing else can serve as much. As we find this and that
unavailable we find ourselves subject to the appropriate disorders that belong
to our infatuation and the worse disorders—the order of the contingent or
actual world—which seem to attack us because we think we have no part in
them. The disorders are all familiar; it is the condition of infatuation that
makes it impossible for us to ignore them and undesirable to understand
them: our intimacy with them frights us out of sense, or so to speak raises the
temperature of sense a little into fever. So we find Shakespeare, in his confrontation of the young man, feeling himself the imperfect actor, inadequate
to his role and troubled by himself and the world, and all for fear of trust—of
himself or of others.

> So I, for fear of trust, forget to say
> The perfect ceremony of love's rite . . .

The rival poet is in the twelfth line, "More than that tongue that more hath
more express'd"—where "more" becomes an ugly accusation indeed from a
man "O'er charg'd with burthen of mine own love's might." To self inadequacy is added, as if it were a double self, a new, and worse, and inextinguish-

able self-love, which at one moment asserts eternal strength and at the next fears impotence and cries out for fresh "apparel on my totter'd loving." Infatuation does not fill every moment and would not exist at all if one were not half the time outside it. The *miseria* of infatuation is in the work necessary to preserve it *together* with the work necessary sometimes to escape it; and *ennui* is always around the last and next corner—the last and next turning—of *miseria*. It is *ennui* that gives infatuation its sharpest turn. Sonnet 29 ("When in disgrace with fortune and men's eyes") is a poem of *ennui*, but is also (and perhaps consequently) a true monument of self-pity—of ambition, career, profession, as well as infatuation: all places where one finds oneself "Desiring this man's art, and that man's scope." It is in T. S. Eliot's "Ash Wednesday"—*his* monument to self-pity—that this line is used with the word "art" changed to "gift." Love is only a refuge as it was only an excuse for perceiving all this. It may be less Christian of me but I prefer Shakespeare's word and if I had to make a substitution I would use "deep skill." Sonnet 30 ("When to the sessions of sweet silent thought") carries on this theme of self-pity which no writer of the first rank—and I think no composer—has been able to avoid, and makes in the first quatrain a human splendor of it. The splendor was so great that nothing could be done with it; so he made a couplet. One engages in self-pity to secure an action or to preserve a sentiment. The sentiment is in the second quatrain, the action in the third, but the human splendor is in the first. As for the couplet, its force is much better expressed in the third quatrain of sonnet 31, which otherwise fits poorly in this set, unless as a digressive generalization.

> Thou art the grave where buried love doth live,
> Hung with the trophies of my lovers gone,
> Who all their parts of me to thee did give:
> That due of many now is thine alone.

It seems an accident of *expertise* that the next sonnet should be a complaint—the special complaint of the lover as poet—that this poet cannot join the decorum of style with the decorum of love. Who knows better than the man aware of his infatuation that style is impossible to his love? The content of infatuate love, while one is in it, is of a violence uncontrollable and changeable by a caprice as deep as nature, like the weather; which one might not have thought of did not the next sonnet deal with violent change in actual weather and the one after that with changes in moral and spiritual weather. The third (number 35) makes something of both weathers and brings us to the civil war of love and hate, from the sense of which we are hardly again free in

the course of the sonnets, whether those to the young man or those to the
Dark Lady. It is that civil war of love and hate, no doubt, which inhabits sonnet 36 ("Let me confess that we two must be twain") but appears in the form
of the perennial guilt felt in any unrequited love. This kind of guilt is what
happens to the motive for action that cannot be taken.

> I may not evermore acknowledge thee
> Lest my bewailed guilt should do thee shame.

The next batch of sonnets (37 through 40) makes something like a
deliberate exercise in poetics on the analogy of substance and shadow, with
love (or the young man) as the tenth Muse who brings presence to the other
nine. But they also show (in 40) the first dubious form of the jealousy that is
about to rage at large, quite as if it had been what was being led up to all
along. Jealousy is perhaps the tenth Muse, and has the advantage that she can
be invoked from within, the genie in the jar of conscience, needs no help
from outside, and operates equally well on both sides in the civil war of love
and hate, outlasting both. *Jealous,* it should be remembered, was once an active verb in English (as it still is in French), having to do with an intense,
usually unsatisfiable craving, especially in its defeated phase. It is the right
verb for infatuation in its later and virile stages when all but the pretence of
the original force of love is gone. It is of this sort of thing Thomas Mann is
thinking when he speaks (in *The Story of a Novel*) of "the motif of the
treacherous wooing" in the sonnets, and of their pattern, "the relation of
poet, lover, and friend"—a relation made of jealousy.

Indeed from sonnet 41 on there is little left truly of love but infatuation
and jealousy in a kind of single distillation, sometimes no more than a flavor
and sometimes the grasping substance of a poem. Jealousy becomes a part of
clear vision and by the special light it casts alters the object of the vision. The
threefold relation makes jealousy thrive and encourages her to create. There
is an intermittence of life as well as of the heart, and it takes place in those
moments when jealousy reigns absolutely, which it succeeds in doing more
frequently than any other of the emotions under love. But the moments of
sovereignty are never long; she never rules except by usurpation, and by pretending to powers and qualities not her own—as truth and necessity. In her
bottom reality she is a craving, zeal without proper object, and indeed as
sometimes in English the words *jealous* and *zealous* have been confused; so
have what they signify. In the sonnets the occasional return to the purity of
infatuation is almost like becoming whole-souled. Again, as before, the accidental order of the sonnets provides a fresh reticulation. After the jealousy

of 41 and 42, there is the invocation of dreams and daydreams in 43 and the invocation of thought in 44 and 45, with, in 46, "a quest of thoughts, all tenants to the heart." These remind us that there is a desperation of condition, deeper than any jealousy.

Dreams are a mode and daydreams are the very process of creation. Nathan Sach's remark, which ought to be famous, that "day-dreams in common are the form of art" can perhaps be amended to read "the form of life"—especially when connected with an infatuation which, as in these sonnets, takes over so much else in life than its asserted object. There is much to be said about daydreams as the poetic agent of what lasts in poetry, but not here; here the point is to emphasize that dreams and daydreams—"darkly bright, are bright in dark directed"—show a deep poetic preference at work; this sonnet does not wish to *change* reality so much as to rival it with another creation. Similarly, addressing ourselves to sonnet 44 ("If the dull substance of my flesh were thought"), there is a great deal to be said about the way the poetic process illuminates the nature of thought; here the immediate interest, and it should not be pushed much out of its context, is in the ninth line: "But, oh, thought kills me that I am not thought." May not this be pushed just enough to suggest that thought and daydream are in the very closest sort of intimacy? Shakespeare seems to grasp what I assume to be the fact that thought takes place elsewhere than in words, though there may be mutual impregnation. I believe there is some support for such a notion in Prospero's phrase (*Tempest,* IV, i, 164, New Cambridge Shakespeare): "Come with a thought; I think thee, Ariel: come." This is rival creation triumphant.

The three sonnets 49-51 could be taken to represent that awful ennui in infatuation when both thought and daydream fail. The idea—image, not thought—of suicide seems at hand, the only refuge from the ennui of the unrequited. The idea lurks between the words, lending a thickness. But the ennui itself gets bored into a return to the old actions and the old patterns of action, together with the doubts and stratagems appropriate to each, in the contrary stages—the breathless ups and exhausted downs—in the history of any grasping infatuation. Consider the variety—the disorder pushing into order, every created order dropping away—in sonnets 53 through 65. The paradox of substance and shadow presides, but is constantly recognizing other speakers. It is essential to infatuation that it cannot feel sure of itself except by assertion, and every assertion carries its own complement of doubt and therefore its need for reassertion. In one's love one makes, or finds, the ideal; and at once the ideal draws on, breathes in, everything in the lover's mind; then the beloved, so to speak, is surrounded, attended, or ignored as the case may be. It is certain among all uncertainties that when Shakespeare speaks of the constant heart (at the end of sonnet 53), what is signified is the pulsing shadow of the veritable ideal. But, to repeat, consider the variety of these assertions. There is the poetics of beauty and truth, where my verse distils your truth, and with this belongs the immortality of ink. Then there is the feeling of apathy in perception, that slipping out of infatuation where one *knows* it to be self-sustained if not self-created; but to know this is to feel the pinch that sets one going again, when we get infatuation fully occupied *and* conscious of itself. This releases the possibility, which sonnet 57 seizes, that one may so rejoice in jealousy that it becomes a masochistic generosity, a martyrdom for love of the enemy and the self—not God. Surely then there is the need to ad lib at the edge of love, playing with eternal recurrence, with the poetics of time, and risking the assertion of self-love (in arguments to the beloved) as a form of objective devotion. Then comes the most familiar recurrent assertion of inky immortality, with the poetics of history and ruin and the mutability of nature herself (as we might say in the second law of thermodynamics) as new modifiers. Such is a summary account of the variety of pattern and shifting pattern. The next sonnet (66) speaks sharply to the whole procession, what is past and what is to come. It is the center of the sequence.

It is better at the center than it would have been at the end, for as it is now the reader can put it in wherever he arrests a particular reading of the sonnets. It is a center that will hold, I think, wherever it is put. "Tir'd with all these, for restful death I cry." In form it is not a sonnet, nor is it so as a mode of thought, but it exists formally to the degree that it is among sonnets, and as mode of thought it depends on, and is in answer to, the feelings that inhabit these sonnets: it is like a principle issuing order for their values. It is an advantage that the poem has also an independent existence as a catalogue and a naming of the convertibility of goods and ills in the world that makes us—a convertibility to downright domination. The lines are in the Roman sense classic in their modelling and so familiar in their sentiment that we can nearly ignore them as one more cry: All that's upright's gone! But let us look at the lines not as familiars but as strangers—or if as familiars, familiars we detest. Each line from the second to the twelfth exhibits clichés for what in any other form we could not tolerate and as clichés can dismiss if we read lightly. But once we bend our attention we see that these are insistent clichés, like the ornamental dagger on the desk which suddenly comes to hand. The cliché insisted on resumes its insights, and perhaps refreshes and refleshes itself as well. To re-expand the cliché, so that it strikes once again upon the particular and the potential experience it once abstracted and generalized, may well be a part of the process of wisdom; it is certainly the business and use of serious poetry—a business and use of which Shakespeare was prime master. Our sense of his mastery only redoubles when we remember what we can of the powerful clichés his work has germinated in our language. In the present poem the clichés were not germinated by him but were modified by the order he gave them and by the vocabulary—mastery of the force in words— of the last four in the catalogue.

> And art made tongue-tied by authority,
> And folly, doctor-like, controlling skill,
> And simple truth miscall'd simplicity,
> And captive good attending captain ill.

Do not these items precipitate us at once from the public life which presses us so much but in which we are actually so little engaged directly into the actual life which absorbs both our private momentum and all our free allegiance? These are lines where our public and private lives meet and illuminate, even judge, each other. They strike our behavior down with all its inadequacies to our every major effort; yet this behavior, and its modes, are how we keep alive from day to day—though it is how we should die lifetime to lifetime. The reader may gloss as he wills the generals of these lines into the privates of his life; but I think he might well gloss in the light they cast on the secret form of the mastering infatuation we have been tracing in these sonnets. These are the circumstances of any love which makes a mighty effort. Here it seems better to gloss only the apposition of "simple truth miscall'd simplicity." What is truly simple is only so to those who are already equal to it; a simple is a compound, like a compound of herbs, of all that we know which bears into the nearest we can manage of a single substance. Here, in this line, a truth achieved is miscalled perception not begun. Hence the rightness of Shakespeare's couplet.

> Tir'd with all these, from these would I be gone,
> Save that to die, I leave my love alone.

Love is the simple truth achieved, and not to be able to love is to be in hell. This sonnet is a critique of love infatuated.

It is a pity not to arrest these remarks now, but there are other themes, and new developments of old themes, in the remainder of the sonnets, both those to the young man and those to the Dark Lady, which will fatten further into fate the truth of the love and of the infatuation here paused at in "Tir'd with all these." A few will do for comment, and the first will be one of the sonnets (number 73, "That time of year thou may'st in me behold") having to do with the imminence of death. I remember H. Granville-Barker talking at great length about the first quatrain of this sonnet. It illustrated his notion of why we need no scene painting when producing the plays. I do not know if these remarks got printed, or I would send the reader to them. Here are lines two through four:

> When yellow leaves, or none, or few, do hang
> Upon those boughs which shakes against the cold,
> Bare ruin'd choirs, where late the sweet birds sang . . .

The reader will remember that the second quatrain is an image of sunset fading into dark and sleep, and that the third develops the notion that the ashes of our youth make our death bed and ends with the trope that haunted Shakespeare throughout his work, the trope that something may be "consum'd with that which it was nourish'd by." These two quatrains have no particularity in their imagery or their syntax, and are indeed vague generally, a sort of loose currency. But these quatrains are lent particularity and the force of relations by the extraordinary particularity (barring perhaps the word "choirs") and syntactical unity of the first quatrain. If the reader cannot see this, and see where he *is,* indefeasibly, let him read the lines over till he does, noting especially the order of "yellow leaves, or none, or few." Perhaps it will help if he remembers an avenue of beech trees with nearly all the leaves dropped, and the rest dropping on a late November afternoon toward dusk; then even the "bare ruin'd choirs" become enormously particular. These words are the shape of thought reaching into feeling, and it is the force of that thought that was able to achieve particularity and order in the words. It is to achieve the eloquence of presence, and it is this presence which interinanimates the whole poem, so that what was merely set side by side cannot now be taken apart. I suggest that this is a model in something near perfection for how the order and particularity are reached in the sum of the sonnets if they are not counted but taken by the eloquence of full presence as one thing.

In support of this, the set of eleven sonnets (numbers 76 through 86), which are frankly on poetics, may be brought into consideration as studies of the interinanimation of poetry and love. One begins to think one of the things to be said about poetry is that it makes an infatuation out of life itself: the concerns of the two seem identical. At any rate these sonnets are concerned with style—where "every word doth almost tell my name"—with style whereby we both invoke and control the violent talents of the psyche. *Grammar* and *glamor,* as the dictionaries will tell you, are at some point one and the same; the one is the secret art, the other the public show; the one is the Muse, the other the Love. The rival poet—the "other" way of writing—also inhabits these sonnets, and I think his shadowy presence suggests that he never existed save as an aid to Shakespeare's poetics.

He makes possible, this rival poet, along with the mistress shared by the lover and the young man, the seeking of humiliation and hatred and personal falsity, and that very grace of shame (sonnet 95) which discloses what Dostoevsky's Dmitri Karamazov calls the beauty of Sodom together with the harshness of love in action. But he does not make possible, except as something to turn aside from, as a prompt to a reversal of momentum—the deepest change of tide, yet only possibly its fall—these two sonnets of transumption (I will not say transcendence; it is not a word that belongs in Shakespeare's poetics. I prefer Dante's Latin adjective *transumptivus* to describe this aspect of Shakespeare's sonnets.) I mean sonnets 105 ("Let not my love be call'd idolatry") and 108 ("What's in the brain that ink may character"). The first sonnet is a Phoenix and Turtle poem, with these last six lines:

> "Fair, kind, and true," is all my argument,
> "Fair, kind, and true," varying to other words;
> And in this change is my invention spent,
> Three themes in one, which wondrous scope affords.
> "Fair, kind, and true," have often liv'd alone,
> Which three till now never kept seat in one.

I will not gloss the three words, except that they have to do with belonging and that together they make a mood which does not gainsay or transcend but is a crossing over from other moods by the ritual of repetition. The ritual is necessary and superior to the mere words—like Pascal's unbeliever who if he takes the devout posture may find belief—and when ritual is observed the distinction disappears between the hysterical and the actual. This, in effect, is the commentary sonnet 108 makes on the text and practice of sonnet 105:

> like prayers divine,
> I must each day say o'er the very same.

To cultivate one's hysteria and to cultivate the numen may often turn out to be the same thing, and the ritual for the one may be the observance of the other. In the end how far can the human need be from the power that moves it? And how different should be the approach? We repeat and repeat—almost as much as in music in the elsewhere of poetry we repeat—for the secret presences in words are felt, if not revealed, in repetition, and this is so whether it is the Lord's Prayer or the prayer that intensifies personal infatuation. As the good father who would convert us says, we cannot escape prayer. The immediate object of the prayer tends to disappear as the presence presses: fair, kind, true.

Only one other sonnet (number 116, "Let me not to the marriage of true minds") makes a comparable transumption, and again it comes with a reversal of the tide that has been flowing. That tide was undermining and reductive, subduing the lover's nature to what it worked in, reducing love at last to a babe in the couplet of number 115, as if this were the last form the hovering, transmuting eye of infatuation could show. But from Love is a babe we come in number 116 to "Love's not Time's fool." Like Cleopatra's speeches in Acts IV and V of her play, we need the right syntax of feeling to see how this sonnet escapes nonsense: It is a nonsense we would all speak at the next epiphany, whether of the same person or another. Such nonsense is the only possible company for the mighty effort to identify the ideal of love in the individual. It is the last accommodation of man alive, its loss its deepest discomfort. The second quatrain knows both:

> O no! it is an ever fixed mark,
> That looks on tempests and is never shaken;
> It is the star to every wandering bark,
> Whose worth's unknown, although his height be taken.

Some say the star is the North star, but I think it may be any star you can see, and lose, and find again when you use the same way of looking, the very star "Whose worth's unknown, although his height be taken." It is only the angle of observation that we have learned of the one thing always there. The pang is in the quick.

Beyond this there is nothing in hope or faith; but in cheated hope and bankrupt faith there are the sicknesses and nightmares of love infected by the infatuation it has itself bred. So it is with the remaining sonnets addressed to the young man. It is not the sickness of love longing; it is the sickness when the energy has left the infatuation, though the senses are still alert and vanity still itches, and indifference has not supervened. The nightmare is double: the trespass of the actual beloved on the lover, and the trespass of the actual lover upon the beloved. These are the trespasses that bring us to ruin—if anything of the ever fixed mark can still be seen—and the amount of ruin in us is inexhaustible until *we* are exhausted. "O benefit of ill!" Nightmare is how we assess the trespass of one individual upon the other (which is why "trespasses" in the Lord's Prayer are nearer our condition than "debts"), and if we have dreams and daydreams in common, as Montaigne and Pascal thought, then it may be that in the terminal stages of an infatuation we sometimes have nightmares in common. Then the general becomes our particular. Let the first quatrain of sonnett 119 stand for these trespasses:

> What potions have I drunk of Siren tears,
> Distill'd from limbecks foul as hell within,
> Applying fears to hopes and hopes to fears,
> Still losing when I saw myself to win?

Number 126, the last of the verses to the young man, is not a sonnet but six rhymed couplets. Had it become a sonnet, or even added a couplet, it must have become a curse or even an anathema. Nothing is so mortal as that which has been kept too long in one stage of nature; we have horror even of a beauty that outlasts the stage of nature to which it belonged. Not even an infatuation can be maintained more than one and a half times its natural life. There is no relief so enormous as the surrender of an infatuation, and no pang so keen as the sudden emptiness after. Such is the curse, the anathema, upon Pygmalion and Narcissus these sonnets show; but they would show nothing were it not the presence among them of the three sonnets—"Tir'd with all these" (number 66), "Let not my love be call'd idolatry" (number 105), and "Let me not to the marriage of true minds" (number 116). The first gives the condition of apprehension, the second the numinous ritual, and the third the limits beyond us in hope and faith for the mighty effort, which in one of our traditions is the highest of which we are capable from the *Symposium* and the *Vita Nuova* through these *Sonnets,* the effort to make something last "fair, kind, and true" between one being and another. There is a trinity here. What wonder then, as we find ourselves short of these powers, if in vain hope we resort to infatuation?

And not once but again, with what we call the Dark Lady as our object, and this second (second or hundredth) time with a prophetic soul for abortion and no hope of children at all. One knows at once one is among the mistakes of life which, unless we can make something of them, are the terms of our central failure in human relations. Where with the young man it was a question of building something, if necessary with other means short, by the cultivated hysteria of infatuation, with the Dark Lady there is a kind of unbuilding going on, the deliberate exchange of pounds of flesh for pounds of spirit. It is like drinking too much. Every morning the rewards show as losses, and the more they show so, the more one is bound to the system. One's private degradation is the grandest Sodom. If it were not for the seriousness of the language and its absolute jarring speed, a sonnet such as 129 ("Th' expense of spirit in a waste of shame") could have been written of any evening begun in liquor that did not come off well; but there is the language and its speed, and apprehensions from the central lonely place that this lover must seek what he must shun. The two sonnets, number 133 ("Beshrew that heart that makes my heart to groan") and number 134 ("So, now I have confess'd that he is thine"), together with 129, make a dread commentary on *philia*. In this lover's triangle, where each pair shares the third, mere sexual force—that treachery which moves like an army with banners—is superior to the mightiest effort *philia* can make alone. Once infatuation is simply sexual it is the great swallower-up of friendship or love. Sonnet 134 exacts not Shylock's pound of flesh, which he was refused because it would have cost spirit, but is sexuality exacting, and receiving, since it does not harm the body, the pound of spirit.

> The statute of thy beauty thou wilt take,
> Thou usurer that put'st forth all to use,
> And sue a friend came debtor for my sake;
> So him I lose through my unkind abuse.

The two sonnets are two maws for over-interpretation. Let us say sexuality is indeterminate and undeterminable; a force that has too much left over to absorb into its immediate end; or a force of which the sexual is only a part, but which sex raises to its extortionate ability. In the impasse of these sonnets, it would help nothing that the Dark Lady can be thought a third man, but it would hinder only those who wish to improve Shakespeare's reputation. But I suggest this only to return to the possibility, with which I began this paper, that the poetics of infatuation move among the coils and recoils of the various selves that thrive and batten upon the Psyche. This is the sixth line of number 133: "And my next self thou harder hast engross'd." Add to this only what evidence there may be in the two "Will" sonnets (135 and 136) where, other matters being present by chance, Shakespeare paid attention chiefly to the clenching of his wills in the general field of sexuality. Has no one suggested that this clenching of wills was Shakespeare's way of declaring his uncommitted anonymity? There is Thomas Mann's realm of the anonymous and the communal between us all. "Swear to thy blind soul that I was thy *Will*."

Dark Lady, Third Man, Next Self, or the Anonymous One, there is no question of the sexuality and human infatuation pressing to find form within and under and among the words of the sonnets. In this second set, without the mighty effort to lift us that was in the first set, without Pygmalion and Narcissus and the Immortal Ink, the spirit wrestles in the flesh that engorges it, and the flesh—one's own flesh—is convulsed in the spirit that engulfs it. The two journeys are remarkably the same—as are the tower and the abyss—both in itinerary and target. Deceit, distrust, humiliation, jealousy, the plea for annihilation, and self-pity, with occasional glories in general disaster and with the world of the real senses—like the light and sweet air in Dante's Hell—always at hand; these are the common itinerary, with all the other "tender feeling to base touches prone." The common target is repudiation—repudiation without an ounce of renunciation in it. "I am that I am." To say it once more, the sonnets illustrate the general or typical as the poetic, but there is a force under the words, and a force drawn from the words, which compels us to apprehend what had been generalized.

With that force in mind let us look at two sonnets just before the end. Number 151 ("Love is too young to know what conscience is") has perhaps as one of its points that love asserts a special form of conscience by escaping its general form (as we use the word in English) into what we know now as consciousness. (The reader who delights in such matters should read the chapter on *conscience* and *conscious* in C. S. Lewis' *Studies in Words;* he does not touch on this sonnet's conscience, but he does discuss several other Shakespearean usages which help us to apprehend our present mystery.) I myself think that the two sets of meanings are deeply present here, on the simple rule of thumb that a poet can never know exactly which power or powers in his words he is drawing on, and the clearer the intention (what was to be *put* into words, not what was already there) the greater the uncertainty of his knowledge must be; and besides, the words may modify and even correct his intention, as well as ruin it—else there were no reality in words and no rush of meaning either from, or to, or among them. When I say the two sets of meanings are present, I do not intend to mark an ambiguity, but to urge that two voices are speaking at once which can be heard at once. This is the compacting power of poetry, which commands us so far as we hear it. Love is too young to know what true consciousness might be, Love is too young to know the pang of judgment as to the good and evil nature of an act or thought or condition, "Love is too young to know what conscience is." The second line, "Yet who knows not conscience is born of love?" suggests that intimate consciousness leads to the pang of judgment, just as the pang illuminates the knowledge one did not know that one had. Children and saints, said Dostoevsky, can believe two contrary things at once: poetry has also that talent. Our common idiom, "I could (or couldn't) in all conscience," keeps the pair alive in what seems a single approach. The phrase "in all conscience" generalizes several sorts of behavior in a convenient singleness of form, so that none of them can be dismissed. I remember the anecdote a sociologist told me about an inmate in Trenton State Prison. When asked why he had stolen a car, he promptly answered that his conscience made him. "Yet who knows not that conscience is born of love?"

As we go further into this sonnet the voices thicken with tumescence, both of the body and of "the nobler part" as well. Priapus, rising, empties the rest of the body and drains something of the spirit ("tender feeling to base touches prone"); there is a physiological and spiritual disarray for the sake of a momentary concentration where it would be out of order to call for order.

This, then, is the priapic parallel, the comment of consciousness and conscience together; now that Pygmalion and Narcissus are in another limbo, for all the sonnets, whether to the young man or to the Dark Lady. Pygmalion and Narcissus made human efforts, but Priapus is a god and undoes all efforts not his own. His comments are in his searching actions. We can see this in lines seven and eight:

> My soul doth tell my body that he may
> Triumph in love; flesh stays no farther reason . . . .

The Greeks had a word for the bitterness of things too sweet, but Shakespeare has the verbal power for the sweetness of things too bitter. The soul in these lines cannot be taken as reason (the habit of ratio or proportion), and is unlikely to be the immmortal soul which in the end must want another lodging and deserts the body it has used. I think rather of the "blind worm" in Yeats's very late poems and of the stubbornness of dreams prompting, prompting, prompting—for lines forgotten and stage business impossible. The lines may return to mind and action ensue. Because I think of the blind worm I think the soul here is the Psyche, who is much older than the soul and is so much further back in the abyss that she is prepared to identify life with the blind stubbornness of the worm if necessary. It is the Psyche that gurgles in the words of this sonnet. When the Psyche speaks, and is heard, everything merely personal collapses—all that the Psyche must regard with the disdain owed to the mere artifact. One hunts for a grave that is not an artifact, not even the headstone. It is the Psyche's voice, then, in the couplet, where

Whitman or *The Prophetic Books* of Blake, where the feeling for catalogue and syntactical pause are in continual resort. It is not that Holmes is ignorant of the habits of verse in English; he refuses the aids those habits offer. Nor is he using the habits of prose, measured or otherwise; he makes no advantage of Melville, Hearn, Wilde, Yeats,—or Baudelaire. His line structure, so far as I can see, indicates only a slight lift in the tone of voice and a special care for articulation of syllables as compared to street-corner speech. The mere fact that a flow of words is set forth in lines not wholly controlled by the margins of the page—that mere fact must do something to the way in which we hear and read these words. This help Holmes' poems accept, and it must if Holmes uses lines at all, but I expect he would have liked better no help whatever.

At least his practice suggests as much. John Hall Wheelock in his Introduction to Holmes' *The Harvest and the Scythe* is reminded by Holmes' line of Robert Bridges' line in *The Testament of Beauty;* and it may be so, even though Bridges' line is the result and carries the weight of a lifetime's metrical experiment and (as Holmes does not) gives the reader a whole set of precise instructions as to how the lines are to be read. Mr. Wheelock does not press his own point and quotes Holmes, evidently from a letter. " 'The long line,' he explains, 'was the result of two concerns: a wish to speak in them the language I speak as a person—perhaps because this is the only one I feel I have a chance to speak really well—and a respect for the line of poetry as a unit of expression, with a totality and a meaning, however much a part of the rest of the poem it may be. . . . In most cases, before I can say very much using the language I do, the line requires some length. I feel that the image should be as totally expressed as is compatible with the associations of the poem. . . . As I look back, it seems that the way was opened for me to do this kind of poetry through my readings of Rilke's *Elegies* . . . Eliot's *Quartets,* and translations of Homer and Virgil that impressed me. I think they brought me to form, through what they led me to understand about poetry: that the bottom value of poetry lies not in the maximum demand it makes on language, but in the minimum. They led me to see that poetry derives its power from that phase of its language that corresponds to its most plain and simple use; where the words become transparent, and mediums through which we read the relationships between the objects, concepts and feelings they stand for. It is in this knowledge that I have sacrificed some of the traditional value poets have found in words, rhyme, pun and meter, to get at a greater amount of the potential for expression that lies behind the words: the force which the correspondences between us and the world have to illuminate our life. It is a language which man has found he has in common with man at most times;

and, when written as words, is as nearly translatable as verbal language can be.'"

I have quoted all that Mr. Wheelock quoted, so that Holmes may stand on his own sea-legs of prosody and diction. It is in general the argument of Wordsworth but made by someone who has breathed—I do not say studied—the notions and desires of French symbolist poets and their successors. Holmes wants a language free of other people's controls. He has a natural resistance to imposed form in prosody or in any other aspect of composition; he wants, if not a one-man religion, a one-man language which by lucky universal accident will be understood by other men. He has a natural will towards permissive form; he wants shapeiness rather than shapeliness. Rejecting, or avoiding the practice of his masters, he would seem to accept nearly at face value every accidental achievement—as if the ephemeral were the very substance of the eternal, the accidental the substantial. Yet he has a profound desire for form.

As to diction or the relation of existing words to his use of them, the story is much the same. He would out-Wordsworth Wordsworth: where the very language of men becomes the very language of the man writing. Coleridge would have had more fun with Holmes than he had with Wordsworth, and Holmes would have been as impervious to the annotation as Wordsworth was. Holmes, like Wordsworth, is free of experimentation: his independence arises from certainty—even conviction—at the moment of composition that the words unite with his intent. There is none of us who does not believe as much in every moment of practical urgency of defence, attack, persuasion, or justification. We are all solipsists when the urgency is great enough; and otherwise when we are lazy. Take this from Holmes.

> The important part of me has passed into the realm of form,
> that realm of preterite being, of virtual happening—
> where the flares that broke in the night on the fourth of July
> now light up their own skies.
>
> The dwelt-in predication of this house about me—what is
>   all else?

Since Holmes has chosen the poem containing these lines to represent him in this token collection, the reader can think of them in their whole context with only the trouble of turning a few pages. It will correct any overemphasis on my part when I say take from the lines the three words: preterite, virtual, and predication. Each of these words wears an air of oddity, something in-

cognito which we yet might know, something inviting like masks at a ball—
but also with a blankness of expression. What is preterite is past, is bygone—
but also with a blankness of expression. What is virtual is what *is* such (virtual
death, virtual hope) for practical purposes though not in name or strict definition. Predicated is what is asserted or affirmed as true or existent. Perhaps
Holmes is some sort of Platonist. Perhaps the words made their annunciation
in a random day-dream, a kind of side-dream while he was making his poem.
Many possibilities invite us in this dance. Nobody knows where his words
come from and one is always surprised where they go. Most people guess
their language; and as readers or listeners we must guess *their* guesses or substitute favored guesses of our own. The art of poetry commands our guesses:
and in Holmes' sort of poetry the guess is provoked (as in much symbolist
poetry) by omitting the signified object and emphasizing the signifying subject. Or let us say that the habits of his language are enthymemic: that is, he
writes poetic syllogisms with one of the premises omitted. I would suppose
that the enthymeme is unconscious in him as a device but is lively on the very
tips of his writing fingers: he writes so as to feel the pressure of the missing
premise, the attraction of the signified object. When there are omissions, the
things that are left get very near together. If you will take these abstractions
as the account of a fundamental skill you will see how near things get, in this
poem, between preterite and virtual and predicated—between what was,
what cannot quite be, and what is promised true. Each of us knows where he
is and must needs think each other in the same place.

Again, as with the prosody, what Holmes is doing with his diction is
natural enough at the present day, and is in part an effect of some three centuries of the malicious criticism of knowledge. There have been painters
paint white on white, concert virtuosi in total silence, ballets without movement, buildings barren of space or lift; and in literature, never so pure as the
other arts, we have what goes with solipsism, expressionism, the revolution
of the word first noticed by Heraclitus: the rejection, so far as possible, of any
skill not one's own, and the flight from any meaning not one's own. Holmes
cares little about purifying the language of the tribe; but he cares vastly about
the words of his private language. Do I say what I mean? Do I mean what I
say? Holmes does not distinguish these directions of meaning much more
than Alice did. But, as for form, he has a profound desire for meaning.

Meaning and form are both in some sense—it may be only hallucina-
tion—inescapable. Form is the limits of the thing we see, and meaning is the
action form takes on us. Similarly, no matter how much one tries to escape
them, some elements of pattern and measure persist in the most independent

prosody, and part of the history and metaphor-making power of our words persist in each use of them. Some of E. E. Cummings' most typographical poems read best if you also think of them as the sonnets they are—in some cases actually were, and Spenserian sonnets at that. W. C. Williams offers us no hidden sonnets (to him a form of suicide) but his poems often read themselves as iambic pentameters with the caesura represented as the end of a line and with the irregularities less varied and vivid than in *Hamlet* or *The Winter's Tale*. Metre is the motion of meaning, and it has no other. Similarly again, in any difficult place in a poet who attracts us we cannot help bringing the central power (often far from the initial power) of a word to bear. This is how we feel the "rightness" of a word even when we do not know the word in any dictionary or doctrinal sense. We could not otherwise *put* meaning into our words; that is, find and emphasize it there. Thus in Holmes, we find his lines running towards the anapest or the dactyl (something you will also find, where it is deliberate, in the *Pisan Cantos*) and I have seen other places where the lines could be freed into blank verse with minimal rearrangement. One cannot entirely get rid of the skills one has absorbed. And so in diction, wherever his natural piety towards the senses is at work, we find a created accuracy of observation and notation. I say created because the accuracy did not exist until he put his observation into words. I say observation because by repeating it we can make corresponding things accurate for ourselves. And I say natural piety—again a Wordsworthian term—because it is the duty of tender care he feels by nature towards the forces that move him and move within him. Here in variety are a number of observations and notations taken, as they are best taken, in isolation.

Some seem like proverbs either Chinese or from a lost prophetic book by William Blake and some spring from a more immediate nature. "The water that lightens the seed in the womb springs from the same place as tears. . . . The old feel a kind of youth in what they come to after having lived out their years. . . . A broom in the corner of the subway and a lamp in the corner of the study. . . . A baby hides in his carriage the softness of the night he was conceived. . . . Each day we are out traveling in the weather of our soul. . . . Life stripped of consciousness remains the last form of love. . . . The leaves that fall from the tree keep the frost from reaching the root. . . . The house sits up on the hill; and has that satisfied look of a head taking credit for the comfort the body enjoys in bed. . . . The poor in bed at night find that their heart grows great. . . . [Prayers] that, at night, are like the foliage of the trees we look through to see the stars. . . . The bloom of pure pain that somehow always gets stifled in the bud. . . . Only on earth has

there ever been found a prediction in the stars of a life to come. . . . A thinker often feels his thoughts like animals made to stand on their hind legs."*
Holmes' poems are full of lines and phrases like these; a yield uncommon to say the least of it in contemporary poetry. If, as I think, they are characteristic of the poetry he wants to write, then the reasons for his long line prosody become plain: any other prosody would disturb his thought and would also commit him more closely to other people's thought and diction than seems convenient to him. His independence leaves him with more work to do by himself than has hitherto seemed possible for an ambitious poet. One's genius is doubtless one's own, but is fragmentary if stuck to, and I do not know that a poet of the meditative mode would wish to be more fragmentary than his times compel him to be. There is nothing so stifles identity as its fragmentary expression; I mean, of course, for others' knowledge of it: We are all pure bird-song, so long as none listen. I would say there are two ways to read this last quotation from Holmes: "It is the child that must bear the weight of his father's accomplishments." The dactyls are almost perfect. I hope very much that, dactyls and all, Holmes will read it both ways at once. The accidents of one reading give him the right to the greater reach of both.

---

*These quotations are from *The Harvest and the Scythe, Poets of Today IV,* New York, 1957, pp. 75-103.

Afterword to
"The Celestial Railroad" and Other Stories

Perhaps Hawthorne's clearest statement about the mode in which he wrote most of his tales comes at the beginning of "The Threefold Destiny, A Faëry Legend." As this tale is not here reprinted, the opening paragraph may be quoted entire.

> I have sometimes produced a singular and not unpleasing effect, so far as my own mind was concerned, by imagining a train of incidents in which the spirit and mechanism of the faery legend should be combined with the characters and manners of familiar life. In the little tale which follows, a subdued tinge of the wild and wonderful is thrown over a sketch of New England personages and scenery, yet, it is hoped, without entirely obliterating the sober hues of nature. Rather than a story of events claiming to be real, it may be considered as an allegory, such as the writers of the last century would have expressed in the shape of an eastern tale, but to which I have endeavored to give a more lifelike warmth than could be infused into those fanciful productions.

Hawthorne's allegory, then, is meant to touch at least the diaphragm of the quick, to raise at least the qualm of recognition if not the shock. (It was in a letter to Hawthorne that Melville used the phrase "the shock of recognition.") Yet I would suppose most readers coming to Hawthorne at any time after the age when belief is not a problem—say after fifteen—would find him as remote as he found the eastern tale. We do not like the "faery legend," and the less so if we do like the fairy tales of Kafka and Camus, of Faulkner and Hemingway, or if we have been taught to like the allegory of Melville or Dante. Hawthorne seems thin in comparison to any of these writers—thin in mind, thin in prose, and thin in the conventions by which he foreshortens his vision. This is partly a judgment of Hawthorne, partly a judgment of ourselves; it is also altogether a historical matter. Our histories no longer coincide. Hawthorne does not command us what to bring with us to find his "lifelike warmth," and what we would bring by instinct and experience does not seem to fit. We do not tell quite the same lies in order to find or escape the truth. Yet at one stage we did. Hawthorne's "Snow Image" haunts me from the age of six, and "The Great Stone Face," too, and as deeply as the letter A in *The Scarlet Letter* did later on, and I recognize both the image and the face in the last lines of Wallace Stevens' poem "The Snow Man." It seems to me that Hawthorne and Stevens and I are all one—

> the listener, who listens in the snow,
> And, nothing himself, beholds
> Nothing that is not there and the nothing that is.

Coleridge was right enough that some literature requires the "willing suspension of disbelief," but for writers like Hawthorne we must come nearer Keats's negative belief; indeed, we must make the belief positive and immediate so far as Hawthorne will persuade or permit us. The mind, the prose, and the conventions will all richen a little, even if they do not thicken solid, if the preliminary belief is there, reaching for what is meant to be there.

One way to reach is to take the paragraph quoted from "The Threefold Destiny" phrase by phrase, as if we were commenting scripture head by head with every head a revelation and a sermon needed on each; but as this procedure would require twenty-five drowsy and exasperated discourses—a full set of lectures in the fall term of any graduate school—we will not do it here. Let us rather think quickly, agitated only by the temptation to go further, of how some of the heads might appear, and assume the elaboration. "A subdued tinge": I will show you how what is hidden is yet innate; for the wild is within us and the wonderful is what makes the bed squeak. The "faery legend" is the inescapable account when, as always, all others, including the religious, fail; and there is nothing with which we are more intimate than the spirit, nothing to which we are more prone than the mechanism, of the "faery legend." The "sober hues of nature" are, for the given day, the first and last shades in the looking-glass, shaving or powdering, the toothbrush or the salts, the oncoming nightmare or the lapse of virtue. Thus every "story of events" claims immediate reality but must also be considered as going beyond any mere story; it signified what we did not yet know—what indeed had not yet been created until the event had been put together; which is the allegory— where what we think of signifies further than we expected it possible for thought to go—into either the pusillanimous or the great-spirited. It is in this sense, surely, that what seems to us, as other things seemed to Hawthorne, the "shape of an eastern tale" has a "lifelike warmth." To go back toward the beginning of Hawthorne's paragraph, the "spirit and the mechanism of the faery legend should be combined with the characters and manners of familiar life." Spirit and character, mechanism and manners. The words so paired run away with one because the substance in them is alive with its own momentum. It is possible they ran away with Hawthorne, too. To read him we must run with him.

We must believe at the level of serious writing what we commonly believe in our own daydreams: in curses, blessings, miracles, in the magical man of science, in alchemy, and above all in the creation of beauty by art and vision. In "The Birthmark" we must believe both in the fatal flaw of humanity and in the now perfect woman. In "Young Goodman Brown" we must believe that the Devil is in the Forest, but that the forest is within and the devil is ourselves; it is only the Calvinist version of Turgenev's proverb, that the heart of another is a dark forest. We must believe in the frivolity of "The Celestial Railroad" because Bunyan once seriously touched us when we found ourselves, if only for a moment, within the movement of *Pilgrim's Progress*. In "Egotism" we must believe in the Serpent in the Bosom as well as the devil in the heart. We must know that "The Vision of the Fountain" is an adventure of Narcissus, and must feel the Fountain of Youth sink into our own sands in "Dr. Heidegger's Experiment." We must hope that "The Gray Champion" must fearfully rescue us all, and we know that upon at least one of our expressions we should put "The Minister's Black Veil" before we look again in the mirror.

All these matters constantly press into the substance of everyday belief. In Hawthorne they seem to have absorbed belief and left us at the edge of the precipice, ourselves the only obstacle to keep us from falling from ourselves. Is not this what Hawthorne is suggesting at the end of "Wakefield"?

> Amid the seeming confusion of our mysterious world, individuals are so nicely adjusted to a system, and systems to one another and to a whole, that, by stepping aside for a moment, a man exposes himself to a fearful risk of losing his place forever. Like Wakefield, he may become, as it were, the Outcast of the Universe.

In Hawthorne people are constantly stepping aside for a moment—but with something in Hawthorne that always steps back. In each of his twice-told tales there is a withdrawal from the possibility. If I may twist the application a little from Hawthorne's intention, in story after story it is like Roderick's words to the sculptor in "Egotism."

Could I for one instant forget myself, the serpent might not abide within me. It is my diseased self-contemplation that has engendered and nourished him.

One thinks at once of Baudelaire and then of Huysmans and of Pascal behind them all. They are all of the same tradition, with Hawthorne being the New England version and like so much in New England twice told and twice removed. Hawthorne did not know that there was a future for his perceptions.

From the same story, but in Hawthorne's own voice, I draw two further passages in illustration of how his fiction looks at life.

All persons chronically diseased are egotists, whether it be sin, sorrow, or merely the more tolerable calamity of some endless pain, or mischief among the cords of mortal life.

The remainder of the passage says a great deal about Hawthorne's psychology, but the quotation is better arrested on the splendid phrase, "or mischief among the cords of mortal life"; which is what the great masters, and the religious masters, too, have dealt with, and which is where Hawthorne's perceptions seem to lead. The other passage, a thousand words further on, shows where Hawthorne actually drove his perceptions.

Thus making his own actual serpent—if a serpent there actually was in his bosom—the type of each man's fatal error, or hoarded sin, or unquiet conscience, and striking his sting so unremorsefully into the sorest spot, we may well imagine that Roderick became the pest of the city.

The hoarded sin in Hawthorne is what is substituted for the mischief among the mortal cords of life. It is not very different with Faulkner; both are adepts if not masters of a kind of black and blackened Christianity. This psychology, this way of looking at life, is one which cultivates nightmare to the point where true dream—or virtue—is excluded. It would never have been permitted in the temples of Aesculapius, but it seems a characteristic trait of American imagination and the opposite of American action. In Hawthorne the culmination is perhaps reached in "Feathertop," where the scarecrow sees himself . . . and is nothing. "Feathertop" is as humorous as Hawthorne could be; if the reader insists on a "serious" version, he may turn to "Edward Randolph's Portrait" which hung obliterated in the state chamber of the Province House until in the imagination of the beholder he wears "the terrors of hell upon his face."

What I have been saying is that the mode of most of Hawthorne's short stories is that of the daydreams which edge toward nightmare—toward our desire to be pursued, cast out, demolished, damned—daydreams undertaken, I should suppose, so that we may escape the reality of such things and protect ourselves from life. Such daydreams are certainly among the great uses of fiction; for in fiction they become fetishes or amulets, little patron images, more often of devils than saints worn to keep the wind away, which nevertheless blows as it wills and in its own severity. We use them, these fictions, like sympathetic magic or homeopathic medicine, to control our experience of what they represent. It is like sticking pins in the wax model of our disaster; and when we put the model away, we put off, having enjoyed it, the disaster. They make a Mardi Gras of what we would not do if we could. One or another of these phrases should fit Hawthorne's tales.

Take "Ethan Brand." I do not know how it may be now, but when I was a boy the unpardonable sin, the unforgivable sin, or, as I was taught it in church, the sin of blasphemy against the Holy Ghost was a major though intermittent attraction in the short times that seem so long just before sleep. It was a frightening possibility that I might find what it was and how to do it: the frightening thing was that I might then have to do it, as if discovery was actual commission of the sin. The verse in St. Mark (3:19) contained as much potential horror as anything I have ever read or heard said, outside the pitiless words of private life. So when I read "Ethan Brand" I knew where he was, his marble heart turned snowy lime, and in reading escaped where I was: I escaped being the fiend, the satanic, all powerful pride of intellect, and the glory of heartless triumph, and escaped all these by enjoying them in little; though as I think of it now I do not think Ethan Brand ever committed the unpardonable sin, unless it be, which Hawthorne does not tell us, that he committed it by finding that it was the impossible sin. When every possibility is taken away, *then* we have sinned. The theology is doubtless unsound, but there is an agony in the perception.

The bite of the word sin and the notion of unpardonable sin has pretty well gone out: we hardly know what is meant when we say—or hear—that sin gave birth to death; but we experience the perception, and are wooed to imitate the action, when we read "Ethan Brand." It is like being wooed to paranoia—or to all those other states that would be so wonderful if there were no outside world, and it is the kind of wooing we all enjoy because we can fill in all the details ourselves, as no doubt, so far as he was concerned, Hawthorne did when he wrote the tale. His business in this tale was to provide a frame or an armature for things going totally wrong with great pride and inordinate ambition and ability. Each of us is enough of a paranoiac to see the details.

If the reader is not tempted by "Ethan Brand" and unpardonable sin, surely he will succumb to "Rappaccini's Daughter" and her fatal beauty—I mean for the thrills and the shivers, and also to explain why in one's own life one never dared make a total commitment. There is nothing in Hawthorne if not pi-jaw—minatory occasional exhortation where you delight in what you professedly repel: the censor who keeps and shows his dirty pictures. The flagrant morals make the flagrant sinner, as morals absorbed make virtue possible. Here we will skip morals, whether flagrant or absorbed, and stay with the thrills and shivers of fatal beauty at work in a poisoned Italian garden. Gardens are where everything happens which is doubtless why Voltaire said that one must cultivate one's garden, and an Italian garden has the advantage that though mainly walled it is usually accessible from various quarters—one overlooks it, spies upon it, and descends into it. As for the poison, we all know, including the smiling and the wily Italians, that the Italians are master poisoners; Shakespeare, Webster, and all the people who have written about the Borgias have all told us so—arrows, ointment, and rings—so why should we object to poisoned flowers? In our own day we have the residue of fallout in our milk, not to mention other foods; Hawthorne is not out of place in either history or legend in giving us a garden of love where

> There was hardly an individual shrub which a wanderer, straying by himself through a forest, would not have been startled to find growing wild, as if an unearthly face had glared at him out of the thicket. Several also would have shocked a delicate instinct by an appearance of artificialness indicating that there had been such commixture and, as it were, adultery of various vegetable species that the production was no longer of God's making, but the monstrous offspring of man's depraved fancy, glowing with only an evil mockery of beauty.

This is right enough to legend and history, and perhaps Hawthorne is right enough in calling Rappaccini's garden an "Eden of poisonous flowers." It is only the botany that is wrong; all the other excesses—the scar from the touch of the hand, flowers from elsewhere wilting in the grasp—spiders and bees dying from a breath—all these are in the fatality of beauty as we should sometimes—since it hurts us so and will not abide our sentiment—like to see it: the disaccommodation and destroyer of the spirit who made it by perceiving it. The daydream of fatal beauty is only the natural though fantastic protection against the harshness and destructiveness of love in the actual world.

It is of a type, as Hawthorne looks at it, with the serpent in the bosom and the unpardonable sin: the one prefigures the other. The upshot, as Hawthorne puts it when Rappaccini's daughter falls dying:

> To Beatrice—so radically had her earthly part been wrought upon by Rappaccini's skill—as poison had been life, so the powerful antidote was death.

Some say Hawthorne was a great student of evil; I think rather he studied how to avoid and ignore it by interposing the frames of his tales between evil and the experience of it.

As a final example, there is the tale, very well thought of by many critics, called "My Kinsman, Major Molineux." It is a tale wholly without limiting specification, but it provides a frame for any specification you may choose, even the most random, and the signifying power of what you choose will depend on the power or the inanity of your mind. Thus it is open to any interpretation of whose method you—not Hawthorne—are a master. I can imagine someone treating the tale as a late and remote version of the three temptations in the wilderness—but unless you are the Dostoevsky of "The Grand Inquisition" (itself mercilessly exposed both to insane and powerful interpretations) you had better not try it. The general assault of possible evil and the general contagion of woes do not seem to me the result of the pressure of vision—hard or lovely things finally seen—but they are very well adapted to the sentimental use of anyone in need of a parallel for his own adventures not met.

I hope it will not be offensive to quote, for contrast with Hawthorne's allegory, the words Dante gives to Ulysses for his speech to his crew on the threshold of their last adventure beyond man's landmarks.

> "O brothers!" I said, "who through a hundred thousand dangers have reached the west, deny not, to this the brief vigil of your senses that remains, experience of the unpeopled world behind the sun. Consider your origin: ye were not formed to live like brutes, but to follow virtue and knowledge."

In Dante's allegory every adventure is met and what is met signifies further than had been known or intended, in prospect endlessly. Dante commands us what to bring by the authority of what is there. Hawthorne allows us to put in what we will at our own or a lesser level. Dante's allegory gives force to our own words—and thus to our thoughts as they find words—that they never previously had. Hawthorne's allegory lets our words seem good enough as they are, so that at best they only pass for thought. Dante's allegory is constructive, Hawthorne's allegory is reductive. Even the allegory of *The Scarlet Letter* is reductive of the values concerned; it is in the twilit limbo of virtue and knowledge—*virtute e conoscenza*—not in the light and dark of the continuing enterprise.

I find that in these remarks I have repeated a good many times different versions of the judgment of Hawthorne which I now bring to a head when I say that his allegory is reductive, as if allegory could go backward, and is even more likely to do so in him than to go forward. I must also then repeat what I have said less frequently, but as much believe, that Hawthorne's kind of allegory—his whole kind of writing—his whole way of looking at life—is one of the ancestors living within us, not a ghostly or merely haunting ancestor, but an active agent in our perception of things and the way in which we deal with them in the rote and wearing away of getting along. We cannot always be about mastering life; it is altogether sweet to put life off and give it the lie, and it is altogether proper to reduce life to a little less than our own size by the pretense either that we are bigger than life or that we are outcast. Hawthorne is an excellent help to these refuges, the more so if his language and conventions differ from ours. It is like saying, "I love you," in French; it is not so very different and, the first time, much more charming. If, when seen with the other eye and heard with a different voice, Hawthorne seems thin in mind, thin in prose, and thin in the conventions by which he foreshortens his vision, so are we. It is good that he is so remote.

Introduction to
the *Collected Novels* of Conrad Aiken

Aiken is all of a piece within his works, whether you think of his poems, his short stories, or his novels; and I think he is also personally deeply present in his works—of course not all of him but only that part of him which he needs, or which clings to him, as an author aiming at a theme: the finding, declaration, and loss of the self or pysche among the melodramas of love and jealousy, death and immolation, personal power and the frustrate abyss which in their fragments assault his sensibility. The reader can pursue these relations and their phases in Jay Martin's admirable and useful book about Aiken,* which should invite him to the works themselves. Here I mean merely to assert the fact, which has made itself plain with a re-reading of his novels all at once, of the deep relatedness—the necessary reticulation—and the constant theme. Perhaps with this assertion I can divagate and return.

Aiken's novels and stories are full of observations of gesture, of fragmentary conversations, spots of scene, the accidents of itinerary—everything that can be overheard or spied out: everything (in a phrase he used in one of his poems) between the foremath and the aftermath, the early growth and the after growth of the intended harvest. In the novels these snippets of anecdote make minor *éclaircissements* of who-knows-what (a speculative version, two centuries or so further along in the study of what we cannot take hold of, though it takes careless sudden hold of us, the *je-ne-sais-quoi*), and become a part of the permanent ambience of everything we are up to and everything we flee from. It is the ambience of the vaudeville of the psyche. (It is worthwhile noting here that in Aiken the minor people are vaudeville or burlesque, while the major people go in for striptease of the self with uncontrollable drums.) Whatever happens in the city invades and inspirits whatever happens

---

Conrad Aiken: A Life of His Art, Princeton, New Jersey, 1962.

to ourselves. Anyone who has dined often with Aiken must have been struck a livening blow by his restless percipience of the casual that was going on about him in the midst of no matter what genuine preoccupation—of money or marriage or career—concerned both of you. Whatever the roving eye or cocked ear could report was in its circumfusion sponged into the preoccupation, and so becomes part of the declaration of the double self between you. The fresh observation gives ambience to that self.

The recapture—the retention by repetition—of the familiar locus—the place—the naming of buildings, streets, flowers is a strain similar to that of the fresh observation. It is like the dining. Every place is the scene of some crime, and if we can name it we reactivate the crime a little—even when we make mistakes of identity or direction now and then. There is a refuge from our present guilt in the old crime—or even our old guilt. Original sin is never-ending. It is the precision (not the rightness or wrongness) of the observation that counts. Every observation must be made at least twice (though the second may be in memory only) before it presents itself as force, before it *works*. Observations made many times have the effect of creating something afresh that without our knowing it had already long been. There is thus an elegiac effect.

In Aiken's novels, Cambridge, Boston, and the Duxbury part of Cape Cod are full of such observations and recognitions. Anyone who has lived in these places between 1905 and 1940 (as I have myself) knows where he is, and knows within the harder knowledge of change; and each will add his own knowledges of contour and monument; and will perhaps complain because of a different and sometimes contradictory knowledge. My compass, for example, will not permit me to envisage, as Aiken's compass permits him, anything on the *south* side of Commonwealth Avenue near Massachusetts. I suppose Aiken means the side of Commonwealth toward the South End, which I would call the *east* side. Compass needles wobble and deviate upon their point, and the magnetic north is never the true north. Local knowledge is needed in these waters. I know where Aiken meant to place me, though it may not be exactly the same as where he placed himself; in either case I share the intense intimacy of his local knowledge and am therefore drawn along the pattern of physical movement in the Boston and Cambridge of his novels. I walk there, too.

Of course, most people don't dine with Aiken and most of his readers will not have lived in Boston and Cambridge the greater part of the years from 1905 to 1940. The point is, they will nevertheless be *placed*, and with intimacy, in Aiken's ambience of fresh and familiar observation. Local knowledge invites and commands general response reinforced and provisioned by the reader's own alien local knowledge. A "local habitation and a name" are among our most precious objects; possessed and tended they make a faith possible.

These remarks about Aiken's Boston and Cambridge would be an idle if agreeable commonplace if they were not, as I think, in analogy to the intense intimacy of his local knowledge and the flood of creative observation in the psychological territory—the strangely inhabited inscapes—of his novels. I do not mean that Aiken gives us the soul of Boston and Cambridge, only that he has a psychic territory—among many possible ones—of his own in which we find some part of ourselves, I will not say at home but in motion. We are in the two territories together, and as our awareness of one affects our awareness of the other, so the two territories act mutually upon each other's contours. They place each other and the place is a new place, and a place which is changing every minute. Every stop turns out to be a way station which we will reach again tomorow or next year or in some more ancient repetition of pattern of memory and expectation than we yet know.

The place is changing every minute, whether in Cambridge or in the way stations of the psyche; and indeed the names of the novels insist on the change: *Blue Voyage, Great Circle, King Coffin, A Heart for the Gods of Mexico, Conversation*. All invoke journeys, and no pause may be more than a sojourn. Even a conversation, to be a good one, must be the intimate constant change in the exchanges of the speakers; the weaving of the inconsequential along the consequent pattern. The form is very old in our accounts of the novel. It is the combination of the form with the material that makes the innovation. The form is the picaresque, the material that of psychology, or the conditions of life which a particular psychology points at. Let us call the combination the Psychological Picaresque; it may not be the right name (for the right name is always receding, always secret), but it is an indication of what goes on in these novels. Depending on how your mind bends you will say either that you have in each of them a picaresque of conscience streams or, which I take to be the lesser mode, a picaresque of the stream of consciousness. Conscience would seem the better term because there is always in these novels a striking together, a clutching together, even if there is not a uniting, of what is known. It is conscience not consciousness that can make or follow a pattern; and it is conscience that estimates the lies we tell in our search for the truth of self or love in our blue voyage along the great circle of conversation. One does not know if it is the voyage or the great circle that never ends.

In *Blue Voyage* we have as windows to love and to the self, the psychology of virtual death and of virtual crucifixion, where, with the sea all around us, we have death as a condition of life and crucifixion as a specifically human condition. It is the story of the man with the love he cannot have because, or *as if*, it were out of his class, except when he ventures from his own second-class accommodations into the first class where his love, his Cynthia, is. It is a book where everything that is second class in us shrieks in self-crucifixion and everything that is out of class, or out-classed, in us looks for death. The blue voyage is where somebody, or anybody, or even everybody must die. *Amare* and *morire* or *aimer* and *mourir* become somehow *again* a single conjugation throughout to the supervening noise of the sea: *thalassa, thalassa:* to love is *not* to die. Demarest, the hero, is a logolater, an idolizer of his words, and the meanings of his words and of his visions change in him according to his desires—*come amor vuol* as Dante says of his dreaming pilgrim (*Purgatorio* XIX). The horror of identity and the horror of love lie somewhere along the great circle course of this change. No wonder the reaction is self-crucifixion and the coming action death, with damnation equally in acceptance or rejection. Demarest—play with the particles and syllables of this name in what psychology and what Latin of the heart you will—hears still and continuously what at least one of the Sirens sings: as if to love were *not* to die.

This is a vulgar translation, at best a barbarous Vulgate, of what every Aiken hero hears his siren sing: as if to love were *not* to die. It is the sirens, not the mermaids, sing the most human of all songs, and if the sirens fail or we have too hard a wax in our ears, it will be Circe we attend, for Circe we have always within us in Aiken's novels. In *Blue Voyage* Circe is perhaps Faubion, the young woman you can't take your eyes or your hands off, the young woman who haunts you before you have had her and whom you know, if only you get drunk enough, you will have.

In *Great Circle,* the Hero, Andy Cather, is drunk enough both in liquor and in jealousy to create within himself—within his internal panic—the intolerable Circe voice. Memory and hope between them make a muck and in the muck there is Andy's life-long recurrent dream of the crucified pig—as if the pig were continuously stuck and continuously screaming. This is how the pig in us takes to crucifixion in the Aiken psychology that reeks catastrophe and creates disaster by prolonging, by "normalising" our moments of instinctive degradation beyond what the sleeping life can bear. In ordinary life we commonly wake up to our nightmares with a stifled scream, in Aiken's novels— particularly *Great Circle*—the nightmare is carried over and intensified in waking life. No wonder Bill the psychiatrist can listen no longer to Andy's waking nightmare but takes himself to sleep. Yet how tempting the Aiken psychology is to the frustrated or injured psyche as a providential occupation with our illusions. Reality is nothing, this psychology seems to say, anybody can cope with reality, but with our illusions we cannot cope, which is their blessing upon us: to satisfy our deep need for what we cannot cope with, except by martyrdom, crucifixion, degradation—all three in one nightmare.

How far Aiken's Circe psychology carries us in *Great Circle* is evident, I think, when in Sander's Theatre, Andy hears the other voice: Koussevitzky conducting the Boston Symphony in Mozart's overture to *The Magic Flute*. The listening is interspersed with a reading of the Program Notes (I like to think they were still Philip Hale's) and with a watching of his deserted and unfaithful wife far below him in the pit of the theatre with his own proper seat empty next to her. The last of the program notes quoted, to which Andy gives full assent, calls the overture "one of the most perfect instrumental compositions ever produced by human genius." To Andy god and the hurdy-gurdy speak to each other and then together. The Circe within listens to the siren without. This stands as preface to one of those intimate reconciliations that do not quite occur, but which may yet at another time and in an older place. I do not know that I read the end of the book right, and indeed I do not know that Aiken meant any one reading to prevail. Andy goes off to Duxbury, to the edge of the sea on Cape Cod, where as a child he had come on his first catastrophe and on his first knowledge of infidelity: when he found that his mother and his uncle were lovers, and had himself found them drowned. Now he must see for himself his own shattering daybreak on the old pattern repeated in himself; to see how "at a moment of discovery—one loses oneself in order to create oneself: the end that is still conscious of its beginnings. Birth that remembers death." This is of course the Great Circle. But how, in accepting it, does Andy qualify it? As "The wonderful nightmare, the wonderful and acceptable nightmare!" As if for the length of the next lap of the circle the crucified pig will scream again.

Certainly there is very little but that scream, subdued and muffled but penetrating, in *A Heart for the Gods of Mexico,* the scream in someone else not oneself, the scream in any silence listened to. It is in this case the scream in the willful nightmare of the young woman Noni, who has six months to live and eyes like the fringed gentian. Her lover, Gil, does not know of her coming death. Her confidant and as it were her lifetime hidden lover, Blomberg, knows it better than she. The three of them set off from Boston for Mexico—on the "great circle to Mexico," Mexico the death country, the murder country—so Noni can get a Mexican divorce and marry Gil before she dies. What do we say here? To love is *not* to die, as in *Blue Voyage,* or is it the older theme, the gray horror where to love is altogether to die, a bloody heart on the altar of the Plumed Serpent? At any rate the only embrace we feel is of Noni in the arms of death, her own and other deaths surrounding. The book is a lyric fusion of several mythologies, and what the lyric cries, what it *implores,* is the manifest divination of death, and the voice is the voice of a sibyl (I here rearrange for compactness some of Aiken's own words). For the greater part of the book we are on the train, with its motion and pauses and changes, as a kind of parallel to the other motions and changes in the three travelers, each different from the others, each hurrying in its own way, never quite in time or key or gear. Each is on his own journey in the same train, which is on its own journey. It is a décalage on a Blue Train—a décalage of independent neuroses, which are all psychogenic, in a general neuritis, which is a condition of life whenever it chooses an individual form or commits a particularized self to experience. But it is a sibyl's book and I will not undertake to report her. Like Blomberg at the very end there is a misery that wants to laugh and especially when it is so very far from home.

Conversation is much nearer home, is indeed domestic in every detail. Even the screams in tenor and hope: the tenor of keeping things going, like the planting of a hundred lilacs by dusk and night; the hope of recovering—of recouping as they say so falsely on the market, truly in the soul—the accidental and unintelligent losses that constitute the history of a lifetime: the damages of the sojourn. This is Aiken's version of the two wars—or the warring which makes the conflict—of the journey and the pity of life which Dante announces (*Inferno* II) as the subject of his comedy, adding that such an account will show the nobleness of memory. What Aiken adds—what almost any modern poet without a future world in faith must add—is the other nobleness of expectation. In faithful days there was no bad end that might not be overcome. We cannot bank on heaven and must keep our expectations near, unless in desperation. Memory and expectation breed in our time, and in their hybrid we dream our safety. Hence our staying powers have shrunk. At the opening of *Conversation,* the man and wife, Timothy and Enid, are so shrunken that they have almost nothing to say to each other unless it can be converted into a quarrel. Looking at and listening to them we have a fresh instance of how so many marriages are only held together by the cement of fresh quarrels, so that if the quarrels stopped, the crazy glaze of the marriage would fall apart. Here is the dilemma for the marriage counselor (I mean the novelist): beware of the spouse who will not quarrel, but beware more of the spouse whose only enthusiasm is to quarrel. Timothy and Enid have not decided upon which horn to impale themselves; the only thing certain, as the story begins to unfold, is that both husband and wife are beginning to act against their own interests. Each informs upon himself to himself; each is marvellously equipped to find, nourish, and develop the evil in the self.

The informer is that blackguard in the soul who would justify only its shortcomings and who has nothing but contemptuous distrust, and even spite—diseased chagrin—for the importunate hope for magnanimity and compassion between persons. It is as if there were a heraldic motto for this family of mankind: Every Man and Woman their own Cad, as an apt translation of *Honi soit qui mal y pense,* or God angers Himself in Vain. We see this in dinners unprepared, in failing water pumps, in Earth closets that are no more, in falsified careers, in the waiting for contact in dark rooms, and in that anarchy between people which could not exist without the supervening order which the anarchy denies. This last perhaps needs translation. A shop-lifting anarchist has come to the Cape Cod town (another version of Duxbury) with a troupe of those who call themselves artists but who have no requirement of craft or talent, and the good fun of this anarchy becomes in argument the horror between man and wife. The man has brought them here, though there are no shops to lift, from love of the possibility; the wife cries out because they show up the strange fact of the impossibility. The scandal of that impossibility becomes the horror between them, as the possibility or impossibility of anarchy—of uncontrolled or uncontrollable life—is always the terror of people in deep relation. That the shoplifter and his friends are in themselves only freaks does not matter. The freaks that irritate are most easily made the monsters who sack our citadels. In *Conversation* husband and wife use the freaks to break each other's peace, but something else would have done as well; for the husband, a visit from the wife's family; for the wife, the discovery of her husband's affair with Nora, just now terminated by a lovely lyric letter of conscience from Nora. Indeed nothing at all but their sense of their martyred selves was needed; for their marriage had reached that stage, that interlude, where indifference becomes a malevolent force, which must end either in mutual hatred or new love, in the silent scream or the new conversation. I will not say that the conversation which ends the long quarrel of the book makes an affirmation; it may or may not, and if so it will have to be repeated; I would say rather than affirmation that it makes a compassionate annunciation. Annunciation is the everlasting possibility, and conversation is the compassion in which we feel it.

Thus in four of Aiken's five picaresque novels of the psyche, we have had differing but converging versions of his two themes: the declaration of the self and the accomplishment of love, with a teetering balance between the psychology of Circe and the psychology of the sirens, and with death a multivalent measure of every effort. All Aiken's people are in the troubles which we would like to be ours, or, even if we did not like them, into which we could slip as we slip into a vice or a heroism or a martyrdom or an ambition of love. Exactly in the middle comes *King Coffin,* in which love is discarded and the self asserted to the point of destruction. There the hero is megalomaniac, determined "to exit outside society" in "a deeper and darker world of which a pure terribleness would be the principle." This is the refuge we are all of us born to see when love fails and the self collapses and anonymous murder becomes the only possible act. If *King Coffin* must be taken in series with the other four novels, it is something like this which we must say about it: It is the lyric of our insane selves which frightens us out of the fear of love and the loving self.

Other than the insane self I would rather take the book as a splendid, gay, and entrancing venture (with the very best actual local topography) into the psychology of the gangster self (in Christian times more often the satanic self). Indeed, I am rather sorry that Jasper Ammen should be made explicitly insane, for it impairs the credibility of his thoughts and acts. I would, for the joy of reading, take him as one of the condottieri of the Psyche, a good companion on the domestic scene for Gide's Lafcadio, Dostoevsky's Stavrogin, Balzac's Vautrin, or even Mann's Felix Krull, with all of whom I feel much personal sympathy. Some part of us is most at home in the idea of pure crime. Which of us would not rejoice in the prospect, as Jasper Ammen did, of a pure and random murder as the most magnificent form of mastery available to us—magnificent because also spontaneous. Ammen was right when, once having conceived the idea of murder, he decided that neither an enemy nor a friend would do; the victim must be a stranger. Our purest intimacies are with strangers, especially those we spy on and never talk to, and intimacy without the taint of interest or conflict. And who has not seen, if by accident we meet the stranger, the instant pollution of intimacy with knowledge. No. Ammen was indeed right to master everything about his victim possible without acquaintance. In the anonymous is the truly communal, just as every ultimate action is a tour de force quite without love and altogether free of any notion of the shared self. Very few of us can maintain such purity to the end, but for those interested in pursuing the idea of such purity the venture of Jasper Ammen is exemplary if you stop short of the last pages. Regrettably, at the last, the mighty hero does not topple into insanity and kills himself instead of his victim. Or should we rather say that he relinquishes one mastery for the sake of another?

It is right, though, that *King Coffin* should stand as a reminder between the two pairs of the other novels. It comments both with the primitive and more terrifying form of the same psychology that inhabits those efforts of love and self. If you look over any human shoulder *King Coffin* is there, where the nightmares in human relations come from.

Sources

"Notes on the Criticism of Herbert Read." *Larus* 1 (1928), pp. 45–58.

"Politikon." *Hound & Horn* 2 (1928), 49–60.

"A Postscript to Politikon." *Hound & Horn* 2 (1929), pp. 149–54.

"T. S. Eliot." Cambridge, Mass.: *Hound & Horn,* 1928. Published separately as "T. S. Eliot," *Hound & Horn* 1 (1928), 187–213, and "T. S. Eliot: II," *Hound & Horn* 1 (1928), pp. 291–319.

"The Discipline of Humanism," in *The Critique of Humanism,* ed. C. H. Grattan. New York: Brewer and Warren, 1930.

"Psyche in the South." Tryon, N.C.: Tryon Pamphlets, 1934.

"Chaos Is Come Again." *Southern Review* 6 (1941), pp. 658–74.

"The Enabling Act of Criticism," in *American Issues,* ed. Willard Thorp. Philadelphia: Lippincott, 1941. [Rpt. in *Critiques and Essays in Criticism, 1920-1948,* sel. by R. W. Stallman (New York: Ronald Press, 1949), pp. 412–17.]

"The Undergraduate Writer as Writer." *College English* 3 (1941), pp. 251–64.

"The State of American Writing." *Partisan Review* 15 (1948), pp. 861–65. [A symposium, pp. 855–94, with John Berryman, Robert Gorham Davis, Leslie Fiedler, Clement Greenberg, John Crowe Ransom, Wallace Stevens, Lionel Trilling, and H. L. Mencken.]

"The King over the Water: Notes on the Novels of F. M. Hueffer." *Princeton University Library Chronicle* 9 (1948), pp. 123–33.

"The Substance That Prevails." *Kenyon Review* 17 (1955), pp. 94–110.

"The Language of Silence: A Citation." *Sewanee Review* 63 (1955), pp. 382–408. [Rpt. in *Language: An Enquiry into its Meaning and Function,* ed. Ruth Nanda Anshen (New York: Harper, 1957), pp. 134–51.]

"Emily Dickinson's Notation." *Kenyon Review* 18 (1956), pp. 224–37.

"Introduction," in *American Short Novels.* New York: T. Y. Crowell, 1960, pp. 1–17.

"Religious Poetry in the United States," in *Religious Perspectives in American Culture,* ed. A. L. Jamison and J. W. Smith. Princeton: Princeton University Press, 1961, pp. 273–87.

"Afterword," to *"The Fall of the House of Usher" and Other Tales* (New York: Signet, 1960), pp. 375–83.

"The Chain of Our Own Needles," in *The Critical Matrix*. Washington: Georgetown University Press, 1961, pp. 36–48.

"A Poetics for Infatuation." *Kenyon Review* 23 (1961), pp. 647–70. [Also in *Venture* 3 (1963), pp. 38–59; and in *The Riddle of Shakespeare's Sonnets*. New York: Basic Books, 1962, pp. 131–61.]

"Theodore Holmes: Dactyls and All." *Princeton University Library Chronicle* 25 (1963), pp. 44–50. [Also in *Seven Princeton Poets,* ed. Sherman Hawkins, Princeton: Princeton University Library, 1963, pp. 44–50.]

"Afterword," to *"The Celestial Railroad" and Other Stories* (New York: Signet, 1963), pp. 289–97.

"Introduction," in *Collected Novels* of Conrad Aiken. New York: Holt, Rinehart, and Winston, 1964, pp. 5–11.

Index

Note on the Author

Richard Palmer Blackmur was born January 21, 1904, in Springfield, Mass. He was expelled from Cambridge High and Latin School in 1918, after a quarrel with the headmaster; the incident marked the end of his formal education. He educated himself by clerking in Cambridge bookstores, and supported himself through the 1930s by writing critical essays. He was associated with the Harvard magazine *Hound & Horn* as both contributor and editor. He married the painter Helen Dickson in 1930. His first book, a collection of essays called *The Double Agent,* was published in 1935. In 1940 he accepted a position as associate to Allen Tate in the Creative Arts program at Princeton University. During the years 1937–47, Blackmur published three volumes of poetry. He held the Hodder Fellowship at Princeton and the Rockefeller Fellowship in Humanities, and from 1944 to 1946 he was a fellow at the Institute for Advanced Studies. He inaugurated the Christian Gauss Seminars in Literary Criticism at Princeton in 1949, and in 1951, the year he was appointed full professor with tenure at Princeton, he and his wife divorced. During the remainder of his academic career, Blackmur devoted himself to study and travel. He was elected to the National Institute of Arts and Letters in 1956, and in that same year lectured at the Library of Congress. He served as Pitt Professor of American History and Institutions at Cambridge University in 1961–62. In 1964 he was elected to the American Academy of Arts and Sciences. R. P. Blackmur died February 2, 1965, in Princeton, New Jersey.

Note on the Editor

James T. Jones was born in Decatur, Ill., on April 5, 1948. He was educated at St. Teresa High School, Eastern Illinois University (B.A. 1971, M.A. 1973), and Southern Illinois University (Ph.D. 1980). He served as instructor of English at Millikin University from 1980 to 1983, and has taught American literature and literary criticism at Southwest Missouri State University since 1983. His first book, *Wayward Skeptic* (University of Illinois Press, 1986), was the first full-length treatment of the critical theories of R. P. Blackmur.